THE GLORY OF CHRIST

Apostles of the churches, the glory of Christ.

— *2 Corinthians 8:23*

The Glory of Christ

A PAGEANT OF TWO HUNDRED MISSIONARY LIVES FROM APOSTOLIC TIMES TO THE PRESENT AGE

BY MARK L. KENT, M.M.
AND SISTER MARY JUST OF MARYKNOLL

THE BRUCE PUBLISHING COMPANY
MILWAUKEE

CB
Ke G

NIHIL OBSTAT:

John A. Schulien, S.T.D.
Censor librorum

IMPRIMATUR:

✠ Albert G. Meyer
Archiepiscopus Milwauchiensis
April 15, 1955

Catholic University of America Classification:

Lynn: BQT3244 Dewey: 922.2

Library of Congress Catalog Card Number: 55–7863

Made in the United States of America

The Glory of Christ

A PAGEANT OF TWO HUNDRED MISSIONARY LIVES FROM APOSTOLIC TIMES TO THE PRESENT AGE

By MARK L. KENT, M.M.
AND SISTER MARY JUST OF MARYKNOLL

THE BRUCE PUBLISHING COMPANY
MILWAUKEE

NIHIL OBSTAT:

JOHN A. SCHULIEN, S.T.D.
Censor librorum

IMPRIMATUR:

✠ ALBERT G. MEYER
Archiepiscopus Milwauchiensis
April 15, 1955

Catholic University of America Classification:

Lynn: BQT3244 Dewey: 922.2

Library of Congress Catalog Card Number: 55–7863

MADE IN THE UNITED STATES OF AMERICA

Preface

SUPPOSE that, at any given period in the history of Christianity, the Holy Father desired to obtain a comprehensive view of the living Church founded by Christ. He would always be informed of men and women whose sole aim has been and is to maintain the Faith in its integrity in regions where it already exists, and ceaselessly to push outward the rim of Christendom. As a pageant of two hundred missioners passes through this book, we can glimpse a partial vision of what the popes from St. Peter to the present Holy Father have more widely perceived—the gradual unfolding of God's plan for the salvation of all nations.

Pains have been taken to make our pageant of missioners as representative as possible of various nations and religious institutes, but of necessity many great names have been omitted. Even if space permitted the inclusion of every known missioner, the pageant would be incomplete. Neither history nor tradition has recorded the names of all those who, since Apostolic times, have led others to Christ.

Some of our missioners labored for Christ until old age and baptized thousands of converts; others died as martyrs before their apostolate had fairly begun. The Venerable Francis Libermann, saintly missionary founder and organizer, never saw Africa, the continent of his apostolic desires. Pauline Jaricot, the foundress of the Society for the Propagation of the Faith, spent all her energies in organizing financial aid for the spread of the Kingdom of God.

Most of the men and women in this pageant were not considered of great account by their secular contemporaries; but in the light of the eternal destiny of humanity, they were and are the most important persons who ever drew the breath of life. "There is nothing more divine, among all divine things, than to co-operate with God in the salvation of souls," wrote Dionysius the Areopagite many centuries ago.

Our missioners were all alike in one respect: they loved Christ so much that they could not bear that souls for whom our Lord died on the cross should remain ignorant of the Lord of Glory and withhold, in consequence, their due share of praise and thanksgiving. The story of these missioners is proof that every Catholic who loves God more than all else can find ways and means of joining the company of those of whom St. Paul wrote: "Apostles of the churches, the glory of Christ" (2 Cor. 8:23).

Contents

THE GLORY OF CHRIST

PART I

The Church of the Catacombs

(BIRTH OF CHRIST TO A.D. 312)

UNTIL the victory of Emperor Constantine at the Milvian Bridge, in A.D. 312, the Church was outlawed and persecuted. Christianity nevertheless survived, and even began to spread widely. The fortitude of the early Christians was sustained by the Holy Eucharist and by the promptings of the Holy Spirit. No one has ever determined the number of the martyrs in those centuries; but the pagan historian, Tacitus, referred to them as being an "immense multitude."

In its advance from the Holy Land, the religion of Jesus gained an increasing number of adherents in Samaria, Asia Minor, Macedonia, Greece, Illyria, and Dalmatia. St. Peter arrived in Rome in A.D. 63 or 64. From Rome, the Faith was transported to southern Gaul and to Spain. Tradition tells us that its light even reached out as far as distant India.

The Christian apologist, Tertullian, wrote in the third century: "Afflict us, torment us, crucify us. In proportion as we are mowed down, we increase; the blood of Christians is a seed."

On this and the following pages are glimpses of a few among the heroic early messengers of the Word. Impelled by the love of Christ, they set out dauntlessly to take the tidings of salvation to a pagan world, heavy with darkness and the shadow of death.

ST. PETER, *Vicar of Christ* (*d. c.* 67)

Why did the Saviour choose the impetuously rash Peter, as the rock upon which He would found His Church? The answer is that our Lord knew from the beginning that the very richness of Peter's love and loyalty for his Master was the source of the fisherman's impetuous imprudence. Christ knew also that, under the action of the Holy Spirit, Peter's impetuosity would later be transmuted into an unshakably generous solicitude for the infant Church.

At the time of our Lord's Passion, Peter's character was strengthened and refined by the tremendous sorrow he experienced, after he had three times denied his divine Master. His new and touching humility endeared him yet more to the Saviour and to the other Apostles. After Pentecost, the precedence of St. Peter in the Church was never disputed. He ruled with the authority given him by the Holy Spirit, but his rule was one of love. He was nobly willing, for instance, to be guided by St. Paul's experience in the apostolate among the Gentiles.

Herod Agrippa I (A.D. 42–44) began a new persecution of the Church in Jerusalem. He cast Peter into prison and planned to put him to death after the Jewish Pasch. But an angel of God delivered the Prince of the Apostles from captivity. The Acts tell us that Peter then left Jerusalem, to go to "another place."

Tradition relates that St. Peter's missionary journeys in the Near East took him into various provinces of Asia Minor. It is a historical fact that the Vicar of Christ eventually established his residence in Rome, the capital city of the ancient world. From then until now, each successor of St. Peter has been, in turn, the Bishop of Rome.

During the bloody persecution of the Church by Emperor Nero, St. Peter was imprisoned and condemned to death. According to tradition, the Prince of the Apostles was martyred on June 29, in the year 67, on the same day that St. Paul went to see Christ face to face. Because St. Paul was a Roman citizen, he was beheaded. But St. Peter had the joy of suffering the same death as his Master, the ignominious torture of the cross. For a last time, all the impetuous love of that great heart welled up in thanksgiving, when Peter was granted the additional shame of hanging on the cross head downward.

BELIEF IN THE DIVINITY OF JESUS

St. Peter was the spokesman of the Twelve in proclaiming that Jesus is God: "We have believed and have known that thou art the Christ, the Son of God" (Jn. 6:70).

ST. PAUL, *Apostle of the Gentiles* (*c.* 3–*c.* 67)

On June 29, in the year 67, St. Paul was taken from his prison and led out to a country place called "Healing Waters," three miles from Rome. As the old man walked obediently to his death, his thoughts traveled back over the years to another road, bathed in the fierce radiance of a Syrian noontide. There, on the way to Damascus, Christ had appeared in dazzling effulgence to Saul the persecutor, transforming him into Paul, the Jesus-loving missioner.

Now the great missioner's journeys were over. The weary feet of the worn Apostle, once so swift and sure in the service of Christ, trudged down their last stretch of dusty highway. But his thoughts hastened joyously on to the end of the journey, for he was about to offer for the salvation of souls all that yet remained for him to sacrifice — his own life.

After the martyr had been beheaded, the persecuted Christians of Rome spoke of St. Paul wherever they met. "He could well say to his converts that he was their father in Christ," affirmed an old man. "What did he not suffer, in order that they might be reborn to Christ? He was seven times cast into prison. More than once, he was beaten with rods, stoned, and compelled to flee. And while he was laboring to bring souls to the true God, he lived in the utmost poverty, supporting himself by the toil of his own hands."

"Yes. And did not he himself say that he had often been in peril from shipwreck, in peril from robbers, in peril from waste places, toil, and weariness of every sort?" recalled an eager lad.

"Think of his tremendous missionary journeys! He preached in the principal towns of the Mediterranean, both in the east and in the west," added a merchant. "And it must not be thought that Paul neglected the Jews. He gave them the first chance of listening to the gospel story — but most of them returned his love with bitter hatred. Then Paul gave himself to the Gentiles."

"The life of Paul will be a model for Christian apostles as long as the world exists," stated a priest. "And his writings will continue to reveal to men's hearts the splendor of God. All this we know. But the dying of Peter and of Paul on the same day has, indeed, left us orphans."

"Still, we must rejoice for them," said a young girl softly. "I hear constantly in my heart the words of the Apostle of the Gentiles: 'For me, to live is Christ; and to die is gain.'"

THE GOAL OF SANCTITY

To his converts, St. Paul wrote: "With Christ I am nailed to the Cross. It is now no longer that I live, but Christ lives in me" (Gal. 2:19, 20).

THE SAMARITAN WOMAN (*First Century*)

One of our Lord's very first missioners was a Samaritan, who before she met Christ at Jacob's well was a woman of ill repute. She was surprised that the gracious stranger, a Jew, should talk with her, because the Jews habitually looked down on the Samaritans and held no communication with them.

Jesus, being God, saw the generosity of that despised woman's soul. At that time in the world's history, almost no one knew that Jesus Christ is the son of God; but He chose to reveal this stupendous truth to the Samaritan woman. She did not remain at the well, indulging in her newly found joy and faith. The first thought of this selfless convert was for others, for neighbors who had only too often spoken ill of her.

Entirely of her own free will, she hastened with apostolic zeal into the streets of nearby Sichar, announcing to the townspeople what she had just heard from the lips of Christ Himself. St. John tells us in his Gospel that many of the Samaritans of that town believed in Jesus, because of the word of the woman who bore witness. In all the apostolic annals of the Church, it would be hard to discover a more poignantly moving missionary story.

A TRULY CATHOLIC HEART

A truly Catholic heart cannot be selfish. Jesus was pleased when the Samaritan woman hastened away, to lead her townspeople to her newly found Saviour. When charity calls, Christ will be closer to us in the highways and byways among our fellow men, than if we remain engrossed in the pursuit of purely personal spiritual consolations.

ST. PHILIP THE DEACON (*First Century*)

Soon after Pentecost the twelve Apostles found that their serving of the poor consumed so much time that they were hindered in the preaching of the Gospel. So, with the approval of the faithful, the Apostles ordained, for the service of the poor, seven deacons, men "full of the Holy Ghost and wisdom." Among those seven deacons were Stephen, the first Christian martyr, and Philip, who was to prove himself an ardent missioner.

While Saul (the future St. Paul) was persecuting and scattering the Christians of Jerusalem, St. Philip the Deacon journeyed into Samaria. He preached Christ to the Samaritans, and he performed many miracles in their midst. After Philip had baptized numerous converts, he sent word to the Twelve of the success of his ministry. Then the Apostolic College appointed Peter and John to administer the Sacrament of Confirmation to the baptized Samaritans.

Afterward, an angel of God told Philip to journey southward, to the desert of Gaza. The missioner obeyed. He encountered south of Jerusalem an Ethiopian, who was returning from a pilgrimage to the Holy City. This stranger was a man of great authority, the treasurer of Queen Candace of Ethiopia. As the pilgrim journeyed homeward, he was reading the Book of Isaias.

The Holy Spirit inspired Philip to approach the stranger's chariot. "Do you understand what you are reading?" the missioner asked the Ethiopian.

"How can I, unless someone explains it to me? If you are able to help me, come up and sit with me in my chariot!" pleaded the pilgrim.

Then Philip perceived that Candace's treasurer had been reading the sublime prophecy in which Isaias foretold the Passion of Christ. The zealous deacon told the seeker after truth in what manner the ancient prophecy had recently been divinely fulfilled. After a while, the chariot drew near to water, and the pilgrim asked for baptism.

"You may be baptized, if you believe with all your heart," said Philip.

"I believe that Jesus Christ is the Son of God," answered the noble convert.

So Philip baptized the treasurer of Queen Candace. Surely that convert, expressly desired by God, must in his turn have baptized many neophytes in distant Ethiopia. The last glimpse the Acts afford us of the apostolic labors of St. Philip the Deacon shows us the valiant missioner evangelizing the coast of Palestine from Azotus to Caesarea.

NO THOUGHT OF SELF

Eagerness to obey the promptings of the Holy Spirit freed Philip the Deacon from all hampering self-consciousness in his approach to the noble Ethiopian. Modern Catholics could imitate Philip to great advantage in their contacts with those outside the Church.

ST. JAMES THE GREATER (*d. A.D. 43*)

St. James the Greater, a Galilean fisherman, was the brother of St. John the Beloved Disciple, and was a near relative of our Lord. Like his brother, St. James the Greater was chosen by Jesus as a member of the Apostolic College. Christ called James and John "Sons of Thunder," no doubt because of their impetuous zeal. But before the Holy Ghost had descended on the brothers on the first Pentecost, their zeal often lacked patience.

When some Samaritans refused to receive Christ in their town, James and John wished to call down fire from heaven upon them. Jesus rebuked the two brothers, saying: "You know not of what manner of spirit you are; for the Son of Man came not to destroy men's lives, but to save them" (Lk. 9:56).

Christian tradition has long held that St. James the Greater evangelized Spain. The shrine of St. James at Compostella became in the Middle Ages, after Jerusalem and Rome, the most famous place of pilgrimage in Christendom. In the eleventh year after our Lord's Ascension, James returned to Jerusalem, where Herod Agrippa was on the throne.

Herod Agrippa sought to please the Jews by persecuting the Christians. St. James the Greater was delivered into the hands of Agrippa by an informer, and the Apostle was sentenced to be beheaded. The informer was so struck by the courage and the holy joy of his victim, that he repented of what he had done and declared himself publicly a Christian.

"Peace be with you!" said St. James, embracing the traitor who was to die a saint.

The Apostle and the repentant informer were beheaded together, in A.D. 43. St. James the Greater was the first of the Twelve to suffer the glorious death of martyrdom.

PERFECTED IN CHARITY

St. James the Greater never forgot the words in which his divine Master had once rebuked his lack of charity: "The Son of man came not to destroy men's lives, but to save them." So, on the eve of his martyrdom, St. James saved the soul of the wretched man who had betrayed him.

ST. ANDREW, *Apostle* (*d. A.D. 60*)

St. Andrew and St. John the Beloved Disciple were the first two Apostles chosen by our Lord. They were both followers of St. John the Baptist. One day, while they were listening to the preaching of the Precursor, Jesus approached. Seeing Him, the Baptist cried out, "Behold the Lamb of God!"

At once, Andrew and John followed Jesus. The Saviour turned and said to them, "What seek you?"

They asked Him, "Master, where dwellest Thou?"

Jesus said to them, "Come and see."

Andrew was the brother of Simon Peter. They were both fishermen, and lived together in Capharnaum. Because Andrew had found Jesus and recognized Him as the Messias, he ran joyfully to bring Simon Peter to the Master. After that day, Peter and Andrew were to become fishers of men.

Early Christian tradition tells us that in the years following the first Pentecost, Andrew was a great missioner. He preached in Asia Minor, and among the savage Scythians north of the Black Sea and east of Lake Aral. Then he labored in Byzantium (Constantinople), Thrace, Macedonia, Thessaly, and southern Greece. It was in civilized southern Greece, and not among the wild Scythian nomads, that the brother of St. Peter was martyred.

Andrew was put to death during the reign of Emperor Nero, in A.D. 60. It is generally agreed that the glorious Apostle was bound, not nailed, to the cross, in order to prolong his sufferings. In memory of St. Andrew's apostolate among the Scythians, Christian Russia honored him as a special patron. He is, also, the patron saint of Greece and of Scotland.

A TRUE BROTHER

We all have a God-given obligation to love and aid in a special manner those of our immediate family. St. Andrew was a true brother to St. Peter. No sooner had Andrew found the Expected of the Nations, than he hurried with eager joy to bring the loved Simon Peter to the Saviour.

ST. BARTHOLOMEW, *Apostle* (*First Century*)

St. Bartholomew, a doctor in the Jewish law, was an intimate friend of St. Philip. After Christ had called Philip to His service, the young Apostle could not rest until he had brought Bartholomew to his Master. When Jesus saw Philip's friend coming to Him, He said, "Behold a true Israelite in whom there is no guile!" (Jn. 1:47).

This is the only glimpse that the New Testament gives us of the character of St. Bartholomew. But it is surely enough for us to know that the God of Truth saw the heart of this Apostle unstained by any shadow of deceit.

After the first Pentecost, St. Bartholomew evangelized Asia Minor, northwestern India, and Greater Armenia. While he was preaching in the latter country, the Apostle was arrested and condemned to death. An ancient tradition relates that Bartholomew was flayed alive.

In the midst of his awful sufferings, the martyr must have heard in his soul the echo of the glad, triumphant words with which he had first saluted the Master so many years ago: "Thou art the Son of God, Thou art the King of Israel!"

THE MAN WITHOUT GUILE

The innocent soul of St. Bartholomew was open to the truth. Though he did not think it likely that the Messias would come out of Nazareth, he did not adhere to preconceived ideas. Instead he went willingly to see Jesus, and recognized Him forthwith as the Son of God. "Blessed are the clean of heart: for they shall see God" (Mt. 5:8).

ST. THOMAS, *Apostle* (*First Century*)

A very ancient legend describes how our Lord appeared to St. Thomas in Jerusalem, and told him to go and preach the Faith in India. "Lord, send me anywhere, except to India!" implored that Apostle.

But our Lord said to Thomas: "Go, I will watch over thee; and when thou shalt have converted the Indians, thou shalt come to Me to receive as a recompense the crown of martyrdom."

The legend goes on to relate how St. Thomas accordingly journeyed to the far country of India, converting many infidels and performing frequent miracles along the way. Everywhere in India, the people flocked to hear him speak of Christ.

At last a certain King Mesdeus, a worshiper of the sun, ordered his soldiers to seize the Christian teacher and to put him to death. Four soldiers took St. Thomas to a neighboring mountain and, in a lonely spot, pierced him through with their lances. The town from which the Apostle was led to martyrdom was Calamina, in southern India, afterward called "Mylapore," or "Town of Peacocks."

This ancient legend contains a sound kernel of truth. The apostolate of St. Thomas in India is confirmed both by the most remote Christian tradition and by modern archaeological discoveries. St. Jerome, who died in the year 420, speaks of the labors of St. Thomas in India as of a fact universally known at that time. In the early Middle Ages, French and Anglo-Saxon pilgrims journeyed to the tomb of St. Thomas at Mylapore. The Saracens, too, held the spot in profound veneration, saying that the holy Apostle was a great prophet.

In India itself, many native families still glory in the belief that their ancestors received the Faith from the Apostle St. Thomas. Chaldean books found in India affirm that St. Thomas carried the light of Christianity even into China. In any event, we have ample evidence that the doubting Thomas became a missioner of strong, vivifying zeal.

CONFORMITY TO GOD'S WILL

As the ancient legend tells it, St. Thomas experienced a strong human repugnance to mission labor in India; but after he had conformed his will to that of Christ, he became the venerated and wonder-working Apostle of that great subcontinent. Throughout the centuries, Catholics have found that conformity to God's will reveals as being for our eternal good what we hitherto humanly dreaded.

ST. MARK THE EVANGELIST (*d. A.D. 75*)

The mother of John Mark was a wealthy and prominent member of the infant Church at Jerusalem. Her home was a meeting place for the brethren; and it was to this haven that St. Peter turned, on his release from prison in the Holy City (Acts 12:12–17).

In A.D. 47, when St. Paul and St. Barnabas were evangelizing the island of Cyprus, they took with them as their helper the young John Mark, who was a cousin of Barnabas. Paul planned to penetrate next into Galatia, in Asia Minor; but John Mark drew back, appalled before the prospect of labor among the rude mountaineers of that region. This defection wounded Paul intensely.

St. Mark soon surmounted his youthful timidity, and he became in due course the beloved companion and secretary of St. Peter in Rome. Tradition tells us that the Christians of Rome asked Mark to set down in writing the many sermons of the first Pope about the sayings and the public ministry of our divine Lord. Mark did as the Christians requested, and so was written the second Gospel of the New Testament. It is a terse, direct, and picturesque document, in a language that must have been very close to the words of Peter, the former fisherman of Galilee.

In his later Epistles, St. Paul referred to John Mark as one of his fellow workers and said, "He is profitable to me for the ministry." When St. Paul was imprisoned in Rome, Mark visited the Apostle of the Gentiles and cared for his wants with loving kindness.

The writings of both St. Peter and St. Paul give evidence that John Mark, in his mature years, evangelized many districts of Asia Minor. Tradition also represents St. Mark as the founder of the Church of Alexandria, and claims for him the glory of martyrdom in that Egyptian city. Certain it is that until his death, St. Mark was always obedient to the great command transmitted to him by St. Peter and set down in the final chapter of his Gospel: "Go ye into the whole world, and preach the Gospel to every creature" (Mk. 16:15).

PATIENCE WITH YOUTH

The development of St. Mark's character shows us the need of patient caution in judging young people. Hasty harshness can warp the growth of a soul.

ST. ONESIMUS (*d. A.D. 95*)

The slave Onesimus belonged to one of St. Paul's converts, a certain Philemon, a wealthy citizen of Colossae, in Asia Minor. Onesimus robbed his master and escaped to Rome. He must have planned his crime well, for he was not stopped anywhere along the way.

On his arrival in the capital, the slave soon found himself in want. He heard that Paul was imprisoned in the city, and he remembered how the Christian leader had gone out of his way to be kind to the slaves when he had visited Philemon's home. So Onesimus went to see Paul.

Without too much prodding, the slave related the full story of his robbery and escape. Paul thought it was a shame that such cleverness should be wasted on crime, and he told Onesimus as much. The great missioner used all the eloquence of his burning love for souls to win the poor thief for Christ.

"Now I have an errand for you," said the saint to his new convert. "I am sending you back to your master, as the bearer of a letter from me. Do not be afraid. Philemon will forgive you, after he will have read my letter."

If we take the New Testament and turn to St. Paul's Epistle to Philemon, we see why that noble convert could not refuse the Apostle's request. "I plead with thee for my son, whom I have begotten in prison, for Onesimus," wrote Paul. "I am sending him back to thee, and do thou welcome him as though he were my very heart."

Onesimus went back to his master, and Philemon did forgive him. The generous master did even more: he gave Onesimus his freedom. Onesimus became a missioner, and found special joy in preaching Christian doctrine to slaves. In the year 95, Onesimus proved his love for Christ by a martyr's death.

FAITH IN CHRISTIAN FRIENDSHIP

When St. Paul asked his loved Christian friend, Philemon, to forgive the converted slave, the great Apostle wrote: "I know that thou wilt also do more than I say." Philemon could not but respond to such greathearted trustfulness.

ST. LUKE THE EVANGELIST (*First Century*)

A young man by the name of Luke became St. Paul's disciple when the Apostle of the Gentiles was in the harbor of Troas, in Asia Minor, near the entrance to the Strait of Dardanelles. Luke was a physician, and a native of Antioch in Syria. He used his pure Grecian language to become the evangelist and the historian of his leader; and until St. Paul's martyrdom, Luke was a faithful co-worker of his master.

The essence of St. Luke's Gospel is Paul's intense love of the Gentiles and his special revelation of the universality of the Church. Often Luke employs the selfsame forms of speech as his master, but his own serene Greek genius softly illumines the austere heights of Paul's theology.

All over the world, priests read at Mass on Christmas morning St. Luke's simple and touching account of the Saviour's birth. The young physician must have talked with the Blessed Virgin herself, in order to obtain the true story of the very first Christmas. Otherwise, how could he have learned and passed on to us the many warm and intimate details of that tremendous event in the little town of Bethlehem?

Almost nothing is known about St. Luke's life after the martyrdom of St. Paul. But we do have in the New Testament a second masterpiece from his gifted pen, in the Acts of the Apostles. The Acts give us invaluable information about the early years of the Church, and especially about Paul's missionary journeys. St. Luke's inspired account of the love of Christ for all men proves that he himself must have been a very great missioner.

CHRIST LOVES THE LOWLY

The Christ of St. Luke's Gospel is the Saviour of the lowly ones of the earth. Luke alone recorded the words of Christ's prayer for His unwitting murderers, and of the soul-stirring dialogue between the dying Saviour and the Good Thief. The third Gospel is, above all, the Gospel of the Merciful Heart of Jesus.

ST. JOHN, *Apostle and Evangelist* (*d. c. 100*)

St. John, the youngest of the twelve Apostles, was about twenty-five years of age when our Lord called him away from his fishing nets in Galilee, to become a fisher of men. John was in a special way the Beloved Disciple of his Master. At the Last Supper, he leaned on Christ's breast. On Calvary, he alone of the Twelve stood under the cross and shared the agony of his Master's Passion. To the care of John, the dying Jesus entrusted His Blessed Mother.

St. Paul tells us that, after Pentecost, St. John was venerated as one of the pillars of the Church at Jerusalem. Paul was martyred in the year 67, and then John continued the great work of the Apostle of the Nations in Asia Minor. St. John made Ephesus his chief residence. As the years passed, he meditated ceaselessly on the divine riches of the Heart of Jesus.

The fourth Gospel was the fruit of the Beloved Disciple's meditations. He wrote it after the other three Gospels had been composed. St. John stressed with moving splendor the divinity of Christ, and he set down many of the Saviour's words that the other Evangelists had not recorded.

According to a very ancient tradition, St. John was cast into a caldron of boiling oil at Rome, during the reign of the Emperor Domitian. God preserved the saint unhurt, and he was banished to the island of Patmos. In that exile, the aged Apostle wrote the sublime Book of the Apocalypse.

After St. John returned to Ephesus, he was so feeble that he had to be carried on the shoulders of his followers. In his closing years, his preaching consisted of a single sentence, repeated over and over again: "Little children, love one another!" It was the echo of his Master's words after the Last Supper: "A new commandment I give you: That you love one another, as I have loved you" (Jn. 13:34).

As the first Christian century was ending, St. John completed his earthly apostolate of love and went to see his divine Master in the eternal joys of heaven.

A FUNDAMENTAL LIKENESS

Our Lord gave to two of His Apostles especially sacred trusts. The forthright Peter He made His Vicar on earth; and in dying, He entrusted the care of His Mother to the beloved John. These two Apostles were alike in the greatness of their love for Christ. The blunt Peter could manifest surprising tenderness; and John was at times so ardently impetuous that Jesus called him "Son of Thunder."

ST. IGNATIUS OF ANTIOCH (*d. c. 107*)

"Let him be put in chains and taken to Rome – there to become the food of wild beasts and a spectacle to the people!" commanded the angry Emperor Trajan in the year 107.

Trajan had won splendid military victories in Asia Minor, and he had determined to complete his conquest by forcing the Christians of that region to worship the Roman gods. The greatest obstacle to his purpose had proved to be the aged Christian leader now standing fearlessly before him.

St. Ignatius, Bishop of Antioch, was a living link with the first Apostles of Christ. He had been appointed by St. Peter, the first pope, to govern the see of Antioch, and he had heard St. John preach at Ephesus. The holy bishop lived only to keep his people faithful to our Lord. For himself, he desired ardently the grace of martyrdom; the threats of Trajan merely filled him with joy.

St. Ignatius had much to suffer during the long journey from Antioch to Rome. In a letter to the Christians of Rome, he compared the cruel soldiers who guarded him to "ten leopards." In spite of that, the journey of the venerable bishop was a triumph. The soldiers traveled mostly by land, and everywhere the faithful of the young Christian communities flocked to listen to the inspiring words of the illustrious prisoner.

"Be obedient to your bishops and shun the leprosy of heresy," the saint told them. "As for me, did not Christ give me His Body and Blood in Holy Communion? And is it not, then, a joy to me to give my flesh to the lions, for the love of Jesus?"

There were pagans, too, in the crowds that gathered around the old bishop; and in the last days of his apostolic life, he spent himself utterly to win new followers for his Master. Then, at the journey's end, St. Ignatius died gladly for Christ in the Roman arena.

AN ATHLETE OF CHRIST

St. Ignatius of Antioch eagerly ran the "course" spoken of by St. Paul. He was devoted to his apostolic duty, ardently loved self-sacrifice, and fearlessly defended Christian truth. This strong athlete of Christ merited the triple honor shown him by the Church, as apostle, bishop, and martyr.

PART II

Barbarians Overrun the Roman Empire

(312–496)

AFTER Constantine's victory at the Milvian Bridge, Christianity was upheld by the Roman Emperors, except during the brief rule of Julian the Apostate. During the fourth and the fifth centuries, successive waves of barbarians overran the decaying Roman Empire. In the year 476, Odoacer, from the Danube, exiled the last Roman Emperor.

As the Empire was shrinking, the Church was expanding. Early Christianity was, it is true, plagued by numerous heresies and schisms; but the refutation of those errors served to define more sharply the fundamentals of Christian belief. Christian monasticism arose in Egypt in the third century, and rapidly made its way into almost every province of the Roman world. Monks became the spearhead of missionary expansion.

By the closing years of the fifth century, Christianity was the religion of practically the whole population of the former Roman Empire; German tribes were accepting the Faith; and the teachings of Christ had been taken to Persia, Arabia, Armenia, the Caucasus, the west coast of the Red Sea, and Ireland.

The baptism of King Clovis of the Franks, in 496, emphasized the course the Church was taking. By the conversion of barbarian invaders, she was giving birth to European Christendom – a new world. At the same time, she alone was salvaging the noblest elements of the ancient civilization.

ST. NINO (*d. c. 320*)

When Joseph Stalin was a boy, Georgia, the Russian province of his birth, was a region of devout Christians. That was before the time of the Bolshevik victory in Russia and the subsequent Communist persecution of Christianity. Georgia had been evangelized over sixteen centuries earlier by the slave girl, Nino.

Nino grew up in Cappadocia, in Asia Minor. One day some pagan marauders from Georgia descended on Nino's native town of Colastri, and they took the Christian girl back to their country as a slave. Nino did not lose faith in God in that alien land, and soon she had made a deep impression on her captors by her holy life and the long hours she spent in prayer.

Once the slave girl prayed over a sick baby, and the little one got well instantly. Word of the miraculous cure reached the Queen of Georgia, who suffered from a grievous ailment. The royal lady went to ask the aid of Nino; and she, too, was cured.

"What can I do to reward you?" asked the grateful sovereign.

"But I did not cure you," answered the Christian girl. "Jesus did. He is the Son of God. You must thank Him."

The queen told her husband about the wonderful little slave, and urged him to find out more about the Son of God, who had restored her to health. But the King of Georgia did not pay much attention to his wife's story. He thought that women were always too ready to believe in wonders.

Some time later, the king was out hunting and lost his way in a dense fog. He was in a lonely region infested by robbers, so he became really alarmed. He thought suddenly of the Son of God his wife had told him about. "Jesus, if You are truly God, show me where the road is, and I will believe in You," he said. Instantly the fog cleared.

The King of Georgia was true to his word. Nino instructed the royal couple in the Faith; and they asked her to teach their subjects, too, about Jesus. The leading architect was called in and given orders to build a Christian church. Then an embassy was sent to the Emperor Constantine, to tell him what had taken place. Immediately the Emperor sent bishops and priests to Georgia, to minister to the converts that Nino had made.

After the arrival of the missioners, the holy girl retired to a cell in the mountains. There she spent the remainder of her life, praying for the once-pagan land that had become dearer to her than her own home. St. Nino is venerated as the apostle of Georgia-in-Russia. She died in about the year 320.

ST. NINO UNDERSTANDS

When we ask the saints in heaven to intercede with God for the conversion of Soviet Russia, let us invoke St. Nino. She was once a slave in pagan Georgia, and she converted her captors. With what yearning compassion she must look today on the Russians enslaved body and soul by atheistic tyrants.

ST. MARTIN OF TOURS (*c. 316–397*)

It is strange to recall that Martin, the great saint of the French countryside, was not born in France at all; his native land was the distant country of Hungary, which was then a Roman province. Martin's father was a pagan Roman officer. Soon after the boy's birth, the family moved to Italy, and there Martin learned to love the Church. He longed to be baptized and to become a monk, but a law of the Empire imposed military service on the sons of veterans. As Martin always performed his duty well, he soon became an officer.

He was sent on garrison duty into Gaul (France), first to Rheims and then to Amiens. It was at the latter post, in the year 339, that Martin drew his sword, cut his splendid officer's cloak in two, and wrapped half of it around a naked beggar. That night as he slept, Martin saw the Saviour standing before him, wearing the half cloak with which the officer had covered the beggar. Martin was then still a catechumen; but immediately after that divine favor, "he flew to baptism," as an ancient biographer of the saint tells us.

When he was about twenty-five years of age, Martin was released from military service and became the disciple of the illustrious St. Hilary of Tours. That prelate ordained Martin exorcist, a function of vital importance in those times when Druids still carried on their cruel rites in the depths of Gaul's forests. Later, Martin founded a community of monks, and was ordained to the priesthood. Together with his monks, he evangelized the surrounding countryside. In the year 368, St. Hilary died. The people of Tours made Martin Hilary's successor, virtually by force.

As a bishop, Martin remained a monk, living in the greatest poverty. In caves outside the city he founded the monastery of Marmoutiers, where his monks preserved the literature of antiquity by their work as copyists. A seminary and a school for the Christian laity developed at Marmoutiers, under Martin's fostering care. Soon St. Martin's monastery became the mother house of similar foundations throughout Gaul.

But Martin was not merely an episcopal abbot of genius. He was, also, one of Europe's greatest missioners. In his time, most of the cities and towns of Gaul were already Christian; but Martin determined to root out the paganism of the French countryside. Tirelessly he journeyed all over Gaul. Prayer was his weapon, and no pagan stronghold was proof against it. Martin organized parish life throughout his diocese and far beyond. He assigned a priest to each country parish, and established the custom of episcopal visitations. The saint's Touraine became the model diocese for all of Gaul.

The beloved Bishop of Tours continued the marvelous works of his charity until he was past eighty years of age. His apostolic zeal was then as strong as ever. As he lay on his deathbed, St. Martin was so moved by the sight of his disciples' grief that he cried out, "Lord, if I am still necessary to my people, I do not refuse the labor."

A GREAT PRIEST

The Gradual of the Mass of the feast of St. Martin contains a sentence that says all: "Behold a great priest, who in his days pleased God."

ST. JOHN CHRYSOSTOM (*c. 344–407*)

In his *Studies in Saintship,* Ernest Hello wrote of St. John Chrysostom: "He was a universal man. He spent himself always, under all circumstances, for the benefit of all, in the cause of all. . . . Very few of the saints have been so beloved."

Fourth-century Constantinople thrilled to the eloquence of St. John, and the people called their great bishop "Chrysostom," or "Golden-Mouthed." But in his sermons, the Bishop of Constantinople condescended to the ordinary details of human life, with a tenderness that recalls the parables of his divine Master. No class of society was too lowly for St. John's loving solicitude.

Near his episcopal residence, the Bishop of Constantinople owned a house, the front door of which was always open to the poor and to wayfarers. One day a traveling Scythian decided to sample the Christian prelate's hospitality. Bishop John dropped in to visit with his guests, and soon noticed the stranger. He went over to get acquainted with him.

"Tell me, kind sir, why do you feed all these poor people, and even strangers like myself?" asked the Scythian.

"Remain as my guest for a few days, and I will endeavor to answer your questions fully," said the saint.

The Scythian was quite willing to remain, so the bishop told the stranger all about Christ. Before he left, the traveler asked for baptism. "I am returning to my country, and I will tell my people all about your house of hospitality and your Christian religion," he declared.

Of course St. John Chrysostom sent a missioner with his new convert. History records that the zealous prelate also sent missioners to the Persians in the south and to the Goths in the north. New

Catholics in pagan lands, as well as St. John's diocesan flock, mourned the death of the Christlike Patriarch of Constantinople, in the year 407.

REVERENCE FOR THE INDIVIDUAL SOUL

St. John Chrysostom esteemed every human being, however lowly his estate, because Jesus Christ suffered and died for the salvation of each man's precious soul. This great Churchman would have found ridiculous and fallacious, indeed, the concern of Marxian Communists for "collective humanity."

ST. AUGUSTINE OF HIPPO (*354–430*)

In North Africa, in the second half of the fourth century, St. Monica wept for the sins of her son, Augustine. A holy bishop consoled the grieving mother, saying, "Go your way, with the blessing of God; it cannot be that the child of those tears should perish."

God had endowed Augustine with a brilliant intellect and with lively and deep emotions. From his infancy, his mother had instilled into his heart the truths of Christian belief. But the lad fell into bad company while he was pursuing secular studies. The subsequent impurity of his life so dulled Augustine's keen intellect that he was drawn to the errors of the Manichaean heretics. In manhood Augustine became a professor of rhetoric; and in 383, he went to teach in Rome. In the following year, he went to Milan; and there, under the influence of the great St. Ambrose, the son of St. Monica was at length converted.

Augustine was then thirty-two years of age. His joy and repentance found utterance in the cry: "Too late have I loved Thee, O Beauty so ancient and so new! . . . O Love which always burnest and art never extinguished, true charity, my God, set me all on fire!"

St. Monica died soon after the conversion of the son of her prayers. Augustine returned to North Africa, where he was ordained to the priesthood at Hippo in the year 391. Later he was consecrated bishop and placed over the see of Hippo. Augustine became one of the most illustrious Churchmen of all the Christian ages. He was the author of a rule of religious life that greatly influenced the development of Western monasticism. Augustine was an inspired writer, and two of his works, the *Confessions* and the *City of God,* are reckoned among the world's classics.

It is not commonly realized that this brilliant Doctor of the Church was likewise an ardent missioner. In his personal experience, St. Augustine had known what it was to be plunged in the darkness of error and of sin. As Bishop of Hippo, the saint invited heretics, pagans, and Jews to his episcopal board. While he broke bread with those misbelievers, the saint spoke to them with burning charity of the peace of Christ.

"From my own experience, I can tell you, dear friends, that the heart of man is restless until it rests in God," the zealous apostle would say to his guests. No wonder that many of the guests later became converts!

St. Augustine left this earth on August 28, 430, while the fierce Vandals were besieging Hippo. He welcomed death, as a means of eternal union with Christ. "What love of Christ can that be, to fear lest He come, Whom you say you love?" asked the apostle on his deathbed.

ON MOURNING

In a letter of consolation to a member of his flock, St. Augustine wrote: "Because of Christ, death is no longer to be looked upon with fear as the destruction of human life. Nor should any one of those for whom very Life died, be mourned as if at death he had lost life. Before such divine consolations as these, human sadness blushes and melts away."

ST. NINIAN (*d. 432*)

In the fourth century, the northern provinces of Britain were still largely pagan, and there were no beautiful churches in that region. Early in life, Ninian, the son of a British prince, resolved to evangelize his native land. He made the difficult journey to Rome, and there the young Briton studied for the priesthood.

"If only we had beautiful churches like these in northern Britain, they would draw my people to the Faith," Ninian often said to himself, as he visited the stately ecclesiastical edifices in Rome.

In due time, Ninian was ordained to the priesthood. Later the Holy Father consecrated the Briton bishop, and sent him to labor in his native country. On the way back, Ninian stopped at Tours, in Gaul, where he and the great St. Martin became fast friends.

St. Martin shared Bishop Ninian's love for beautiful churches, so he said to his friend: "I'll lend you some of my stonemasons. They will direct your workmen, so that you may be able to erect a fine episcopal center in Britain."

Bishop Ninian established his center at Whithorn, in the south of Scotland. With the aid of St. Martin's stonemasons, he erected a striking cathedral, built of the white stone that was so abundant in the nearby hills. Close to the cathedral, a monastery was built and dedicated to St. Martin. Ninian called his episcopal center *Candida Casa,* or "White House." Then from the "White House," Bishop Ninian and his monks evangelized the northern Britons and the Picts in Scotland. So many converts were made that the pagan priests of the region moved away.

Until his death, in the year 432, St. Ninian told the people who came from far and near to admire the "White House": "You see how beautiful this cathedral is! But its beauty is as nothing, compared to the splendor of the God whom Christians worship there."

HE STUDIED THEIR NEEDS

It was not for his own prestige or that of his priests, that St. Ninian desired a fine episcopal center in Britain. His zeal for the conversion of his countrymen led him to choose a mission method adapted to their needs; and he knew that the splendor of God's house would lift up their aspiring souls to the Christians' beautiful God.

POPE ST. CELESTINE (*d. 432*)

St. Celestine never went on a missionary journey in search of souls, but he was a missioner nonetheless. He could not very well leave Rome, for he was Pope; but he spent much time planning the conversion of Ireland.

Even then, there must have been a few inhabitants of the green island who were Catholics, because we are told that Pope Celestine I sent the missioner, Palladius, as bishop "to the Irish who believed in Christ." But St. Palladius found mission work among the ancient Irish too difficult, so he crossed over into Scotland.

Pope Celestine was not discouraged. He selected another man to do the work that he could not perform himself. The second missioner whom Celestine sent to Ireland was St. Patrick. That great event in missionary annals occurred just three days before the Holy Father died.

But from heaven, St. Celestine saw his envoy winning the whole of Ireland to the Faith. Many churches and great monasteries soon covered the fair island, so that Ireland became known as the Land of Saints and Scholars. Then Celestine beheld hundreds of Irish missioners setting out for Scotland, England, and the continent of Europe. Surely we can say that Pope St. Celestine had a share in the wonderful results of the mission work done by St. Patrick.

THEY SEND THE MISSIONERS

The supreme planners of the campaign to make all men members of the Kingdom of God have always been the popes, Christ's vicars on earth. Catholics should be aware and justly proud of this glorious role taken by the successors of St. Peter.

ST. PATRICK (*c. 389–c. 493*)

Britain, Scotland, and France have all laid eager claim to "Succat, son of Calpurnius," as St. Patrick was called in his youth. Patrick himself tells us in his *Confession* that his father was a member of the municipal council of a Roman town and was prosperous enough to own a farm. Although Succat's nationality is not definitely known, the fact of his capture by Irish pirates is. When not quite sixteen years of age, the lad was taken from the grounds of his father's villa, carried overseas to Ireland, and there sold as a slave to a petty chieftain.

During six years, Succat herded the swine of his pagan master. In his lonely vigils, the slave "said a hundred prayers by day and almost as many by night." The resolution to serve God perfectly became the "fixed purpose of his soul," from which no subsequent obstacle was able to deflect him. When Succat was twenty-two years of age, he escaped and eventually made his way back to his family.

But the heart of the young man found no rest for thinking of the pagan Irish. Night after night he thought he heard them calling to him to come over and help them. Succat resolved to become a priest and a missioner to the Irish. He studied for the priesthood in France; but for a long while, his ecclesiastical superiors opposed his desire to evangelize Ireland. Succat was forty-five years of age when he was consecrated a bishop and commissioned to carry the Gospel to Ireland. Pope St. Celestine gave the new prelate the name of Patrick, or "Father of a People."

From his memories of the Irish, Bishop Patrick knew that bold methods of evangelization would serve best. He advanced on Tara, the residence of the High King, Laoghaire. In the presence of the proud pagan ruler, the saint dispelled a magic darkness caused by the Druid priests. "They can bring darkness, but they cannot bring light," Patrick told the amazed pagans.

King Laoghaire thought so highly of Patrick that he gave the apostle the freedom of his realm, to preach Christianity where and to whom the missioner would. Shortly afterward, the saint addressed vast multitudes at the national Fair of Taillte. He won thousands for Christ, and "all who looked on the face of Patrick loved him."

Thereafter, during nearly three decades, St. Patrick journeyed ceaselessly throughout Ireland. He labored with burning passion, and to us his works appear superhuman. He baptized hundreds of thousands with his own hands. Everywhere he left behind him churches, schools, and monasteries. One after another, the tribes of Ireland were reborn to Christ.

The apostle took with him on his endless journeys a group of likely candidates for the priesthood; these he trained simultaneously in practical mission work and in priestly studies. When Patrick founded a new church center, he nearly always had one member of this "hedge seminary" ready to become its pastor.

St. Patrick had an extraordinary zeal for the promotion of learning. He introduced the Roman alphabet, and he made the Latin tongue the ecclesiastical language of his adopted land. He taught his monks and nuns how to read and write. He sent young Irish overseas to study in France. It was the missionary genius of St. Patrick that made the Christian Irish the foremost scholars of the early Middle Ages.

As death was drawing near, Patrick installed his favorite disciple, Benignus, in the see of Armagh; then he gave himself wholly to prayer. One day he saw in a vision his beloved island entirely enveloped in heavenly brightness. God revealed to him that the fire of the love of Christ, which the missioner had kindled in the hearts of the Irish, would burn for all time. With this immense consolation in his soul, the Apostle of the Gaels passed to his eternal reward.

THE POWER OF EXAMPLE

The simple pagans of Ireland did not always understand St. Patrick's words; but they were invariably drawn by the most powerful sermon the saint ever preached, the example of his selfless life. He was "not deterred by cold, not possessed by hunger or thirst, sleeping on a bare stone, enduring great toil."

ST. SEVERINUS (*d. 476*)

Severinus was a hermit in the Eastern Empire, and he might have spent his days in peaceful contemplation. But his apostolic heart was stirred when he heard how the Christians in the West were suffering in the disorders caused by the decline of Rome. So Severinus journeyed far from his hermitage, and became a missioner in Austria.

The Eastern saint founded several monasteries in Austria. He led so severe a life that in winter he journeyed barefoot over the ice of the frozen Danube River. One day his errands of mercy took him to a town in the grip of a terrible famine. Severinus assured the people that, if they would do penance for their sins, God would send help. The saint's prayers moved God. Soon afterward the ice broke up on the Danube, and relief barges laden with food hurried from nearby cities.

Even the barbarians respected Severinus. When King Odoacer set out on his march against Rome, he went to the saint and asked for his blessing. "Go forward, my son," said Severinus. "Today you are still clad in the worthless skins of animals, but soon you will make gifts from the treasures of Italy."

After Odoacer had overthrown the Roman Empire of the West, he did not forget the missioner in Austria. The barbarian sent a messenger to Severinus, inviting the apostle to request some favor. The saint asked only Odoacer's pardon of an unfortunate man who had been condemned to banishment.

The holy life and many miracles of Severinus in Austria had but one aim: that more men should come to know, love, serve, and praise God. In the year 476, the saint lay dying in a monastery he had founded near Vienna. The weeping of his monks interrupted their prayers, so St. Severinus himself began to recite the psalms. With the words, "Let everything that breathes praise the Lord!" he passed away.

DEEPER UNION WITH GOD

The Imitation of Christ tells us that he who has true and perfect charity does not "desire to rejoice in himself; but above all things he wishes to be made happy in God." So it happened that after St. Severinus had sacrificed the peace of his hermitage in order to save the souls of others, he entered into a deeper and more joyous union with God, who is Charity.

ST. BRIGID (*c. 450–c. 525*)

St. Brigid, who became the beloved woman apostle of Ireland, was born while St. Patrick was converting her people. The child's father was a pagan of royal descent; her mother was a Christian bondmaid in her father's household. Soon the chief wife of Brigid's father became jealous of the bondmaid. "You pay too much attention to that slave and the daughter she bore you!" complained the spiteful woman daily.

In order to have peace, Brigid's father sold the little girl's mother into the service of a Druid priest. As Brigid grew into maidenhood, the Druid came to esteem her so greatly that he set free both the girl and her mother. Brigid returned to her father's house. What the chief's wife thought of that, we are not told.

Suitors came from far and near to woo the beautiful maiden, but she would accept no one. Brigid had a way of bestowing on the poor her father's most treasured possessions. Consequently that worthy chieftain did not object too much when Brigid gave up the world and built for herself a little habitation under a mighty oak tree. The people called it *Kil-dara,* or "Cell of the Oak."

There, under the direction of St. Patrick, St. Brigid founded a Sisterhood, whose object was to be teaching and other works of charity. In that early period of Christianity in Europe, Brigid began a great development of education for women. Not far away a monastery for men was established; and it, too, was under the rule of St. Brigid and her successors, the abbesses of Kildare.

Chieftains and illustrious Churchmen often sought the saint's advice, but Brigid remained unchanged by fame and honor. She founded schools for poor children and taught in them herself. She worked in the fields of the abbey, showing villagers improved methods of farming. Her name is associated with beautiful illuminations for books and also with Irish lacemaking.

Before St. Brigid's death, in 525, a sizable city had developed around the original little "Cell of the Oak." The fame of the great schools of Kildare had traveled to Britain and across the channel to Gaul. In Kildare's schools were trained those intrepid nuns who became co-workers of the seventh-century Irish missioners laboring among the Teutons on the continent of Europe.

THE HANDMAID OF THE LORD

The people of Ireland venerated in St. Brigid most of all her beautiful humility. At the height of her fame, she delighted to work in the fields and to help the poor in person. Thus Brigid merited her most glorious title, "Mary of the Gaels."

PART III

The Fertile Feudal Age

(496–1000)

THE migrations of peoples continued in the Feudal Age; and from the ninth century onward, fierce Norsemen raided the coasts of western Europe and the British Isles. But the greatest menace to European Christendom in its formative period arose in Arabia, which Mohammed (570–632) won over to his new religion. His fanatical followers, the Moslems, began a "holy war" immediately after his death. They overran Palestine, Syria, Mesopotamia, Persia, Armenia, Cyprus, and northern Africa.

In 711, the Moslems invaded Spain, pushing the Spanish Catholics who escaped massacre or serfdom into the foothills of the Pyrenees. Yet even before the end of this period, the heroic Spaniards began the Christian reconquest of their peninsula. The onrushing Moslem tide in western Europe was stemmed at Poitiers, in 732, by Charles Martel, ruler of the Christianized Franks.

As compensation for the loss of old centers of Christianity to the Moslems, the Faith spread rapidly among the vigorous semi-barbarians of Europe. Hardly had the Anglo-Saxon invaders of Britain been converted in the seventh century, than they sent missioners to the continent to join the Irish apostles. The Germanic peoples were brought into Christendom; even the conversion of the Norsemen was begun. Intrepid missioners also carried the Faith to the Slavs of central and eastern Europe. In these years, the Benedictine Rule superseded the harsher regulations of the Irish monasteries, and was recommended by Rome for western Europe.

The Christian Empire formed by Charlemagne (A.D. 800) decayed under his successors; but the attempt was revived by Otto I of Germany with the foundation of the Holy Roman Empire of the German Nation (A.D. 962). The times were so troubled in the closing years of the tenth century, that many persons lent credence to a prophecy which foretold the end of the world at midnight, 999. Nevertheless, these so-called Dark Ages were brimful of missionary zeal, and it proved difficult to make the following selections among a host of singlehearted apostles.

ST. CLOVIS (*d. 511*)

"Bow thy head," said St. Remy, Archbishop of Reims, to the royal convert. "Adore what thou hast burned, and burn what thou hast adored!"

It was Christmas Day, 496, and the great prelate was about to pour the waters of baptism on the Frankish King Clovis, the first Catholic sovereign of Gaul (France). At the same time, were baptized the sister of the young ruler and three thousand of his warriors.

Clovis looked about him at the hundreds of candles burning in the cathedral and the swirling clouds of incense. "Is this Paradise?" he asked.

The strong and courageous Clovis had been chosen as ruler of his people when he was only sixteen years of age. He had been lifted upon a shield by four warriors, while all the men made a great din on their armor with their lances, to signify their joy in having a brave, young leader to go before them in battle. Though King Clovis was at first a pagan, he was friendly to the Catholic bishops in Gaul. The bishops brought about his marriage with Clotilde, a devout Catholic Princess, because they hoped that she would convert her royal husband.

Clovis loved his beautiful, gentle wife; and to please her, he consented to the baptism of their son. As for himself, the young Frank hesitated to abandon the gods of his ancestors. Finally, in the course of a battle with the Alamanni, Clovis saw that his warriors were on the point of giving way. He prayed to the God of St. Clotilde, and promised to become a Christian if victory should be granted to him. The prayer of Clovis was granted; and so, on the anniversary of Christ's birth into this world for the redemption of mankind, the Frankish ruler was reborn into the Kingdom of Heaven.

A SINCERE CONVERT

The conversion of Clovis was humble and sincere. Upon the ruins of the Roman Empire, the first Catholic sovereign of France built a powerful Christian system, the influence of which dominated the civilization of western Europe during many centuries.

ST. BENEDICT, O.S.B. (*c. 480–c. 550*)

During his lifetime, St. Benedict foretold that his monastery on Monte Cassino would be destroyed by the fierce Lombards in the year 580. In the twentieth century, during the fury of World War II, that archmonastery of the West, founded by the gentle "Father of Peace," was again laid waste.

Benedict was born in about 480, in central Italy, in an age when barbarian invaders were plucking the feathers of the once-mighty Roman eagle. He was sent to Rome for his studies, but he was sickened by the decadent vice he encountered in the great city. So the fifteen-year-old youth fled to the lonely mountain region of Subiaco, where he lived in stark austerity in a cave. The fame of the young hermit's sanctity spread abroad, and many disciples flocked to Benedict. The saint built for them twelve small monasteries at Subiaco.

The founder of Western monasticism soon perceived that the manner of living of the Eastern monks was not suited to the Christianity of western Europe. He concluded that his subjects should live, not as solitaries, but in community, sanctifying themselves by obedience and by labor for the common good of souls. With the marked success of St. Benedict's monasteries at Subiaco came the inevitable jealousy and persecution on the part of neighboring clergy. So when Benedict was about forty-eight years of age, he left Subiaco for the region of Naples. There, on the crest of Monte Cassino, he founded his famed monastery to unite all his monks in one large abbey.

Before the saint was able to erect his monastery, he had to destroy the ancient temple of the god Apollo, on the summit of the mountain. The rustic and ignorant inhabitants of the countryside were still plunged in pagan superstition. By his preaching and his miracles, Benedict converted the pagan devotees of Apollo to the worship of the true God. Then the walls of his monastery arose, to overlook and bless the whole surrounding countryside.

At Monte Cassino, Benedict ruled his monks with discretion, "the mother of virtues." "He so tempered all things, that the strong might have something to strive after, and the weak nothing at which to take alarm." The beloved founder died in about the year 550.

The Rule of St. Benedict was one of the most potent factors in building the civilization of Christian Europe. After having raised Europe from the darkness and ruin that followed the downfall of the Roman Empire, St. Benedict's missionary monks went forth into the whole world to combat paganism with the light of Christ. Ever since the foundation of their ancient order, the Benedictines have been among the foremost missioners of the worldwide Church.

STRAIGHT IS THE WAY

In his *Holy Rule,* St. Benedict warned his novices that there is no wide and easy way to heaven. "By the hard and rugged ways alone, lies the journey to the pastures of God," he wrote.

ST. MARTIN OF BRAGA (*d. 580*)

In God's plan, it fell to St. Martin of Braga to make Christ's words known in the sixth century to the people of Gallaecia (Galicia), in northwestern Spain. When Martin arrived in that region as a missioner, he preached the message of the Gospel with such power that it filled every corner of the land. And the apostle's life was so well patterned after the teachings of his divine Master that he convinced his listeners. The Suevi of Gallaecia had been half pagan, or else plunged in Arian heresy; but they heeded Martin's preaching and became members of the true Faith.

Where did Martin come from? He was a native of Pannonia (Hungary), in central Europe, and when a young man, he had gone to Palestine on a pilgrimage. While Martin was in the Holy Land, God called him to the monastic life. After the young man had become a monk, he met some pilgrims from Gallaecia, who persuaded him that Spain had greater need of his labors than had Palestine.

Martin arrived in Gallaecia in 550, and he introduced monasticism throughout northwestern Spain. He was a learned scholar, and several of his highly interesting writings are still extant. St. Martin became the first Archbishop of Braga. Centuries later, Braga was a city in the new country of Portugal. Portuguese Catholics look up to St. Martin of Braga as their patron. Who could watch over them better than the apostle who first brought the Faith in its purity to their land?

UNSTINTED GIVING

St. Martin of Braga was happy in his monastic life in Palestine; but when he heard of needy souls in the far-distant Iberian peninsula, he knew no rest. Unhesitatingly he offered himself to Christ for this new, more arduous service, and thus he laid firmly the Catholic foundations of a nation then unborn.

ST. CADOC (*d. c. 590*)

Have you ever wondered what became of the Christians of Romanized Britain when the fierce Anglo-Saxon invaders overran their country to the accompaniment of fire, sword, and sacrilege? The story is a sad one.

The Britons who were not either slaughtered or enslaved were driven into the mountain fastnesses of Wales, into Cornwall, or across the Channel into Brittany. The Anglo-Saxons burned churches, broke the sacred stones of the altars, and murdered the pastors along with their flocks. In the year 586, the last two bishops who had remained among the invaders, those of London and of York, fled from their churches to the sanctuary of Wales. East of Wales and Cornwall, Britain was in the power of idolators.

Within Wales, as if in compensation for the destruction of Catholic life in the Anglo-Saxon kingdoms, the sixth century was one of great monastic foundations. Among the most renowned of the abbots was St. Cadoc, founder of the illustrious abbey at Llancarvan, where the sons of kings and chiefs were educated. The subjects of the venerated abbot were thrown into consternation when their founder announced his imminent departure for Anglo-Saxon regions.

"Who will minister to the other parts of Britain, if all the priests remain in Catholic Wales?" asked the saint. "And how shall any of the pagan invaders learn about Christ, if missioners do not go to them?"

So, the intrepid abbot went to minister to Britons of the Saxon settlements in the county of Northampton. There, while he was celebrating Mass, St. Cadoc was martyred by a band of Saxon cavalry, around the year 590.

THE MANY NOT OF CHRIST'S FOLD

St. Cadoc knew that the Good Shepherd is solicitous above all for the many sheep not yet of His fold. The great Welsh monastic founder accordingly laid down his life to hasten the day when there will be One fold and One Shepherd for all mankind.

ST. COLUMBA (*c. 521–597*)

In the hearts of the Irish, St. Columba is enshrined with St. Patrick and St. Brigid. Columba was of royal stock. He studied under St. Finian in the great school of Clonard. After his ordination to the priesthood, Columba undertook extraordinary missionary activity. He journeyed and preached incessantly; and in addition, he founded in northern Ireland thirty flourishing monasteries.

When the saint was forty-two years of age, he was exiled for political reasons. A small wicker boat, covered with hides, carried Columba and his twelve companions northward. They landed on the island of Iona, in the southern Hebrides, and there St. Columba founded what was to become the most celebrated of his monasteries. Many recruits went to Iona from Ireland. Eventually Columba's monks carried the gospel message to the most remote regions of Scotland, and he himself shared in that work of evangelization.

When Columba was in the monastery at Iona, he wrote much, chiefly copying Scripture. Thus the holy missioner lived to the age of seventy-six. On the last day of his life, in the year 597, the saint ascended the hill that rose above the monastery. He looked long on the Christian stronghold he had founded – and perhaps he had a vision of his glorious sons who were to convert the northern English.

From that hilltop, St. Columba blessed his monastery, saying: "Small and mean though this place is, yet it shall be held in great honor, not only by the Irish kings and people; but also by the rulers of foreign and barbarous nations, and by their subjects."

HOLY IN WORK

Adamnan, abbot of Iona, wrote his vivid biography of St. Columba while eyewitnesses of the founder's life still survived. Adamnan recorded of the Irish apostle that he was "angelic of aspect, clean in speech, holy in work, and great in council."

ST. KENTIGERN (*d. A.D. 603*)

When St. Kentigern was a young man, he journeyed far into the mountains of Scotland and fell in love with the hardy Picts. For many months, he planned ways to bring these scattered people into the Church.

One day the apostle came upon a cave located near a spot where two rivers met, and he took up his dwelling there. His furniture consisted of leaves and grasses, heaped up on the stone floor for a bed. He wore the skins of the animals that he had killed for food. Most of his days were spent in prayer, and many of his nights, too.

Curious passers-by stopped to speak to the stranger. Kentigern greeted them all kindly. Soon through the hills sped news of this amiable stranger who lived in a cave. Many rough mountaineers visited Kentigern. They discovered that he was a teacher of religion. What he said did not make a great impression; but the holiness of his life, and his kindness, convinced the Picts that the hermit was close to God.

Several of Kentigern's admirers built simple shelters near his cave. Gradually more and more people followed their lead. Before long, a small town grew up around the missioner's dwelling place. Every town has to have a name, so Kentigern's disciples asked him to name their settlement. The saint named the little town near the two rivers *Glasgu,* which means "dear family." Today, when we hear of the famous city of Glasgow, it ought to remind us of the "dear family of souls" that St. Kentigern brought into the Church of God so long ago.

THE CAUSES OF DECAY

Many place names in Europe are a clear indication of the Christian origin of Western civilization. The mother continent of our culture is in sore straits today, because the noxious pests of materialism and atheistic Communism have attacked its life-giving Christian roots.

POPE ST. GREGORY THE GREAT, O.S.B.
(*c. 540–604*)

It was characteristic of St. Gregory that he should have been the first pope to sign himself habitually, "Servant of the servants of God." Gregory had the simplicity of true greatness, which the average man can readily understand, admire, and strive to imitate. For that reason, he set his stamp on a whole era of European history.

Bossuet, the renowned seventeenth-century French Churchman and orator, summed up St. Gregory's achievements as follows: "This great Pope subdued the Lombards, saved Rome and Italy though the Emperors gave him no help, repressed the upstart pride of the patriarchs of Constantinople, enlightened the whole Church by his teaching, governed both East and West with vigor and humility, and gave to the world a perfect pattern of pastoral rule." But strangely enough, Bossuet forgot to mention the chief labor of love of Gregory's whole life, that is, the winning of the Anglo-Saxons to Christ.

Gregory came of an ancient, wealthy, and deeply Catholic Roman family. On his ancestral estates, he founded seven monasteries. In one of them, St. Andrew's on the Coelian Hill, Gregory himself became a Benedictine monk, in the year 575. Thereafter the monk's works of mercy took him often to the Roman market place; and there one day he saw, exposed for sale, three fair-haired, rosy-cheeked, blue-eyed boys from faraway Yorkshire, in England. From that day onward, Gregory was haunted by the bright faces of a people who dwelt in spiritual darkness.

By incessant pleas, the saint wrung from the Pope permission to become a missioner to the Angles. He was actually on his way, when the Roman people discovered the departure of their favorite monk. They hastened to St. Peter's and clamored for Gregory's return. The Holy Father yielded to their desire and recalled the would-be missioner.

In the year 589, St. Gregory himself was elected Pope. He had not ceased to think of his Angles; and in the sixth year of his pontificate, he was informed of conditions in England that appeared favorable for the realization of his long-cherished hopes. Pope Gregory chose as the pioneer missioners to the Anglo-Saxons forty monks of St. Andrew's; and he appointed as their leader Augustine, the prior of that monastery. The missionary monks set out bravely for the unknown perils of a totally unexpected apostolate. However, on their journey across Gaul, they became terrified by gruesome tales of the savage cruelty of the Anglo-Saxons; and they persuaded Augustine to return to Rome, to plead with the Pope for their recall.

Gregory sent Augustine back to his monks with a strong letter of encouragement. "The more you have to suffer, the brighter will be your glory eternally," wrote the saint. "If I cannot share your toil as your fellow worker, I shall at least be able to rejoice in your harvest. For God knows I lack not the good will to work."

In 597, St. Augustine sent word to Pope Gregory that the Faith was firmly planted in Kent, the southeastern kingdom of the Anglo-Saxon heptarchy. "Glory be to God in the highest!" exulted the great Pope to whom history has accorded the title, "Apostle of the English."

CONCERNING MIRACLES

Pope St. Gregory the Great wrote of miracles: "The true value of life is in works of virtue, not in miracles; and there are many saints who, though they do not work miracles, are just as good as those who do."

ST. AUGUSTINE OF CANTERBURY, O.S.B. (*d. 604*)

Nothing is known of the early life of St. Augustine of Canterbury; but unless he had been a man of outstanding sanctity and ability, Pope Gregory would never have entrusted to him the initiation of the conversion of the Anglo-Saxons. Augustine was to manifest a perfect obedience to his great master, and a prudently firm judgment in the execution of Gregory's directions.

In the year 597, King Ethelbert of Kent went to the Isle of

Thanet, off the northeastern corner of his kingdom, to receive the Benedictine monks sent by Pope St. Gregory.

"The leader of the monks is a fine, stately man," said Ethelbert to his consort, Queen Bertha, the Christian daughter of the Frankish ruler of Paris. "Why, he is a head taller than most of my people!"

Ethelbert provided shelter and food for the Italian monks, and he gave them liberty to preach everywhere in his kingdom. After he had been convinced by the fervor and the holy simplicity of the monks' lives that the Christian religion was the real Faith, Ethelbert sought instruction and was baptized. Many of his subjects followed their ruler's example, but this noblehearted convert would not force anyone to change his belief.

On their first Christmas Day in England, Augustine and his monks baptized in the Thames River more than ten thousand inhabitants of Kent. Ethelbert transformed his own palace into a monastery for the Benedictines; and he built nearby a basilica called "Christ Church." That basilica was to become the metropolitan church of England. When Pope Gregory received word of the success of his monks in Kent, he sent to Augustine new missioners, church supplies, and books for the beginning of an ecclesiastical library.

Gregory counseled Augustine to show a wise and generous indulgence toward his new converts. "It is impossible to change all at once all the habits of the savage mind," wrote the missionary Pontiff.

Until his death, St. Augustine, the first Archbishop of Canterbury, continued his arduous journeys on foot, adding to his preaching, good works, and frequent miracles. With the aid of St. Ethelbert, the Faith was introduced into the neighboring realm of Essex. One of Augustine's monks was consecrated Bishop of London.

St. Augustine died in the year 604. A century and a half later, a synod of English prelates directed that Augustine's name should be invoked in the litanies after that of St. Gregory: "Because it is he who, sent by our Father Gregory, first carried to the English nation the Sacrament of Baptism and the knowledge of the heavenly country."

STRONG IN OBEDIENCE

The apostolate of St. Augustine among the English was blessed by God because of the Italian missioner's entire obedience to Pope St. Gregory, the vicar of Christ. Thus Augustine built in England according to the precept of his divine Master, who said: "Thou art Peter, and upon this rock, I will build My Church."

ST. COLUMBAN (*c. 545–615*)

"Must you cross over into Gaul and go roaming about in its vast forests?" a princely relative asked St. Columban. "We need, right here in Ireland, scholars who can write in faultless Latin."

"Ireland does need such scholars," admitted Columban. "But as for me, my heart will never be at rest until I cross the waters and become a wanderer for Christ."

So, in the sixth century, St. Columban and twelve other monks carried the torch of their Faith over into Gaul. At that time, the Christianization of the Franks was merely dawning. The country was covered by immense new forests, under which the ruins of the Gallo-Roman settlements had all but disappeared.

The greatest of the monasteries founded in Gaul by St. Columban himself was the illustrious one at Luxeuil, near the modern city of Besançon. After the saint's death, his disciples at Luxeuil founded a chain of monasteries stretching from the Lake of Geneva to the coast of the North Sea. Candidates for the monastic life flocked to Columban's monasteries, and the cloisters became training schools for Frankish priests. Peasant settlements sprang up around the monastic centers of religion, civilization, and agriculture, so that devastated Gaul began to flourish.

St. Columban was fearless in reproaching the semibarbaric Merovingian rulers for their vices. This led to the banishment of the intrepid Irishman. He and all his Celtic brethren were ordered to go back to Ireland.

"No," replied Columban. "After having left my country for the service of Jesus Christ, I cannot think that my Creator means me to return."

Columban led his little band of exiled Irish monks into the wilds of Germany and Switzerland. As they journeyed, the missioners preached and made converts. On the shores of Lake Constance, St. Columban felt a strong desire to go farther east, to carry the light of the Gospel to the pagan Slav nations. But instead, an angel of God directed his steps into northern Italy, where dwelt the Lombards, at that time fierce Arian heretics.

In spite of his heresy, Agilulf, the ruler of the Lombards, received the venerable exile with respect. He bestowed upon Columban the territory of Bobbio, in a secluded gorge of the Apennines, between Genoa and Milan. The old missioner carried enormous beams of fir wood along the perpendicular mountain paths, for the building of his last monastery. Columban made Bobbio a citadel of the Faith against the Arian heretics. For over a thousand years, Bobbio remained the light of northern Italy.

After completing his final monastery, the aged St. Columban discovered near Bobbio a rock cavern, which he transformed into a chapel dedicated to the Blessed Virgin. There he fasted and prayed; and there, on November 23, 615, the tireless wanderer for Christ rested in the Lord.

PRAYER FOR ENEMIES

In the time of St. Columban, the fierce, corrupt members of the Merovingian royal family were murdering one another. A Frankish monk asked Columban to pray for one king, and against this king's murderous rival. The saint replied: "Your counsel is foolish and unholy. Nor is it according to the will of God, who bade us pray for our enemies."

ST. ISIDORE OF SEVILLE (*c. 560–636*)

Fourteen years after the death of St. Isidore of Seville, the bishops of Spain were gathered in council, and part of their meeting was devoted to the praise of the deceased prelate in these words:

"Isidore, the late ornament of the Catholic Church . . . the most learned man given to enlighten our times . . . he is to be named with reverence."

Bishop Isidore was indeed a man of uncommon learning, for he compiled an encyclopedia that stored up for future ages the rich treasures of the fallen Roman Empire. Having mastered Latin, Greek, and Hebrew, St. Isidore was the best scholar of his day. He introduced the study of Aristotle; and in 633, he was responsible for the decree of the Council of Toledo that there should be a liberal arts school in every diocese of Spain.

The Bishop of Seville also originated much of the ecclesiastical legislation of the period. A contemporary of the saint declared that Isidore was the man who saved Spain from barbarism.

This learned bishop was likewise a great missioner. He had succeeded his elder brother, St. Leander, in the see of Seville; and it was during the episcopate of Leander that the Visigothic conquerors of Spain had renounced Arian heresy in favor of Catholicism. St. Isidore labored untiringly to complete the conversion of the tall, blond barbarians. The saint did his work so well that when the Mohammedan Moors overran Spain in the year 711, they were unable to uproot the Faith from the hearts of its people.

Bishop Isidore also concerned himself with the conversion of the numerous Jews in the peninsula. He nobly protested the use of force in leading the Jews to baptism. St. Isidore is one of the great Doctors of the Church, and a glory of Roman Catholicism in Spain.

TRUE CHRISTIAN DEMOCRACY

In his writings on the religious life, St. Isidore of Seville said that not even slaves were debarred from admission to the monasteries. "God has made no difference between the soul of the slave and the soul of the freedman," he stated. True Christian democracy renounces, also, all manner of racial and social discrimination.

ST. GALL (*d. c. 640*)

"Suffer me, dear master, to remain in this country. Since I am able to preach in the German tongue, I have hopes of winning many of these idolators." So, in the year 612, St. Gall pleaded with his leader, St. Columban, after the latter had informed his disciples that he was about to pass over the Alps into northern Italy.

There can be no doubt that Columban was loath to part with one of his most talented and faithful monks. Gall was one of the twelve original disciples who had accompanied St. Columban to Gaul. In 610, when Columban had been banished from Gaul for having vehemently condemned the vices of the Merovingian rulers, Gall had followed his master on the voyage up the Rhine into Switzerland. But finally, after performing together so many labors for souls, the two Irish missioners had come to the parting of the ways.

Our Lord blessed St. Gall's decision. The Irish apostle converted many pagans of the country we know today as Switzerland. After the saint's death, a church bearing his name was erected on the spot where the Irish missioner had established his hermitage. Before the middle of the eighth century, the church erected to the memory of St. Gall became a monastery. Many benefactions were bestowed on the new monastery by the Frankish ruler, Charles Martel, and by his son, Pepin. Before long, the Monastery of St. Gall became one of the most famous in all Christendom, and so it remained up to the time of the Protestant upheaval.

The town that grew up around the monastery is now one of the chief manufacturing centers in Switzerland. It still bears the name of the Irish wanderer for Christ who, more than thirteen centuries ago, ended in that far country his amazing journey in quest of souls.

GOD'S CALL COMES FIRST

There was no self-seeking in St. Gall's decision to remain in Switzerland. Indeed, had he followed his natural inclination, he would have gone with the spiritual leader he loved so dearly. But he had heard unmistakably God's call to mission labors among the Swiss, so he found the courage to hurt his best friend on earth.

ST. PAULINUS OF YORK, O.S.B. (*d. 644*)

In the year 601, Pope St. Gregory sent to Canterbury, as additional helpers of St. Augustine, the monks Mellitus, Justus, and Paulinus. Mellitus was later consecrated Bishop of London; and Justus, Bishop of Rochester. The pious King Ethelbert of Kent died in the year 616. He left a daughter, whose hand was sought in marriage by King Edwin, pagan ruler of Northumbria, the largest kingdom of the Anglo-Saxon heptarchy. The monk Paulinus was consecrated Bishop of York and was sent north to keep guard over the Christian bride.

King Edwin was quite content to leave his Christian wife to the practice of her religion. The ruler was, moreover, attracted to Bishop Paulinus, an ascetic whose worn face was full of spiritual light and fire. But Edwin was not easily persuaded to abandon the gods of his forefathers hastily. It was only after prolonged instructions that Bishop Paulinus won his royal convert. King Edwin was baptized on Easter Sunday, in the year 627. For thirty-six days previously, Paulinus had been instructing hundreds of Edwin's subjects and baptizing them in the Rivers Glen and Swale.

There followed a time of great prosperity for Northumbria. King Edwin was at peace with all men, and he ruled in a most Christian spirit. Paulinus was made Archbishop of York, and received the pallium from Pope Honorius. It seemed as if St. Gregory's hopes for the Angles were at last about to be fulfilled.

But the very prosperity of Edwin's realm aroused the jealous hatred of Cadwallon, the Welsh ruler, who was Christian in name only. Cadwallon allied himself with Penda, pagan ruler of central England; and the two proceeded to attack King Edwin. The armies met in Yorkshire, in the year 633; and St. Edwin fell in the first encounter. The Church honors him as a martyr. Penda and Cadwallon then cruelly ravaged Northumbria.

It was not safe for Queen Ethelburga to remain in her dead husband's realm. Archbishop Paulinus entrusted to his faithful deacon, James, the care of his scattered and decimated flock; then he conducted back to Kent the royal widow. At that time the see of Rochester was vacant, so Paulinus administered it until his death, in the year 644. To this day, the English nation venerates St. Paulinus as one of its principal Fathers in Christ.

THE FACE OF A SAINT

The words of an old Northumbrian pagan have come down to us, telling us why the people of northern England took so strongly to St. Paulinus: "His worn face was full of spiritual light and fire."

ST. AIDAN (*d. 651*)

"What does it matter if you cannot yet speak well the language of the Anglo-Saxons?" said King Oswald of Northumbria to Bishop Aidan. "I will translate to the earls and thanes of my court all your sermons in the Celtic tongue."

Oswald and Aidan were rivals in ardent zeal for the conversion of souls. As a prince, King Oswald had been baptized at the great Monastery of Iona, founded in the Hebrides Islands by the Irish monk, St. Columba. When Oswald had ascended the throne of Northumbria, in the year 635, he requested the abbot of Iona to send him Celtic missioners for his kingdom. Aidan, a gentle and lovable Irish monk from Iona, was then consecrated Bishop of Northumbria.

Bishop Aidan chose, as the monastic capital of Northumbria, the small, barren island of Lindisfarne, not far from the Firth of Forth. The "cathedral" at Lindisfarne was built entirely of wood, and its roof was covered with coarse sea grasses. The dwellings of the monks were primitive, and the community had neither money nor cattle. St. Aidan refused the offer of a horse and journeyed constantly on foot. The Irish missioner was zealous in rebuking the sins of the powerful, but he was tender and loving to the lowly oppressed. Indifferent to worldly goods, he gave away in alms all that he received from rulers and rich men.

Aidan redeemed innumerable slaves. He instructed those freedmen and raised a number of them to the priesthood. The saintly missioner took special interest in the education of English youths in the monasteries founded by him. One of his first cares was to train twelve young Englishmen for the priesthood. Of those twelve, at least one later became a bishop.

After a while the prosperity of King Oswald's Christianized kingdom excited the rage of the pagan Penda, ruler of Mercia, in central England. King Penda again made war on Northumbria; and in the ensuing fierce battle, St. Oswald was slain, in the flower of his years. But the pitiless Penda was not satisfied: he continued to ravage Northumbria for thirteen years longer.

One day, when Bishop Aidan was at prayer, he saw black smoke and jets of flame above the royal fortress of Bamborough. Lifting his eyes to heaven, the saint cried, "My God, behold all the evil that Penda does us!" At the same moment the wind changed, and the flames whirled around upon the besiegers. Penda thereupon abandoned the siege of a fortress so evidently under the protection of the Christian God.

In the year 651, St. Aidan suddenly fell ill during one of his countless mission journeys. The heroic monk-bishop died with his head resting against a buttress of a church that he had just completed. After the death of their great leader, the Celtic monks of Lindisfarne continued the evangelization of a large part of Anglo-Saxon England.

A PASSIONATE LOVE OF GOODNESS

In his *Ecclesiastical History of the English Nation,* St. Venerable Bede wrote of St. Aidan: "He was a pontiff inspired with a passionate love of goodness; but at the same time full of a surpassing gentleness and moderation."

ST. DYMPNA (*Seventh Century*)

When the Irish missioners began to evangelize the Germanic peoples on the Continent, they very soon discovered that the men could not be won over unless the women were previously converted. So the Celtic apostles brought over nuns from Ireland. Among those pioneer women missioners was a young nun by the name of Dympna. She loved children, and she had great success in teaching the essentials of Christian doctrine to a group of backward little ones. In the midst of that Christlike work, the children's saint was martyred.

After the missionary nun's martyrdom, the grateful Belgian mothers of the backward children erected a shrine to St. Dympna in Gheel, and there they continued to invoke her aid. It became a custom, which lasted through the centuries, to place backward children in the charge of families who lived near St. Dympna's Church. In our own day, the care of backward children at Gheel is under the supervision of the Belgian Government.

HER CHARITY LIVES ON

No known record exists of how St. Dympna looked, of who her parents were, or of the exact year in which she laid down her young life for Christ. But because her charity was of God, its memory lives on and is blessed today by Catholics invoking her compassionate aid for the mentally ill.

ST. WILFRID, O.S.B. (*d. 709*)

St. Wilfrid belonged by birth to the highest nobility of Northumbria. At an early age, he obtained royal permission to become a monk at Lindisfarne, the famous monastery founded by St. Aidan. In some way, Wilfrid discovered that the Celtic rules and traditions of Lindisfarne did not in all points conform to those of Rome; and he verified his discoveries by a daring pilgrimage to the Holy See. On his return to Northumbria, Wilfrid was made abbot of the monastery at Ripon; and soon afterward, he was chosen Bishop of York and of all Northumbria.

Later the gifted prelate founded other Benedictine monasteries. He introduced into northern England Gregorian music and Continental church architecture. Meanwhile, he made bitter enemies by his unrelenting war on the Celtic customs. A number of his enemies were in high places, so he was obliged to spend much of his life in exile. It was during those painful periods of exile that Bishop Wilfrid became a great missioner.

In 678, while the exiled saint was on his way to appeal to Rome, a west wind bore his ship to the low and marshy shores of Friesland, in Holland. The courageous bishop spent a whole winter sowing the seeds of Christian Faith among the pagan inhabitants of that bleak country. Thus to Wilfrid belongs the distinction of having been the first English foreign missioner.

At one time, the saint extended and consolidated the Faith in the English kingdom of Mercia, but later he was hounded out of Northumbria, Mercia, and Wessex. The pagan Saxons of Sussex then harbored the illustrious wanderer. At once the apostolic prelate undertook the evangelization of his hosts. The whole population of Sussex embraced the Faith, which was also introduced into the Isle of Wight. In this wise, the conversion of Anglo-Saxon England was completed by an intrepid Churchman who was one of her own sons.

Wilfrid died in the year 709. No sooner had the tireless soldier of God completed his good fight, than he appeared to the eyes of all the English in his true light – as a heroic apostle and a great saint.

NATIONAL TRAITS CAN BE SUPERNATURALIZED

Great work for Christ and souls can be accomplished, when national traits are supernaturalized by uniting them with God's will. St. Wilfrid, acting in obedience to the Holy Spirit, put to glorious use his English traits: tenacious courage, patient and indomitable energy, and a dogged resolve to fight to the death for his ideals, his honor, and his Christian rights.

ST. RUPERT, O.S.B. (*d. c. 718*)

St. Rupert was driven out of his German see of Worms, largely because he was a Frenchman. But God had prepared a welcome for the missionary bishop in a neighboring territory. The Duke of Bavaria was a recent convert to Christianity. His dukedom had been long without a sufficient number of priests, and the people had reverted to many pagan superstitions. The duke had heard his sister speak of the holiness and the wisdom of the missioner whom Worms had rejected, so he sent messengers to invite Rupert to Bavaria.

Bishop Rupert was happy to accept this invitation. With power he set about the work of restoring Bavaria's Christianity. As the site for a new cathedral, the Duke of Bavaria gave the saint the old, ruined Roman town of Juvavum. Around the cathedral a new, prosperous town grew up. Bishop Rupert named it "Salzburg."

At Salzburg St. Rupert founded the great Benedictine monastery of St. Peter. He also built, on the site of an ancient Roman fort, the nunnery of Nonnberg, over which he placed his niece, St. Erentraud. The monastery and convent were staffed with monks and nuns from France. Working out from this center, the bishop and his helpers won city after city back to the practice of the Faith. Soon new churches and monasteries were springing up all over Bavaria.

The date of St. Rupert's death appears to have been the year 718. Although it is not certain just when that zealous missionary died, there is no doubt at all that he deserves to be called the Apostle of Bavaria and Austria.

THE CLOSEST TIES

More than once, as was the case with St. Rupert, monastic founders were aided by near relatives in their work for God and souls. The ties thus created by union in God's service were far closer than those of kinship itself.

ST. WILLIBRORD, O.S.B. (*c. 658–744*)

Willibrord, the son of noble Northumbrian parents, was a Benedictine monk in the abbey at Ripon, which had been founded by St. Wilfrid. "I, too, will preach the Gospel to the pagans, after the example of our holy founder," declared the ardent young Willibrord.

When Willibrord was thirty-three years of age, he did realize his missionary longings. He was assigned to lead eleven Benedictine companions in the evangelization of Friesland. The little missionary band placed itself under the protection of Pepin of Héristal, the powerful ruler of the Franks. Then Willibrord journeyed to Rome, to obtain the Pope's authority for his labors.

As the years passed, the Anglo-Saxon Benedictines made numerous converts. In 694, the Holy Father consecrated Willibrord Bishop of Friesland. The saint was installed in the see of Utrecht. He and his priests would have made even greater headway among the pagans, had it not been for the fact that, in the minds of the Frisians, Christianity was linked with Frankish conquests. At one time, Willibrord attempted a spiritual invasion of Denmark. But he found the Danish ruler "more ferocious than any wild beast and harder than any stone."

Bishop Willibrord labored on for half a century in Friesland until his death in 744. When St. Venerable Bede wrote his *Ecclesiastical History,* Willibrord was still living, "venerable for old age, having been thirty-five years a bishop, and sighing after the rewards of the heavenly life, after the many spiritual conflicts which he had waged."

LOYALTY TO ROME

The early English missioners were outstanding in their obedient dependence on the vicar of Christ. St. Venerable Bede tells us that St. Willibrord made haste to Rome at the very outset of his missionary work among the Frisians, to obtain the blessing and the instructions of the Holy Father.

ST. BONIFACE, O.S.B. (*c. 675–755*)

St. Boniface, the Apostle of Germany, was an Englishman, born near Exeter, around the year 675. He entered the Benedictine Order at an early age; and in the monastery, he acquired renown for his learning and his strong, serene character. In the gifted monk's heart, there grew a desire to preach the Gospel to the pagans of "Old Saxony," the land of his forefathers.

When Boniface was about forty years of age, he led a little group of missioners to Friesland. But just then, the Frisians had risen in rebellion against the Franks. Though Boniface made a favorable impression on Radbod, the fierce ruler of Friesland, the Anglo-Saxon missioner saw that nothing could be accomplished for the time being in the disturbed district. The saint and his companions sailed back to England.

In 718, St. Boniface again left England, never to return. He journeyed with his helpers to Rome. There, the apostles from England were warmly received by a mission-minded Pontiff, Gregory II. Gregory blessed the undertaking of St. Boniface, instructed him to conform to the rules of the Roman liturgy, and to refer all difficult cases encountered in his apostolate to the decision of the Holy See.

After having left Rome, Boniface returned for a time to Friesland, where he converted many pagans. Then he founded a missionary center in Germany, in Hesse, where no apostle had previously labored. In 722, Gregory II called Boniface to Rome and consecrated him bishop. Soon after his return to Germany, Boniface made a frontal attack on paganism by boldly cutting down the sacred oak of Thor, near Fritzlar, in Hesse. After the Faith had been firmly rooted in Hesse, Boniface revived Christianity in Thuringia and in Bavaria. He planted monasticism solidly in German soil; and to aid him in that vital undertaking, he summoned to Germany many English monks and nuns.

Gregory III, the successor of Gregory II, ordered Boniface to hold Church councils north of the Alps. The ecclesiastical assemblies over which the great missioner presided as Papal Legate in Germany and in Frankland were of prime importance for the development of the Church in Europe. They restored the fecundity of the Frankish Church; and they opened up, for the hierarchy of both Frankland and Germany, effective channels of communication with Rome.

Boniface never had the consolation of including among his immense labors the evangelization of those Saxons who were "of his own flesh and blood." But in his old age, he did return to the pagans of Friesland. To his sorrowing disciples in Germany, the saint said: "I am going. I cannot give up this long-desired journey. My last day is drawing near; soon, delivered from the prisonhouse of this body, I shall depart to gather the eternal reward."

In Friesland, the apostle and his companions baptized a great number of pagans. On June 4, 755, Boniface was near the sea, at a place named Dokkum. He had arranged to confirm there some of his recent converts. While the missioners awaited the arrival of the neophytes, they were suddenly attacked by fanatical idolaters. Boniface and fifty-two of his helpers were brutally martyred.

In addition to his gigantic labors for Germany, St. Boniface had helped to render cordial the relations between the Frankish rulers and the Papacy. More than any other man, he had prepared the way for the Frankish protection of the Holy See, for the donation by Pepin the Short of the Papal States, and for the Pope's coronation of Charlemagne as Emperor of the West.

MESSENGER OF IMMORTALITY

On the base of the noble statue of the English Boniface at Fulda, in Germany, is the inscription: "The word of the Lord endureth forever" (1 Pet. 1:25).

ST. LIOBA, O.S.B. (*d. c. 779*)

In the eighth century, a young Benedictine nun at Wimburn, England, was writing a letter to her illustrious relative in Germany, the great St. Boniface. With the enthusiasm and simplicity of youth, Sister Lioba begged Boniface not to forget her mother and herself. "May I myself, though unworthy, merit to have you as a brother? There is no other man in my family who possesses my confidence as you do," she said.

Some years later, in 748, St. Boniface requested the abbess of Wimburn to send a group of her nuns to be his co-workers in Germany. In his request, the apostle made special mention of Sister Lioba, his young kinswoman. The talented and gracious Lioba became the best known of all Boniface's women helpers. She had been baptized "Truthgeba"; but she so won the hearts of all who knew her that she was generally called "Lioba" – or "Beloved."

At Wimburn, Lioba had been noted for her diligence, her zeal in the study of Scripture, and her all-embracing charity. In Germany, Boniface made her Abbess of Bischofsheim, on the Tauber River. He also gave her authority over his other monasteries of women, in order that she might train all the German nuns to the correct observance of the Benedictine Rule. With all her gentleness, Lioba was a woman of strong courage. She was careful to impose nothing upon others that she herself did not first practice.

The Anglo-Saxon Lioba died in about the year 779. Her nuns, the German people, and the Empress Hildegarde had for Lioba the greatest love and veneration. Her convents were among the most powerful factors in the conversion of Germany by Benedictine monks and nuns.

IN UNION OF WORK AND DEVOTION

Before St. Boniface set out on the journey that was to end in martyrdom in Friesland, he expressed the desire that, after Lioba's death, her body might be buried near his. As they had in life served God together in work and devotion, he said, so might they await together the Resurrection Day.

ST. STURMI, O.S.B. (*d. 779*)

St. Sturmi was the first German to become a Benedictine monk. His parents, who were members of the Bavarian nobility, confided Sturmi in his boyhood to the care of St. Boniface. The Apostle of Germany placed the promising lad in the abbey of Fritzlar, in Hesse, where he was educated by the English monk, St. Wigbert.

Sturmi was ordained to the priesthood at an early age, and he was sent to evangelize the Saxons. During three years, he preached to the pagans with remarkable success. His Christlike charity was visible in the beauty of his countenance, and even the fiercest barbarians were attracted to the young missioner. But as time passed, Sturmi felt himself irresistibly drawn to a life of contemplation. He confided his longing to his saintly leader.

Boniface sent Sturmi, with two companions, to find a site for a monastery in an immense forest of beeches that grew on either side of the Fulda River, in central Germany. A stone church was begun and dedicated to the divine Saviour. Sturmi then journeyed to Monte Cassino, to study the true Benedictine observance. On his return, the young Bavarian was able to raise the monastic life at Fulda to the level of the most famous abbeys of Christendom.

Boniface wrote to Pope Zachary: "There is in the solitude of a vast wilderness a place, situated amid the nations I have evangelized, where I have built a monastery and assembled monks who live under the rule of St. Benedict. . . . There after my death I wish to sleep."

The Pope granted to the monastery at Fulda the coveted privilege by which an abbey is placed under the sole jurisdiction of the Holy See. Under the leadership of Abbot Sturmi, all the arts flourished at Fulda. It became the most influential center of religious, agricultural, and intellectual life in central Germany. In the year 779, Sturmi, the beloved disciple of St. Boniface, went to rejoin his leader in heaven.

AN APOSTOLIC POWERHOUSE

St. Boniface was filled with joy when his young disciple, Sturmi, confided to him his longing for the contemplative life; and this joy was well justified. The Benedictine monastery founded at Fulda by St. Sturmi became a powerhouse of prayer, ceaselessly sustaining the energies of the missioners actively engaged in the conversion of Germany.

BLESSED WIDUKIND (*d. c. 804*)

In the eighth century, the sword of Emperor Charlemagne and the missioners who followed in the footsteps of the victorious Franks combined to introduce Christianity into Old Saxony. The pagan Saxons fiercely defended their German wilderness between the Rhine and the Elbe, near the North Sea. The Saxon chieftain who gave Charlemagne the most trouble was the intrepid Widukind, who led serious uprisings against the Franks in the years 778 and 782.

Finally Widukind grew curious about the religion of the invincible Charlemagne. One Easter Sunday, the Saxon leader disguised himself as a beggar, and so gained admittance to the Emperor's tent during the celebration of the Holy Sacrifice. The intruder found the setting and the Easter music very beautiful, but he could not understand what the celebrant at the altar was doing. Widukind's astonishment increased when he saw the priest elevate what seemed to be a round wafer. But suddenly, in the Host, there appeared to the Saxon warrior a Child of surpassing sweetness and majesty—and the fierce chieftain's heart melted within him into tender love.

In the year 785, Widukind was baptized a Christian. From a persecutor of the Faith, he was transformed into an ardent apostle among his people; and thereafter his friendship for the Franks never faltered. It was Widukind who founded in Saxony the see of Minden and obtained from Charlemagne its first bishop.

GOD ALONE KNOWS MEN'S HEARTS

To the Franks, Chief Widukind seemed insensible to all tender emotions; but God knew that love alone could draw this noble soul to the truth. In our judgment of others, we should seek the guidance of the Holy Ghost, the Spirit of Charity.

ST. LUDGER, O.S.B. (*d. 809*)

"One of the most gifted and holy clerics that I have ever met was a Frisian youth by the name of Ludger," said the renowned English scholar, Alcuin, to Emperor Charlemagne. "When Ludger studied under me at York, he never wearied of telling how he received the blessing of St. Boniface, as the great missioner was on the road to martyrdom at Dokkum."

"Where is this Ludger now?" asked the Emperor. "I have need

of him, because I trust more to my priests and monks than to my armies for the subjugation of the pagan Saxons."

"After his ordination to the priesthood, Ludger evangelized the Frisians with great success," replied Alcuin. "But then the savage Saxon invaders uprooted the Christian establishments in Friesland as far west as the Zuider Zee. Father Ludger hoped to found a Benedictine monastery on his paternal estate near the mouth of the Rhine, so he journeyed to Rome to consult the Pope. The Holy Father advised the young priest to study the genuine Benedictine observance at Monte Cassino. I believe that Father Ludger is there now."

"I will summon him at once!" declared the imperious Charlemagne. And so it was done.

At the behest of the Emperor, St. Ludger returned to his native land, where he resumed his missionary labors during sixteen years. He won many converts among both Frisians and Danes, and he even succeeded in planting the Faith among the ferocious pagans of Helgoland.

In the year 801, Charlemagne called the zealous apostle to work among the Saxons in Westphalia. The saint cured a blind Saxon bard by the name of Berulef. After his cure, the traveling bard carried the story of Jesus from one Saxon hearth to another; and he steered a succession of prospective converts to the missioner's door.

Catholics of Münster still venerate a well that St. Ludger used as his baptismal font. Toward the close of his life, Ludger was consecrated a bishop. It was he who founded the see of Münster. When the Apostle of Westphalia died, in the year 809, he had accomplished more for the conversion of the Saxons than even Emperor Charlemagne had envisioned.

CHARITY IS MIGHTIER THAN THE SWORD

Emperor Charlemagne could make nominal Christians by military conquest; but in order to lead the Saxons to a true knowledge of the God of Love, the mighty ruler had to depend on the aid of dedicated missioners like St. Ludger.

ST. ANSGAR, O.S.B. (*801–865*)

An old Swedish statue represents Ansgar, Apostle of the North, as a tall, spare man, with piercing blue eyes and reddish-brown hair. The saint's habit is girt up for rough travel, and his staff is in readiness for the long road. It is the representation of a man who would have no fear of the wild beasts and the outlawed criminals lurking in Sweden's primeval forests, and who would quickly master the skill of speeding on skis over the deep northern snows.

St. Ansgar was born in Picardy, in northwestern France. He entered the famous Benedictine monastery at Corbie; and his superior selected him to help found, among the newly converted Saxons in Germany, the monastery at New Corbie, on the Weser River. There Ansgar was at work when King Louis the Pious, Charlemagne's son, was seeking missioners to be sent into Denmark. The abbot of New Corbie designated Ansgar for this arduous pioneering.

It was not easy to lead the fierce Vikings to an understanding of the teachings of "The White Christ." At the request of King Louis, the Holy Father had made Ansgar a bishop and appointed him to the new see of Hamburg. In the year 845, Danish pirates captured Hamburg and burned to the ground Ansgar's cathedral and monastery. But the missioner was not discouraged. He again entered Danish territory and obtained royal permission to erect a church near a commercial center. Many Danes were baptized, and among the converts was the leader of the pirates who had destroyed Hamburg.

Ansgar was sent to Sweden when King Björn II asked Louis the Pious for Christian missioners. The intrepid apostle proved pleasing to King Björn II, but the pagan priests of Odin were not quickly defeated. The temple at Upsala, in Sweden, was the most sacred and powerful shrine of northern paganism. Ansgar withstood all the wiles of the pagan priests; and during his two missionary journeys into Sweden, he set the Church on a firm foundation among the hardy people.

In the year 849, the Pope joined the diocese of Bremen to that of Hamburg, and made St. Ansgar archbishop of the combined sees. Death came to the Apostle of the North at Bremen, in February, 865.

Rimbert, the successor and biographer of St. Ansgar, wrote: "He never ceased to pray for the salvation of the pagans. . . . So filled was he with this zeal that, even during his last illness, he himself attended to the affairs of the mission, and never resigned them until he drew his last breath."

INDOMITABLE APOSTLE

Had Ansgar not been intrepid in his apostolic warfare for Christ, he could not have won the respect and liking of the fierce Northmen. This fearlessly generous and humble missioner lived the words of the Apostle St. Paul: "I can do all things in Him who strengthens me."

SS. CYRIL AND METHODIUS
(*d. 869 and 885*)

In Constantinople, in the ninth century, many people had heard of two gifted brothers. Methodius, the elder, had been the able governor of a Macedonian province while he was still a young man. Then he had become a monk of outstanding holiness. Cyril, the younger brother, was a priest endowed with such a brilliant mind that he was called "The Philosopher." When only twenty-four years of age, he triumphed in debate with learned Mohammedans in Asia Minor.

In about the year 860, Emperor Michael III sent Methodius and Cyril to evangelize the Khazars, a group of Tartar tribes in the Crimea. The missionary brothers won numerous converts, in the midst of continual hardships and perils. No sooner had they returned to Constantinople, than the Emperor summoned them to his presence. They were informed that Rastislav, the ruler of the newborn Moravian Empire, in central Europe, had sent an embassy to the Byzantine Court, requesting missioners who could speak Slavonic.

"I realize that you are tired, Philosopher," the Emperor told

Cyril. "But you must go there, for no one can take care of these matters as well as you and your brother."

Cyril, the gifted linguist, invented an alphabet for the Slavs. With the aid of the new alphabet, the brothers then translated the Gospels and the liturgy of the Mass into Slavonic. In 863, Methodius and Cyril arrived in the Moravian capital, in present-day Czechoslovakia. The Moravians were quickly drawn to these apostles who taught them in their own Slavic tongue. Christian life was soon flourishing in Rastislav's realm.

The German bishops still considered Moravia as their missionary territory. They were suspicious of the success achieved by Cyril and Methodius, and they proceeded to make serious accusations against the brothers in Rome. The Holy Father, Pope Adrian II, thereupon summoned the evangelists of the Slavs to the Eternal City. In Rome, the Pope approved of everything the brothers had done, and he consecrated them bishops. The joy of the brothers' triumph was fleeting, however.

Cyril was stricken in Rome with a mortal fever, and he died in 869, saying to Methodius, "Do not abandon the good Moravians, my brother!"

The sorrowing elder brother journeyed back to Moravia, and there labored heroically for another sixteen years. He suffered harsh persecution, and even imprisonment, from the German bishops. On Palm Sunday of the year 885, Archbishop Methodius offered the Holy Sacrifice of the Mass, and blessed his people. "Be attentive to me, my children, until the third day," he told his flock.

On the third day, the beloved missioner died. The Slavs have ever since venerated SS. Cyril and Methodius as the foremost among those who brought them the knowledge of Christ.

APOSTLES OF CHURCH UNION

Though persecuted by German bishops, SS. Cyril and Methodius, the Apostles of the Slavs, did not turn to the Greek Church. They remained unalterably faithful to the See of St. Peter. Today, the Church sustains their use of a Slavonic Liturgy for Catholic Slavs.

ST. ADALBERT OF MAGDEBURG, O.S.B. (*d. 981*)

Princess Olga of Russia had written to Constantinople, begging for Christian missioners to evangelize her people. But none had arrived. So, in the year 961, Olga sent a letter to Otto the Great, Emperor of Germany.

"In my old age, I have experienced the peace and joy of becoming a Catholic," wrote the Russian ruler. "Now, I desire ardently that my people should share my happiness. But how can they learn about Christ, unless missioners arrive among them?"

The energetic Otto replied by sending some Benedictine monks to Russia. The leader of the monks, Adalbert by name, was consecrated bishop. The German monks started out with high hopes on their perilous mission; but they had scarcely set foot on Russian soil, when they were attacked and barbarously slaughtered. Bishop Adalbert alone managed to escape with his life.

After his return to Germany, Adalbert was placed over the new see of Magdeburg. He made his see the headquarters of a great apostolate among the Slavs. Yes, this ardent apostle was determined to take Christ to the Slavs! If he could not convert the Slavs of Russia, he would evangelize the Slavic Wends instead.

Adalbert founded a number of bishoprics in the territory of the Wends in eastern Germany. The Holy Father made Adalbert the Metropolitan of the Slavs, and appointed two legates to assist him in his intrepid pioneering. In 981, when death came to the Bishop of Magdeburg, he was still giving his all for the conversion of the Slavs.

THE CHURCH NEVER DESPAIRS

Though St. Adalbert of Magdeburg could not carry on his apostolate in Russia, he found a way to evangelize the Slavs. So it has been with Catholic apostles in all the Christian centuries. Now that the Soviet Union is closed to Catholic missioners, the Church is training dedicated priests in view of a future, ardently desired apostolate among the Russians.

ST. BRUNO OF QUERFURT, O.S.B.CAM.
(*d. 1009*)

Bruno, born in the tenth century at Querfurt, in Germany, was a member of the Saxon nobility. Ordained to the priesthood at an early age, he became the chaplain of Emperor Otto III. The Emperor was much attached to his young chaplain. Bruno could have wielded great power at the imperial court; but he chose instead to become a Camaldolese Benedictine, under the direction of St. Romuald. The latter gave Bruno the name of Boniface.

When the former favorite of the Emperor was at his prayers and thought of his great namesake, the Apostle of Germany, he would say to himself: "Am not I, also, a Boniface? Why may not I be a martyr of Jesus Christ, as he was?"

After some years, St. Romuald commissioned Bruno-Boniface to evangelize the Slavs in Prussia; and the Holy Father blessed this undertaking. Bruno was consecrated Bishop of Magdeburg. He then set out gladly for Prussia, but his new flock received him with hatred and contempt. One day in the year 1009, St. Bruno-Boniface and his eighteen missionary co-workers were beheaded in the hostile land of their apostolate.

THE VALUE OF A CHRISTIAN NAME

St. Bruno of Querfurt was inspired to become a missioner and a martyr by meditating on St. Boniface, whose name he received in religion. Some Catholics do not pay sufficient heed to the names they receive at baptism. We should ask our patron saints to obtain for us from God the grace to imitate their virtues.

ST. VLADIMIR (*956–1015*)

In Prince Vladimir's youth, no one could have foreseen that he was destined to become the guardian saint of Russia. He resembled far more his father, the pagan Svyatoslav, than his gentle Christian grandmother, the widowed Princess Olga. Indeed, it was generally believed that Vladimir had murdered his own brother and rival,

Prince Yaropolk. After he had mounted the throne, Vladimir offered human victims to the Slavic deity Perun, called "The Thundermaker."

Yet the fierce Vladimir loved and venerated his Christian grandmother. Under the influence of Princess Olga, a divine discontent began to grow in the young ruler's soul. In the year 987, he sought the advice of the elders of his council. They urged him to send envoys to Constantinople to examine the merits of the Christian religion; and he did so.

The Byzantine Emperor ordered that, for the benefit of the strangers, there should be an imposing display of ritual in the magnificent Church of Santa Sophia. "Let them see the glory of our God!" he said.

The Russian envoys were enchanted by the gleaming marbles and porphyries of Santa Sophia, by the gorgeous vestments of the celebrants, by the blazing tapers, and by the superb chanting. "We want no further proof of the holiness of your religion!" they cried. "Send us home again."

Vladimir and his councilors were convinced by the enthusiasm of their envoys; but the Russian ruler wished to prove that, in adopting the Christian religion, he would not thereby constitute himself a vassal of the Byzantine Emperor. He therefore besieged and captured a Greek city in the Crimea. After that he truculently demanded in marriage the hand of the Emperor's sister, Princess Anne.

Out of love for God and souls, Anne consented to the marriage. Prince Vladimir was baptized, and then he proceeded with characteristic vigor to convert his subjects. The great, wooden statue of Perun was thrown ignominiously into the Dnieper River at Kiev. On the following day, Vladimir commanded all the inhabitants of the city to repair to the Dnieper for baptism.

"Anyone who disobeys this order is my enemy!" declared the sovereign.

Under the sway of the royal convert, churches and schools were built in the land. Kiev became the center of Christian influence; and missioners journeyed into the interior of Russia, everywhere instructing and baptizing the people.

"Thus," relates the *Russian Chronicle,* "did Christianity diffuse her light over Russia, like the rising sun, with progressively increasing splendor; and Vladimir rejoiced thereat, and was liberal toward the poor and afflicted, and distributed his gifts among all the people."

In 1015, twenty-seven years after his conversion, St. Vladimir, the royal Apostle of Russia, went to meet the Master he had learned to serve so well.

FROM MURDERER TO APOSTLE

The life of St. Vladimir, Apostle of Russia, reminds us anew that great sinners are potential great saints, if only their strong passions can be directed to the love of God. The mediocre, lukewarm souls are the ones least likely to achieve sanctity.

PART IV

The High Middle Ages

(1000–1300)

THESE three centuries have been called the most Christian period in the history of western Europe; and during the last of them, the thirteenth, medieval civilization reached its apex. The Papacy attained immense prestige. Royal saints adorned European thrones. It was a time of brilliant Christian philosophy, literature, art, and architecture. The Dominican and Franciscan Orders were founded, specially qualified by their freedom of action for apostolic work in the new urban and mercantile society that was arising.

The conversion of the Northmen and of the Slavs continued at an accelerated pace. Western Europe undertook the Crusades, military expeditions to deliver Jerusalem and the tomb of the Saviour from the grasp of the Moslems. In Spain, the Christian monarchs pushed the Moslem Moors steadily southward.

This splendid period was not without its portents of danger and of spiritual decline, however. The long struggle between popes and secular rulers undermined the magnificent ideal of a united Christendom. The Crusaders deviated from their high purpose and went down to ultimate defeat.

During centuries, a rift had been widening between the Holy See and the Greek Church. Its causes were political and cultural, rather than doctrinal. In 1054, the final break sundered the Patriarchs of Constantinople from the Holy See; and the other Eastern Churches, including the vigorous, young Church of Russia, were eventually engulfed in the Greek Schism. The year 1054 was indeed a calamitous one in Christian history.

The Moslem Seljuk Turks waxed strong toward the close of the tenth century, and their cruel treatment of pilgrims to the Holy Land helped to stir up the crusading zeal of Christian Europe. In the thirteenth century, the Mongol tornado of blood and death swept out from the vast plains of Central Asia into eastern Europe. The Ottoman Turks displaced the Seljuks in 1258; then they began a career of conquest which threatened Christendom for nearly three hundred years.

As the thirteenth century was ending, Blessed Raymond Lull, who lived only for Christ and souls, believed that apostolic zeal was declining. "Ah, Holy Catholic Church!" he exclaimed. "Thou seest how many are thy enemies. And how many more thou wilt have, if thou remain in idleness!"

ST. OLAV OF NORWAY (*995–1030*)

Norway was still largely pagan when King Olav Haroldson ascended the throne in the year 1014. The new ruler was a thick-set, redheaded man, whose appearance was redeemed from plainness by the glance of his very piercing eyes. King Olav was renowned for the Viking deeds of his youth. With all the force of his impetuous nature, he determined to convert Norway wholly to Christ.

St. Olav called English and German missioners to his kingdom. He himself sailed in and out of Norway's fiords and marched through its valleys, inviting the most influential of his subjects either to accept Christianity or to do battle with him. He directed the building of churches in places where pagan shrines had for centuries drawn worshipers; and he prepared a new code of laws, in which Christian principles replaced the old pagan tenets.

Meanwhile, this royal Apostle of Norway waged constant strife against his own Viking nature. In renouncing an unlawful love,

King Olav said, "Now it seems to me better that I should live according to God's will, and not after my own evil desires."

Many of Olav's subjects had no wish to abandon the old pagan gods. When Canute the Great, then ruler of England and Denmark, turned his attention to the conquest of Norway, Olav's Norwegian enemies made common cause with the Danish invader. King Olav was slain near Trondheim, in the year 1030.

Scarcely had Olav fallen when even his enemies proclaimed him a saint. Thereafter, as long as the Holy Sacrifice of the Mass was offered in Trondheim Cathedral, the body of Norway's patron saint lay in a golden shrine behind the altar. At the time of the Protestant upheaval, when the people were deprived of the Blessed Sacrament, St. Olav's body was buried – no one knows where.

CHRISTUS VINCIT!

In her account of St. Olav of Norway, Sigrid Undset writes: "The Norwegian missionary kings, who by nature were neither meek nor humble of heart, yet put all their strength into the struggle to convert their people to Him Who has said: 'Learn of Me, for I am meek and humble of heart.'"

ST. STEPHEN OF HUNGARY (*975–1038*)

Many years ago, a group of beggars in Hungary saw a poorly dressed man, carrying a bulging purse. Within a few seconds, the beggars had thrown themselves upon the man, pulled his beard, tugged at his hair, and made away with his purse. Now, the poorly dressed wayfarer was none other than King Stephen of Hungary, going on his daily round of charity, in disguise.

The abused sovereign picked himself up, brushed off his clothes, and made a mild remonstrance to the Mother of Christ: "See, O Queen of Heaven, in what manner I am rewarded by those who belong to your Son!" That was the only complaint registered by King Stephen. He would not permit the rude beggars to be punished.

Stephen was the son of Duke Geisa, the first Christian ruler of the Magyars of Hungary, a people who appear to have been a blend of Finno-Ugrian and Turkish strains. Geisa found in Christianity a powerful aid in the creation of a strong state. He introduced German missioners into his realm, thus binding Hungary to Western Christendom.

After the death of Geisa, in 997, King Stephen continued and consolidated his father's work. This missionary ruler journeyed through his realm as a preacher of Christianity. He brought prominent foreign monks to Hungary, and founded numerous monasteries in his own kingdom. According to the instructions of the Holy See, King Stephen set up in Hungary two archbishoprics and eight bishoprics. Stephen corresponded with the abbot of Cluny, in France, and thus he was in contact with the leading Christian movement of his time.

In 1038, St. Stephen of Hungary went to receive in heaven an imperishable crown of glory. Throughout the centuries, the Magyars have continued to venerate St. Stephen as their greatest national saint and hero.

THE VITAL INFLUENCE OF A CHRISTIAN MARRIAGE

St. Stephen received noteworthy aid in the evangelization of Hungary from his wife, Gisela, a sister of Emperor St. Henry II. The work of this apostolic royal couple was of crucial importance, because the position of the Magyars made them a boundary between the southern Slavs, who were Greek Christians, and the Poles and Bohemians who became Roman Catholics.

ST. GOTTSCHALK OF THE WENDS
(*d. 1066*)

The Slavic tribes called by the Germans "Wends" lived in the regions watered by the Elbe, the Oder, and the Saale Rivers. They hated Christianity, because they associated it with Germanic oppression and conquest. The Wendish Prince Gottschalk had been educated in a Christian school at Luneburg; but he yielded to terrible rage when Germans murdered his father. Gottschalk called his people to arms, and they laid waste the German regions of Hamburg and Holstein.

One day, however, the impetuous prince was struck with remorse at the sight of the havoc he had caused. "The countryside lies desolate, where once fair churches raised their towers to the skies," he mourned. "I vow that henceforth I will support and spread the religion against which I have sinned so grievously."

Gottschalk was crowned ruler of the Wends in the year 1047, and he kept his vow. He invited many German missioners into his kingdom. But he did not leave the whole labor of the conversion of his people to the priests; he himself preached the Faith with all the intensity of his energetic character. For twenty years, he toiled steadily on.

However, the Wends loved their own darkness better than their sovereign's light. They clung to their idols, and they hated Gottschalk because he was friendly to German princes. The few Wendish converts could not resist the rising pagan opposition to their sovereign. At last the storm broke, with dark and savage fury. The royal apostle was its first victim. King Gottschalk of the Wends, apostle of Jesus Christ, died under torture.

THE GREATER LOVE

Love of his murdered father caused Gottschalk of the Wends to become a persecutor of Christianity; but Jesus knew that this generous soul was worthy of a greater love. He called the young sovereign to His service; and from the time of his conversion, Gottschalk knew "only Christ and Him Crucified."

ST. CANUTE OF DENMARK (*d. 1086*)

St. Canute was the grandnephew of Canute the Great of Denmark, who had conquered England and founded a short-lived Scandinavian Empire. While St. Canute was prince, he chased the fierce pirates from the seas around Denmark. Later, by the unanimous demand of the Danish people, he ascended the throne of his country.

King Canute devoted his life to the interests of his subjects and to the promotion of the Catholic Faith. He had a number of churches built in his realm, many of which are still standing. He adorned the cathedral at Roskilde with his own fabulously bejeweled crown. But although Canute was a very just and holy ruler, he had many enemies. In those days, Denmark was still barely Christianized. A rebellion broke out, because King Canute levied a heavy fine on those of his subjects who refused to support their priests.

When the ruler heard that the rebels were marching on his palace, he withdrew to the town of Odense, on Fyn Island. The rebels pursued him. While King Canute was at prayer, a screaming and bloodthirsty mob surrounded the church. The fact that the church doors were barred gave the sovereign time to confess his sins and to receive Holy Communion. Then, as the saint knelt before the main altar, he was mortally wounded by the thrust of a lance.

King Canute was canonized by Pope Paschal II in 1100. He is the patron saint of Denmark. Today, the tomb of the royal Catholic apostle may still be seen in the Protestant cathedral of Odense.

DEFENDER OF THE FAITH

St. Canute knew that he was risking life itself in his undeviating defense and promotion of the Catholic Faith, but he scorned the advice of those who urged him to compromise. God rewarded his total gift of himself with the glory of martyrdom.

ST. ERIC OF SWEDEN (*d. 1160*)

It is the rare ruler who does not tax his subjects. King Eric IX of Sweden was content with the money he had inherited, so he levied no taxes. More than that, he used a great portion of his own wealth in the service of the poor and of religion. When Eric ascended the throne, in the year 1141, the southern part of Sweden was Christianized; but in the vast northern forests the population was still pagan. Eric sent missioners far up into the Arctic regions.

It was this same Eric IX who planted the faith in Finland, also. As a devout Christian, the Swedish ruler loved peace. But when his neighbors, the Finns, made frequent raids into Sweden, he assembled an army and led it against the invaders. Although Eric's forces were victorious, the royal saint wept as he saw on the battlefield the corpses of his enemies. He shed tears because the Finns had died without baptism. King Eric then gave the Finns his dear friend, Bishop Henry, an English missioner in Sweden.

After Bishop Henry had been six months in Finland, one of his converts committed a brutal murder; and Bishop Henry imposed a heavy penance on the criminal. Infuriated, the savage Finn hacked the missioner to death in a frozen marsh. The saint's body was not found until the ice had melted in the springtime. Bishop Rodulfus, St. Henry's successor at Abo, was likewise martyred, in the year 1178; but under Bishop Thomas, another Englishman, the Church began to take firm root in Finland.

King Eric was to win the crown of martyrdom in his own land. Some of his pagan noblemen made a deal with the Prince of Denmark, who wanted to rule both Denmark and Sweden. One day in the year 1160, a messenger rushed up to King Eric as the sovereign was attending Mass. The message was that a Danish army, guided by the Swedish traitors, was closing in on the city.

St. Eric remained in the cathedral until Mass was over. Then he rode out alone to meet the invaders. One of the Swedish traitors knocked Eric from his horse. Then the attacker and the other pagan noblemen beat their sovereign to death. In this manner, the apostolic King of Sweden laid down his life for the Faith he had done so much to spread.

GLORIES OF CATHOLIC ENGLAND

St. Henry, the English Apostle of Finland, was raised to the episcopate in Sweden by Nicholas Cardinal Breakspear, Papal Legate to Norway and Sweden, who was also an Englishman. In the year 1154, Cardinal Breakspear ascended the throne of St. Peter, as Pope Adrian IV. Catholics should pray often for the reunion of the English people with the See of Peter.

ST. DOMINIC, O.P. (*1170–1221*)

In a castle of Castile, in the year 1180, Joanna d'Aza was talking to her ten-year-old son, Dominic de Guzman. "Never forget, my son, that you are descended from an ancient family of Visigothic knights," she said. "Your forebears have always treasured their Christian Faith even more than their family honor."

At that time, Dominic was studying under the guidance of an uncle who was a parish priest. Four years later, he entered the schools of Palencia, then the best in Spain. The young Castilian was ordained to the priesthood in about the year 1194. Soon afterward, he became an Augustinian Canon Regular at the cathedral of Osma. There Father Dominic grew in holiness during nine years of conventual life.

In 1203, the Bishop of Osma requested Father Dominic to accompany him on a diplomatic journey to Denmark. While passing through southern France, the travelers stopped in an inn at Toulouse. Dominic discovered that his host was an Albigensian heretic. All through the night, he argued with the misguided man; and by his charity, he won the innkeeper over to the true, Catholic Faith.

A biographer of St. Dominic has written: "From that time, he cherished in his heart the project of spending himself for the salvation of misbelievers, and of instituting to that end a preaching order to be devoted to the evangelization of the nations."

Pope Innocent III later commanded the Bishop of Osma and Father Dominic to labor among the Albigensian heretics in France. The two missioners converted numerous heretics, by the evangelical poverty of their lives and by religious debates with leading misbelievers. In these debates, the intellectual brilliance of St. Dominic shone out for all to see. In 1206, nine women heretics were converted by the saint. Dominic united those converts in a new religious community at Prouille. Four years later, Dominic obtained Papal sanction for his preaching order of men.

The new religious family adopted the Rule of St. Augustine, since it is flexible enough to allow for the varying conditions incident to a world-wide order. From the beginning and with inspired boldness, the founder dispersed his priests and Brothers, sending them to centers of civilization in Spain, France, and Italy. Dominic had a special interest in the universities; and when scholars were attracted to his order, he sent them to make spiritual conquests at the universities of Bologna and of Paris.

The saint himself was constantly on the road, journeying from one of his rapidly multiplying foundations to another. But his journeys never distracted Dominic's mind from union with Christ, for the great preacher "had a cell in his heart." In the course of one of his journeys, the founder of the Dominicans became ill with a high fever. He died at Bologna in 1221. Only thirteen years later, he was canonized by Pope Gregory IX.

St. Dominic bequeathed to the active members of his religious family a great intellectual ideal: they should lead souls to the freedom of God, by preaching to them the truth. For the Saviour Himself had promised: ". . . the truth shall make you free" (Jn. 8:32).

DOING THE TRUTH IN CHARITY

St. Dominic detested the untruth of heresy; but he loved the heretics themselves. The saint's sympathetic generosity of soul served as the basis of his tremendous power of persuasion. He drew the erring to Divine Truth through his charity enkindled by Divine Love.

ST. FRANCIS OF ASSISI, O.F.M. (*1181–1226*)

St. Francis of Assisi believed that all infidels and pagans would quickly embrace Christianity, if only the Gospel were announced to them in its divine simplicity. Such a conviction was natural in a man who had meditated so deeply on the boundless charity of Christ that "he was all transformed into Jesus."

Francis founded his great religious order in 1209, when he was only twenty-eight years of age. Seven years later, the saint sent some of his Friars Minor to mission lands. He himself had already made two attempts to evangelize the Moslems; but he had been deflected from the first attempt by shipwreck, and from the second by illness. In the year 1219, Francis accompanied Crusaders to the East and arrived at Damietta in Egypt.

The saint first preached conversion to the Crusaders themselves, for he found much immorality in the Christian camp. Then Francis and Brother Illuminatus crossed fearlessly over to the enemy camp and succeeded in gaining admittance to the tent of the Sultan of Egypt. That Moslem ruler asked the missioner his errand.

"I am sent, not by men, but by the Most High God, to show you and your people the way of salvation, by announcing to you the truth of the Gospel," replied Francis.

"We hold that our own faith is the true one," said the sultan. "We believe in Allah and in the Prophet, Mohammed."

Then St. Francis proposed that a fire be kindled, and that both he and a Mohammedan holy man submit to the ordeal of the flames, in order to prove which of them was protected by the true God. But Sultan Melek-el-Kamil replied that he did not think any of his holy men would consent to enter the fire. Many of the Saracens considered Francis mad. Nevertheless, the daring apostle's pure zeal inspired in their ruler real admiration. He sent the two Friars Minor back to the Crusaders' camp in safety.

It is related that the sultan said to Francis, "Pray for me, that God may reveal to me which faith is the most pleasing to Him."

The founder of the Franciscans returned, by way of Palestine, into Italy. There he heard with joy that the five missioners whom he had sent to Morocco had been cruelly martyred by the Moors. "Now I can truly say that I have five real brothers!" exclaimed the saint.

Francis of Assisi did not suffer martyrdom in a pagan land as he had hoped. But the fire of charity that burned in his great heart lived on in his far-flung religious order. Through the succeeding centuries, it has given to the world Franciscan apostles and martyrs. St. Francis himself went to the embrace of his Crucified Lord on October 4, 1226.

BLESSED ARE THE PEACEMAKERS

Praise to Thee for those who forgive for love of Thee,
Sustaining afflictions and tribulations!
Blessed be those who keep themselves in peace!
By Thee, Most High, will they be crowned at last.

– *A Canticle of St. Francis*

ST. ANTHONY OF PADUA, O.F.M. (*1195–1231*)

It would seem, judging from the name of Anthony of Padua, that this popular Franciscan was an Italian; but such was not the case. His baptismal name was Ferdinand, and he was born in Lisbon, Portugal. At an early age Ferdinand became a Canon Regular of St. Augustine in the Portuguese town of Coimbra.

In the year 1220, the bodies of the first Franciscan martyrs were transferred from Morocco to Coimbra. Ferdinand was deeply stirred by the event. He believed that he heard in his soul the voice of Christ, bidding him to follow in the footsteps of the martyrs and to journey as a missioner to Morocco. So Ferdinand sought and received the reluctant permission of his superiors to transfer to the Franciscan Order. As a Franciscan, Ferdinand received the name of Anthony.

Anthony was soon assigned to Africa; but he had scarcely landed on the continent of his desires when he fell desperately ill. The apparently dying friar was ordered back to Portugal. However, on the return journey his ship was carried by a storm to Sicily. From Sicily the young religious traveled to Assisi where he met St. Francis.

After a time, it was discovered that Anthony possessed marvelous power as a preacher. Under the guidance of St. Francis, Anthony began his great apostolate in Italy and in France. Everywhere crowds flocked to hear the inspired missioner. Heretics were unable to resist his ardent charity, and he inflamed the hearts of repentant sinners with the fire of divine love.

St. Anthony spent the last years of his short life at Padua. There he died, on June 13, 1231, when he was only thirty-six years of age. When illness had defeated St. Anthony's hopes for missionary service in Africa, he had placed himself entirely in God's hands. To what superb use God had put this loving surrender!

TREMENDOUS MORAL COURAGE

St. Anthony of Padua, the greatest preacher of his age, drew spectacular crowds numbering twenty, thirty, or forty thousand hearers. But far from seeking popularity, the saint attacked prevalent vices with the utmost vehemence. More than that, he boldly denounced prominent personages to their faces.

FRIAR JOHN OF PLANO CARPINI, O.F.M. (*d. c. 1250*)

In the year 1245, the Council of Lyons decided that the best method of defending Europe against the onrushing Tartars would be to convert those barbarians to the Catholic Faith. So Pope Innocent IV sent ambassadors to Karakorum, the court of the Great Khan himself. The embassy was composed of three Franciscans, headed by Friar John of Plano Carpini, a native of the town of Perugia, Italy.

At that time, Friar John was sixty-five years of age, but he set out with stout heart to face the unknown terrors of the fabulous journey across the vast stretches of central Asia. In Russia, one of the Franciscans fell ill and was obliged to return to Italy. The other two travelers made their way to the headquarters of General Batu on the Volga River. The proud leader of the Tartars of the Golden Horde gave the missioners a haughty reception and sent them on to Karakorum.

The Tartar escorts of the missioners had orders to make the Franciscans travel at full gallop during the terrible journey which lasted several months. After the searching cold of high plateaus, the missioners encountered shimmering heat in the immense Gobi Desert; and often they came near to starvation. But at length,

Friar John and his companion arrived at their destination, and were admitted to the Great Kahn's splendid tent. It was erected on pillars that were covered with plates of gold, joined together with nails of the same metal, and roofed with rich baldachin cloth.

The Great Kahn sent an arrogant reply to the Pope's message. Its gist was that, if the Pope desired peace, he should journey in person to Karakorum to ask for it! Kuyuk did not see any reason why he should become a Christian. The power of God was already with him, he said, and all the earth trembled at the sound of his voice.

The Franciscan envoys began their return journey in November. Often they had to sleep on the ground, and in the morning they found themselves covered by snowdrifts. When they had reached Kiev, in Russia, the whole city turned out to welcome the travelers, as men returned from the grave.

The missioners arrived in Lyons in the autumn of 1247. The Holy Father made Friar John Archbishop of Antivari in Dalmatia; but the valiant old apostle did not long survive his return from the Far East. He had not made any converts in Tartary; but he had blazed the trail for future apostles, by securing detailed and accurate knowledge of the hitherto-unknown interior of a huge continent.

During the following decade, the saintly King Louis of France sent to Karakorum another missionary expedition, headed by Friar William of Rubruck, a French Franciscan. It met with the same heartbreaking lack of result.

IMPELLED BY SPIRITUAL VISION

It seems almost incredible that an old man such as Friar John of Plano Carpini should have undertaken the perilous journey into a then totally unknown Tartary. The stoutest human courage could not have sufficed; but the aged Franciscan was led on by the spiritual vision of millions of souls as yet ignorant of the Lord of Glory.

ST. FERDINAND OF LEON AND CASTILE
(*1198–1252*)

King Ferdinand III was a regal warrior-apostle. In the early years of the thirteenth century, much of Spain still remained in the hands of the Moslems; but Ferdinand freed vast territories from the Saracen yoke. A lust for power was not the motive of his great conquests: this saintly monarch desired only to spread the sway of Christ in the peninsula.

Ferdinand had a tender devotion to the Queen of Heaven. He always carried with him into battle a small ivory statue of Our Lady of Kings. Before each encounter, he spent the whole night in prayer. The valorous champion of the Faith insisted that his soldiers live as good Christians.

This just ruler was always careful not to oppress his people by excessive taxation. Once, a court councilor suggested that a special tax be imposed to defray the expenses of the campaign against the infidels. "God forbid that I should follow your advice!" exclaimed Ferdinand. "I am more afraid of the curse of a single poor woman that would be oppressed by it, than I am of the whole Mohammedan Army."

On all his campaigns, King Ferdinand was accompanied by the Archbishop of Toledo. Together, sovereign and prelate re-established Catholic worship in the territories wrested from the Moors. They founded bishoprics, built churches and monasteries, and endowed hospitals. Ferdinand III was the founder of the illustrious University of Salamanca. After his forces had retaken Cordova and Seville, he had the great mosques in those cities converted into splendid Christian cathedrals.

The warrior-apostle died on May 30, 1252, on the eve of another campaign against the infidels. Clothed in the simple habit of the Third Order of St. Francis, the saintly King Ferdinand was laid to rest in the cathedral of Seville. Popular devotion honored him with the glorious title, "Defender of the Faith."

AN IDEAL CHRISTIAN RULER

In the realm of King Ferdinand III, no problems arose in the relationship of Church and State. The royal saint recognized that the lawful authority of both religious and secular rulers comes from God, and is given in order that all alike may co-operate in the welfare and expansion of Christendom.

ST. HYACINTH, O.P. (*c. 1185–1257*)

Bishop Ivo of Cracow, Poland, and four of his priests journeyed to Rome on ecclesiastical business in the year 1219. Two of the priests with Bishop Ivo – Father Hyacinth and Father Ceslaus – were his nephews. The Polish pilgrims met St. Dominic in Rome, and the Bishop of Cracow asked that some Dominicans might be assigned to labor in Poland.

"I have long desired to send some of my friars to Poland, but at present I have no one to spare for that work," answered Dominic. "Perhaps some members of your retinue might receive the habit of my order. I would return them to you as apostles."

Thus the four priestly companions of Bishop Ivo became Dominicans. Hyacinth quickly outstripped the others in holiness, and an early biographer has written of the saint: "Soon his religious fervor, his austerity of life, and his zeal for God's glory and for the salvation of souls were comparable only to those of St. Dominic himself."

On the way back to Poland, Hyacinth began the great apostolate that was to include many widely separated lands. His missionary journeys finally covered Austria, Moravia, Poland, Pomerania, Prussia, Denmark, Norway, Sweden, Scotland, and Russia. The remarkable success of the Polish Dominican and his confreres was commended by Pope Gregory IX in 1231.

The Holy Father wrote to the rulers and peoples evangelized by Hyacinth: "Follow the instructions of the Friar Preachers, those saintly apostles who have drawn you from the darkness of error into the path of truth and justice."

Everywhere God granted to Hyacinth the gift of miracles. It is evident that the saint was endowed likewise with shrewd common sense. On one occasion, Hyacinth asked the Duke of Pomerania for the gift of an islet in the Baltic, saying that it would one day be the site of a magnificent city and port. The Duke laughed at the prophecy, for the place was then a lonely wilderness. But within a century, the great city of Danzig sprang up as the apostle had foretold; and it became such a Catholic stronghold that it later remained untouched by the Lutheran heresy.

St. Hyacinth was with his friars in Kiev, when the Tartars overwhelmed that splendid Russian city. He rescued from the friary chapel an immense, alabaster statue of our Lady, carrying the great weight easily in his arms. Then Hyacinth led his friars to the Dnieper River, bade them walk out with him upon the water, and so took them beyond the reach of the Tartar hordes. The statue of the Virgin of Kiev became the object of public veneration in Poland.

St. Hyacinth repeatedly refused the episcopal dignity. The illustrious Apostle of the North died in August, 1257. Pilgrims came from far and near to pray at the great missioner's tomb, and it was the scene of frequent miracles, not only immediately after the saint's death, but throughout centuries.

CONFIDENCE IN THE BLESSED VIRGIN

A burning devotion to the Queen of Apostles characterized the zeal of St. Hyacinth. All his astounding success in combating error he attributed to her, "who alone has overcome all heresies throughout the world."

ST. PETER NOLASCO (*c. 1182–1258*)

When Peter Nolasco was urging his rich friends to sacrifice a part of their wealth for the ransom of Christian slaves of the Moors, he would point out some of the miserable captives and exclaim, "Behold eternal treasures that never fail!"

Peter was born of wealthy parents in Languedoc in southern

France. From his boyhood he showed loving compassion to the poor, and was concerned with the eternal welfare of his fellow beings. When grown, he took part in combat against the heretical Albigensians.

Later Peter Nolasco journeyed to Barcelona, as tutor of the young King James I of Aragon. In Spain, the saint agonized over the physical sufferings of the Christian captives of the Moors, and he was still more distressed by the spiritual dangers encountered by those slaves. He had inherited a huge fortune from his father, and he spent it lavishly to ransom captives. But he soon realized that this was not enough, so he formed a confraternity for the rescue of Christian slaves.

The Blessed Virgin inspired King James I and the great St. Raymond of Penafort to come to the aid of Peter Nolasco. King James gave to his former tutor part of his palace, to house the saint's followers. St. Raymond helped Peter to secure Papal approbation for the transformation of the lay confraternity into a new religious order. Thus Peter Nolasco became the founder of the Mercedarians, the Order of Our Lady for the Redemption of Captives.

The Mercedarians made a solemn promise to God that they would devote all their possessions and energies, and even their liberty, should that prove necessary, to the rescue of Christian slaves from the infidels. Peter was one of the first to keep this vow. With a single companion, he set out for enemy territory and purchased the freedom of a great number of slaves. More than that, the spectacle of the saint's Christlike charity led infidels to Peter's divine Master.

The holy founder of the Mercedarians died in the year 1258, but his spiritual sons continued Peter Nolasco's great work. After Spain had expelled the Moors from her soil, and fewer Christians were captured by the Moslems, Peter's Mercedarians turned their zeal to missionary conquests. They won thousands of souls for the Faith in the far-flung Spanish-American Empire.

Thirty-seven years before St. Peter Nolasco founded his Mercedarians, Pope Innocent III had approved another new order for the work of redeeming Christians enslaved by the Moors. This community was the Trinitarians, founded by St. John of Matha and St. Felix of Valois, two apostolic Frenchmen.

AN AMAZING VOW

Liberty is dearer to many noble hearts than life itself; yet the followers of St. Peter Nolasco made a vow to surrender even their liberty, should that prove necessary for the eternal welfare of fellow beings. Only God's Spirit of Love could make the human soul capable of so sublime a sacrifice.

ST. LOUIS OF FRANCE (*1215–1270*)

One day in the thirteenth century, when St. Louis, ruler of France, was crusading in the Holy Land, a knight carried a bundle to his sovereign's tent.

"A wild-looking fellow has just brought this bundle to the camp, Sire," said the knight. "He claims that the Old Man of the Mountain himself sent you this present."

Now, the Old Man of the Mountain was a terrible personage who lived south of the Caspian Sea, in a stronghold called the Eagle's Nest. He kept his followers in a sort of earthly paradise, so that they would always wish to return to it. When the Old Man sent his subjects to murder his chosen prey, he gave them hashish. The henchmen of that strange ruler were consequently called "hashishin," from which name has come our word "assassin."

With some curiosity, therefore, St. Louis opened the bundle. It contained the ominous present of a shroud. The king laughed and said, "I am pleased with this present, for it gives me an opportunity to send a letter by his messenger to that unhappy murderer. I shall tell him about Christ and how He died on the cross to save sinners. God grant that he may yet save his soul!"

The Old Man of the Mountain did not accept Christ; but even he was won to friendship for St. Louis, and admitted that "the ruler of the Franks is a truly holy man."

By no means all the medieval Crusaders tried to convert the infidels. But St. Louis, the noblest of all the Crusaders, was also an apostle. He himself instructed adult Saracen converts for baptism; and he sent their children over the waters of the Mediterranean to receive a Catholic education in France.

In a message that King Louis dispatched to the Sultan of Tunis, he wrote: "I desire so strongly the salvation of your soul that, to secure it, I would gladly spend the rest of my life in chains in a Saracen prison and never again behold the light of the sun."

THE PURE OBLATION

God permitted the two Crusades organized by King Louis IX of France to end, humanly speaking, in failure. On the night before the saint died of fever, in Tunis, he sang snatches of an old French hymn, "We Will Go to Jerusalem." His last words were: "Father, into Thy hands I commend my spirit."

ST. RAYMOND OF PENAFORT, O.P. (*1175–1275*)

When the general chapter of the fairly new Dominican Order met at Bologna, in the year 1221, it was decided that the Friars Preachers should merit their name by going to every country in the world and preaching the Gospel to all men. A remarkable missionary genius of that early period in the order's history was the Spanish Dominican, St. Raymond of Penafort.

Raymond was a kinsman of the kings of Aragon. While yet a young man, he became a distinguished professor of canon law, first at Barcelona and later, in Italy, at the University of Bologna. The future saint joined the Dominican Order in the year 1222, and began to preach to the Moors and to the Albigensian heretics.

Seven years later, Pope Gregory IX called the learned Dominican to Rome. Raymond was appointed confessor to the Pope, and also was entrusted with the tremendous task of systematizing and codifying the canon law. His codification remained the most authentic source of legislation in the Church until the year 1917.

St. Raymond was chosen Master General of his Order in 1238. In the midst of his great honors and heavy duties, he never ceased to think about methods for the conversion of the Moors and the Jews in Spain.

With the support of the kings of Castile and of Aragon, the apostolic saint founded language schools for future missioners in Spain and in Africa (at Tunis). More than ten thousand converts were won by missioners from St. Raymond's schools. When it is remembered that very few converts have ever been made among the Moslems and the Jews, we realize that this number was a rich harvest, indeed. It was at the request of St. Raymond of Penafort that the peerless St. Thomas Aquinas wrote his *Summa contra Gentiles,* an apologetic work for the use of Raymond's mission band.

St. Raymond spent the closing years of his life on the island of Marjorca, where he inspired many of the missionary ideas of Blessed Raymond Lull. A flock of picturesque legends cluster about the missionary labors of the grand old apostle on Majorca. One of the legends relates how St. Raymond spread his cloak on the waves and sailed over to Barcelona, some one hundred and eighty miles away!

PROFESSORIAL DISINTERESTEDNESS

St. Raymond of Penafort condemned the rapacity of professors who demanded exorbitant fees for their lectures. When the citizens of Bologna decreed of their own accord that he should receive a subsidy from the municipal treasury, St. Raymond gave to God and his parish priest the greater part of his earnings.

BLESSED RAYMOND LULL (*c. 1232–c. 1315*)

One summer evening, when Raymond Lull was about thirty years of age, he sat in his room composing a love song. All at once, looking up from his parchment, he beheld the figure of Christ hanging upon the cross. Greatly shocked, the young nobleman tried to persuade himself that he had imagined the vision; but on four later occasions, the silent and reproachful figure of the

Crucified appeared to him. Then Raymond turned away from his petty adventures, and he accepted God's invitation to the quest of the love that has no bounds.

In gratitude for the grace of his conversion, the former playboy resolved "to convert infidels and unbelievers to the truth of the holy Catholic Faith and thereby place himself in danger of death."

Raymond Lull was born into a noble family on the picturesque island of Majorca, to the east of Spain. In his youth, he served as a royal page and plunged into an insatiable quest of adventure and pleasure. Even marriage and the birth of two children had not induced the talented young Majorcan to settle down. Yet three months after his conversion, Raymond set aside such of his possessions as were needed by his wife and children for their support, and then distributed the rest of his wealth to the poor. During the remaining years of his long life, Raymond Lull dedicated himself to the conversion of Moslems and Jews.

The aspirant apostle first devoted nine years to an intensive study of Latin, Arabic, Hebrew, theology, philosophy, and the elements of natural science. He began during that time his prodigious literary activity. Raymond became the author of more than two hundred works of theology and religious mysticism, all of which were planned as "means by which men may learn to love God." In his books, Lull explained his ideas for the conversion of the world. Several of the Majorcan missioner's works rank among the literary masterpieces of the Spanish language.

After the completion of his studies, Lull journeyed ceaselessly. He lectured on mission problems in the great universities and carried on public religious debates with Moslems and with Jews. The Majorcan apostle never was ordained to the priesthood, but he did become a Franciscan tertiary.

Raymond Lull urged the establishment of missionary seminaries, where future apostles might learn the languages and the customs of their flocks-to-be. He advocated the foundation of a specialized mission department in the Holy See, over three hundred years before the creation of the Sacred Congregation for the Propagation of the Faith. This saintly genius accurately foresaw the second great Moslem advance toward Western Europe; and he pleaded for an active campaign to convert the onrushing Mongolian Asiatics, before those pagans should have embraced Islam.

In his old age, Lull made three missionary journeys to North Africa. He preached fearlessly in Tunis and in the town of Bugia, about a hundred miles east of Algiers. In spite of persecution and imprisonment, the aged servant of Christ won numerous converts. One day during his third missionary journey, a shouting mob of fanatical Moslems stoned the octogenarian apostle in the market place of Bugia. In the dawn of Paradise, the martyr saw Christ coming to meet him, "clad in new and scarlet robes."

HIS CONSUMING DESIRE

Like St. Francis of Assisi, Blessed Raymond Lull again and again expressed the desire to accomplish for Christ, "More than I can."

PART V

Renaissance, Great Discoveries, Protestant Revolt

(1300–1555)

CATHOLIC spiritual life declined markedly in the fourteenth and the fifteenth centuries. A rise of nationalism unfortunately coincided with the sojourn of the Popes in Avignon, under French influence (1309–1377). This period was followed by the disastrous Western Schism (1378–1417), during which factions among the cardinals elected Italian and French Popes and antipopes. The heresy of John Wycliff broke out in England and was imported into Bohemia, where it was propagated by John Hus. Inquisitorial methods of suppressing heresy were often not in the true spirit of Christianity.

In the middle of the fourteenth century, the Black Death carried off possibly a quarter of the population of Europe. France was desolated by the Hundred Years' War with England. In the East, in 1453, splendid Constantinople fell to the Ottoman Turks.

From 1431 to 1521, the Popes sponsored the literary and artistic revival of antiquity in Italy. As far as private and public morals were concerned, the Renaissance soon degenerated into paganism. In the closing years of the fifteenth century, the Popes fell into the vice of nepotism, in order to withstand their political enemies in Italy. The low ebb of Papal prestige inclined men to look to secular rulers for leadership in reform.

The Spanish drove the Moors entirely out of their peninsula in 1492, the same year in which Columbus discovered the New World. Four years earlier, Bartholomew Diaz had rounded the Cape of Good Hope, thus opening a sea route to India. The great discoveries of explorers in the employ of Portugal and Spain filled men of the first half of the sixteenth century with adventurous enthusiasm. The heady ideas of the Renaissance, as yet ill-assimilated, were pouring forth from the new printing presses. Hampered by her own inner ills of long standing, the Church was unable to control and direct the white-hot energies of the era.

The powerful Emperor Charles V was a champion of religious unity, but he did not succeed in mastering the disruptive forces of this age of transition from medieval to modern times. The heresies of the Protestant Revolt, backed by aggressive propaganda and armed force, sundered a large part of northern Europe from the Catholic communion. At the Peace of Augsburg, in 1555, Charles had to accept a costly compromise with Protestantism. In place of Christendom as the medieval ages knew it, there arose the modern, competitive self-interest of individual nations.

Apostolic zeal did not die out in these troubled, tumultuous centuries. Archbishop John of Montecorvino carried out his wonderful adventure for Christ in China. In Europe, Lithuania was brought into the Catholic Church. Missioners flocked to the Portuguese and Spanish colonies in Asia and the New World. A new day of great overseas expansion of Christianity was about to dawn. By his founding of the Society of Jesus, in 1534, St. Ignatius Loyola furnished the chief instrument of the approaching Catholic Reformation. The beloved disciple of St. Ignatius, St. Francis Xavier, left behind him the memory of a breath-taking apostolate that has been the admiration and holy envy of all the missioners who followed him.

ARCHBISHOP JOHN OF MONTECORVINO, O.F.M. (*c. 1250–1330*)

Toward the close of the thirteenth century, Father John of Montecorvino, a Franciscan friar, wrote from India: "Here I have baptized about a hundred persons; and here Brother Nicholas of Pistoia, the companion of my journey, died and has been buried."

Father John of Montecorvino was a native of Italy. He had already labored with marked success in Persia. In the year 1291, the Holy Father had chosen the talented Franciscan as his ambassador to the Emperor of Tartary, who then resided in Cambaluc (Peking). In India, Father John had lost his only companion on the tremendous trek, the Dominican, Nicholas of Pistoia.

The intrepid Franciscan journeyed on to Cambaluc. As far as is known, he was the first Roman Catholic missioner to reach China. The Emperor received Father John very graciously, and gave him full liberty to preach the Catholic Faith. But there were already some heretical Nestorian Christians in Cambaluc, and they became furiously jealous of the Franciscan. The Nestorians accused the missioner of being a dangerous spy.

"But at last, by the grace of God, the testimony of a certain individual proved my innocence to the Emperor, and at the same time showed him the malice of my enemies," wrote Father John.

The Franciscan built a church at Cambaluc, and baptized thousands of Chinese. He even won to the Faith the Tartar Prince George, and most of that ruler's Ongut tribe. The zealous missioner devoted special care to the training of one hundred and fifty Chinese seminarians. He taught them how to chant in choirs, and their resulting skill pleased the Emperor very much. During eleven years, the heroic pioneer labored alone in China. Then he was joined by a German Franciscan from the city of Cologne.

The Holy Father was overjoyed to learn of Father John's great work in China. In the year 1307, Pope Clement V appointed John of Montecorvino first Archbishop of Cambaluc. The Pope sent suffragan bishops to consecrate and aid the new archbishop. Archbishop John shared with his helpers the fruits of his long experience in China. The Catholic Faith spread along the coast of the great land, until it had reached Fukien Province, about eight hundred miles south of Cambaluc. When the octogenarian pioneer apostle of China died, in the year 1330, there were in the Chinese Empire approximately one hundred thousand Catholics.

A visiting Catholic archbishop wrote: "All the inhabitants of Cambaluc, without distinction, mourned for the man of God. Both Christians and pagans were present at the funeral ceremony, the latter rending their garments in token of grief, according to their custom on such occasions."

THE SIN OF JEALOUSY

Men of God have often suffered more at the hands of other Christians than from the enmity of nonbelievers. The pagan ruler of China was kind to John of Montecorvino; but the Franciscan apostle barely escaped execution when jealous heretics bore lying testimony against him.

BLESSED JADWIGA (*1371–1399*)

"Surely Your Majesty will not consent to marry the barbaric, pagan ruler of Lithuania?" one of her ladies in waiting asked Queen Jadwiga of Poland.

"Why do you say that Jagiello is barbaric? I have not found him so. And as for his being a pagan – that is precisely why I have decided to consent to the marriage," answered the lovely, young Polish ruler.

"Your Majesty!" gasped the amazed and horrified attendant.

"Has not King Jagiello promised to accept baptism if I marry him?" continued Queen Jadwiga. "And not only that – he has promised to bring into the Catholic Church all Lithuania, the one Baltic country still plunged in gross idolatry. Would you wish me to offend our Lord by refusing a means of saving so many souls? Just think! The poor Lithuanians not only worship lizards and serpents; they also offer those brute creatures human sacrifices! My heart bleeds for such dark ignorance."

The apostolic royal lady was as good as her word, and her Lithuanian suitor redeemed his pledges. On February 15, 1386, King Jagiello was baptized at Cracow. Many Polish priests became missioners in Lithuania, and a Franciscan friar was appointed head of the newly founded see of Vilna. Jagiello assumed the leadership in the destruction of paganism in his native land. The pagan "holy" fires were extinguished; the serpent deities were killed; and the sacred groves were felled.

The zealous Jagiello translated into the native dialects the Apostles' Creed, the Lord's Prayer, and other fundamental Christian formulas. He gave each of the Lithuanian converts a white woolen baptismal robe, and these gifts were highly valued by his subjects. All over the land, great crowds assembled on the banks of rivers to receive baptism.

Blessed Jagiello reigned until the year 1434; and at his death, he left Poland and Lithuania prosperous and powerful. His young consort had died thirty-five years previously. Jadwiga's brief life, wholly consecrated to God and country, made her a regal symbol of the devout and patriotic Polish people.

ROYALTY'S GREATEST GLORY

In the ages of faith, people everywhere recognized that the power of duly anointed sovereigns comes from God. Moreover, many of the nations of modern Europe were first led to the knowledge of Christ by royal apostles.

ST. VINCENT FERRER, O.P. (*1350–1418*)

One Saturday morning, in the fourteenth century, there was a commotion at the entrance of a synagogue in a city of Spain. A man carrying a cross brushed his way past a group of worshipers and advanced up the aisle. The intruder walked right up to the pulpit and motioned for the rabbi to step down. That dignitary was so astonished that he obeyed.

Father Vincent Ferrer mounted the pulpit, and with a commanding gesture stopped the excited whispering of the congregation. We do not know the exact contents of the sermon the Dominican priest preached in the synagogue that day in Salamanca. But what he said so moved those who heard him that the whole congregation desired to enter the Church. After Father Ferrer's sermon, they changed their synagogue into a Catholic edifice and named it the Church of the Holy Cross.

St. Vincent Ferrer publicly condemned persecution as a means of forcing Jews to accept baptism. One biographer claims that the great Dominican's missionary labors in Spain brought twenty-five thousand Jews into the Church.

The fame of Father Ferrer's preaching and holiness traveled to the court of the Moorish ruler of Granada, in Spain, and this sovereign asked the Dominican to visit his realm. Father Ferrer accepted the invitation and preached the Gospel to the Moslems. Soon the saintly missioner had won so many converts that the royal advisers were alarmed. They warned their ruler that before long he would have only Christians as subjects. Reluctantly, the sovereign asked Father Ferrer to leave Granada.

St. Vincent Ferrer lived in the troubled period of the Western Schism, when several candidates at the same time were laying claim to the throne of St. Peter. In addition to his great apostolate in Spain, the saint preached to thousands in France, Switzerland, and Italy. He pleaded for penance, worked miracles, won hardened sinners to the practice of their Faith, and eloquently urged obedience to the legitimate Pope. It was this famous missionary saint who, under God, brought about the end of the Western Schism.

FEW ARE CHOSEN

The Moorish ruler of Granada himself, Mahomet Aben Balva, was disposed to embrace the religion preached by St. Vincent Ferrer, but he was a weakling. He was among the many souls called by God to a higher life, but not chosen, because of their failure to correspond with the promptings of the Holy Spirit.

FATHER JUAN DE PADILLA, O.F.M.
(*d. c. 1544*)

How many American Catholics know the name of the protomartyr of what was later to become part of the United States? Even those who know much about Father Juan de Padilla cannot be sure exactly where or when the Franciscan missioner was martyred.

It is thought that Father Padilla journeyed from Spain to Mexico in the year 1528. In Mexico, he acted as military chaplain to Nuño de Guzmán, and restrained that cruel conqueror in his oppression of the Indians. Afterward, Father Padilla was a zealous missioner in many regions of Mexico. He was also the founder of several Franciscan monasteries.

In the year 1540, Father Padilla accompanied Coronado on the memorable march northward in search of the fabled Seven Golden Cities. The brave Coronado found no mysterious treasures; so after having explored probably as far as what is now central Kansas, the disappointed explorer and the starving members of his expedition returned to Mexico. Father Padilla, however, remained behind, to evangelize the Indians. He won a group of red men to Christ by his intense love for their souls; then he set out to preach to a neighboring tribe.

On the way, the apostle met a band of savages on the warpath. Realizing that the hour of his martyrdom was at hand, the Franciscan knelt calmly to pray. As he was offering to God the sacrifice of his life for the conversion of the Indians, the hideously painted warriors riddled the martyr with arrows. They then threw the dead priest into a pit and covered him with stones.

Some authorities believe that Father Juan de Padilla laid down his life in the year 1542. Other writers claim that the pioneer missioner was martyred later – in November, 1544.

TREASURES IN HEAVEN

The courageous explorer, Coronado, was disappointed in his search for earthly wealth. But Coronado's companion, Father Juan de Padilla, suffered no deception. He found and laid up for himself in heaven priceless treasures – the ransomed souls of red men, and the ineffable grace of martyrdom.

ARCHBISHOP JUAN DE ZUMÁRRAGA, O.F.M. (*c. 1468–1548*)

"I would sooner go to hell than ask an absolution from the Franciscan friars!" declared a sixteenth-century politician in Mexico City.

The politician was a henchman of Nuño de Guzmán, then president of the royal law court; and Guzmán was cruelly oppressing the Indians. The dictator and his followers were furious with the Franciscans because Fray Juan de Zumárraga, the first Bishop of Mexico City, was protecting the red men. The members of the royal law court even threatened the bishop's life. They did not wish Emperor Charles V, in Spain, to find out about their wicked deeds, so they censored all the bishop's outgoing mail. Nevertheless, the intrepid prelate managed to get a letter through to the Emperor. Nuño de Guzmán and his followers were ousted from power, and the great Antonio de Mendoza was appointed first Viceroy of New Spain (Mexico).

Mendoza sought to please God, and he went out of his way to help Bishop Zumárraga get fair treatment for the Indians. The apostolic bishop spent himself in organizing the evangelization and the education of the native people of Mexico. He founded schools and a college for Indian boys, and he brought ladies from Spain to teach Indian girls. Juan de Zumárraga procured for Mexico City the first printing press set up in the New World. It arrived in 1537, and it had been in operation for one hundred years when the Harvard Press issued the *New England Primer.*

Bishop Zumárraga imported from Spain skilled mechanics who trained the Mexican Indians in manufacturing and in improved methods of farming. He consecrated new prelates for Mexico; organized the ecclesiastical life and discipline of the land; and considered the methods for training an Indian clergy. It was during the episcopate of Juan de Zumárraga that Our Lady of Guadalupe appeared to a Christian Indian of lowly birth, Juan Diego. After the bishop had made sure of the authenticity of the apparition, he encouraged the spread of the devotion, which is now dear to the hearts of all Mexicans.

Only death could terminate the labors of the great missionary bishop. "I die very poor, but very happy," he had written to the Emperor, shortly before the end came on June 3, 1548.

Some months before that time, Pope Paul III appointed Juan de Zumárraga to be Archbishop of Mexico City, the capital of New Spain; but the apostle did not live to receive the bull of official notification.

THE TRUE CIVILIZERS

A Mexican authority holds that the true civilizers of Spanish America were the great pioneer missioners, like Juan de Zumárraga. Had it not been for them, he affirms, "Spain would have discovered within a short time that her acquisitions were only deserts which it would have been necessary to repopulate to make them of any use."

FATHER LOUIS CANCER DE BARBASTRO, O.P. (*d. 1549*)

One of the most colorfully heroic missioners in the early history of the Americas is the Spanish Dominican, Father Louis Cancer. He was an apostle who united a keenly vivid imagination with the utmost courage. Both of these facets of his character are evident in his unique evangelization of the Tuzulutlan Indians, in the mountains of Guatemala.

Father Cancer was an enthusiastic supporter of the ideas of Father Bartholomew de Las Casas. He thought, as did his great friend, that the foremost obstacle to the evangelization of the Indians was the oppression exercised by the Spanish colonists. The conquistadors in Guatemala had not been able to vanquish the Tuzulutlan Indians. In the year 1537, Father Cancer obtained from the officials in Guatemala a solemn promise. If the Dominican missioner should succeed in pacifying the fierce warriors in the mountains, then the officials would keep the Spanish colonizers out of the region.

Father Cancer enlisted the help of four Christian Indians of the plains, who were peddlers. The missioner had already mastered the Quiché language of the mountain Indians, so he composed in Quiché a rhythmic catechism. He set the catechism to music, and taught the peddlers how to sing it, accompanying themselves on the crude tribal instruments used by the mountaineers.

When the peddlers had been thoroughly drilled in their musical apostolate, Father Cancer sent them up into the mountains with full packs. The mountaineers were delighted with the peddlers' gifts, and they loved the sung catechism. They soon asked the peddlers to explain what they were singing.

"Only the Christian priests can do that," answered the peddlers. "They are kind and peaceful men, not at all like the white owners of mines and ranches. They only want to teach the Indians about the true God."

So the Indians of Tuzulutlan sent for Father Cancer, and that intrepid apostle went alone into their midst. The country of the mountain Indians had been called the "Land of War." But as time passed, Father Cancer and his confreres made such headway among the red men of Tuzulutlan that the Spaniards changed the name of the region to *Vera Paz,* the land of "True Peace."

In the year 1549, Father Cancer set out northward to evangelize the Indians of Florida who had already been antagonized by the cruelty of Spanish conquistadors. The red men of Florida ambushed and murdered two of the apostle's confreres. Then Father Cancer had himself put ashore alone, at the head of Tampa Bay. He knelt on the beach in prayer; and as he was praying, several Indians seized the missioner and brutally slew him. So was martyred one of the foremost Christianizers of the Americas.

CHAMPION OF THE OPPRESSED

The Dominican Order stands pre-eminent in history as the uncompromising champion of the civil rights of the red men, and

Father Louis Cancer de Barbastro was worthy of these great principles. Before he set out for Florida, he obtained a royal decree restoring to freedom every native of Florida held in bondage in any part of the Spanish dominions in America.

ST. IGNATIUS LOYOLA, S.J. (*1491–1556*)

In the year 1521, Captain Ignatius Loyola, of the Basque nobility, inspired the garrison of the citadel of Pamplona, in northern Spain, to hold out against an overwhelmingly superior French force. But at length the intrepid captain was felled by a cannon ball that fractured his left leg. He was carried to his ancestral castle and treated according to the best knowledge of the time. Then, as the long days of convalescence dragged on, Ignatius realized that his career as a warrior had come to an abrupt end.

"Get me a good tale of chivalry to read," he told his attendant, hoping to distract his mind from his own troubles.

But the only books available in the castle of Loyola were a Carthusian monk's *Life of Christ* and James de Voragine's *Golden Legend of the Saints.* These books gradually worked on the soul of the wounded knight and became the instruments of his conversion. Ignatius understood that he could still serve as a captain in the spiritual army of the King of kings.

As soon as he was able to leave his family castle, Ignatius set out for the town of Manresa. He cared for the sick in the public hospital there, and he spent much time in prayer and penance. In the solitude of a cave outside Manresa, God granted to Ignatius a deep knowledge of divine mysteries and of the science of souls. It was in this solitude that the founder of the Jesuits wrote the major part of his great book of asceticism, the *Spiritual Exercises.*

In 1523, Ignatius made a pilgrimage to the Holy Land. At its close the iron-willed man decided that, if he would carry out his part in God's service, he must first obtain a good classical and theological education. The thirty-three-year-old ex-captain accordingly undertook the study of Latin grammar among boys young enough to be his sons. Later Ignatius attended the Universities of

Alcalá and of Salamanca. But his novel ideas caused the saint to be suspected of heresy; so in 1528, Ignatius left Spain and went to the famous University of Paris.

In Paris, Ignatius Loyola became the roommate of his future permanent disciples, Peter Faber and Francis Xavier. By the summer of 1534, Ignatius had six disciples. On the feast of the Assumption, the seven pioneer Jesuits pronounced their vows, binding themselves to poverty, chastity, and a pilgrimage to Jerusalem. If the pilgrimage to the Holy Land should not prove feasible, they were to place themselves unreservedly under the Pope's orders.

The war of the Turks against Venice did eventually prevent the first members of the Society of Jesus from undertaking an apostolate in the Holy Land. Instead, they were to become the shock troops of the Holy See in the battle against the spread of Protestantism in Europe. Ignatius Loyola and Francis Xavier were both ordained to the priesthood in Venice, on June 24, 1537. The Constitutions of the Society were finally approved by the Holy See on September 27, 1540. The Jesuits took a special vow of obedience to the Pope. Ignatius was elected the first Superior-General of the new spiritual army at the disposal of the Church.

After the Constitutions had been approved, St. Ignatius continued for sixteen years to inspire and direct the amazing expansion of the Society's work. When he died, on July 31, 1556, the irresistible authority of his great spirit had given a permanent stamp to his Society of Jesus. Its members have continued through the centuries to manifest in the service of God the passionate and disciplined devotion that characterized their founder.

INVINCIBLE TRUTH

"Nothing resists the truth for long: it may be assailed, but never overcome." — *St. Ignatius Loyola*

ST. FRANCIS XAVIER, S.J. (*1506–1552*)

St. Francis Xavier, the most renowned of modern apostles, was born of noble parents in the Basque country of Spain. Francis determined to become a scholar, rather than to follow the career of arms. In 1525, the handsome and proudly ambitious young man set out for the University of Paris. At Paris, Francis Xavier soon became popular. He was so fortunate as to have for roommate Peter Faber, a former shepherd from the hills of Savoy and a saint. Peter kept Francis away from the seamy side of university life. In 1530, Francis took the degree of master of arts and was appointed to give lectures on Aristotle; he felt that he was getting somewhere in the world.

Then a third man came to share the friends' university quarters. The newcomer was a middle-aged Spaniard, a former captain of the militia, named Ignatius Loyola. One day, when Francis was talking with enthusiasm about his ambitious hopes and plans, Ignatius interrupted him with the quiet question, "What shall it profit a man, Don Francisco, if he gain the whole world, and suffer the loss of his own soul?"

The question sank deep into the inmost consciousness of the popular young professor, and filled him with a divine disquiet. Both Francis Xavier and Peter Faber became followers of Ignatius Loyola. Francis Xavier served his apprenticeship in caring for the sick in the public hospitals of Venice, and in preaching at Bologna.

Then, in 1540, Father Xavier was assigned to the Orient. St. Ignatius addressed to the beloved son, whom he was never to see again on earth, the great farewell command: "Go and set all on fire!"

On May 6, 1542, Xavier landed at the Portuguese colony of Goa, in India. The saint was shocked by the immoral lives of many of the Portuguese merchants and settlers and the scandal thus afforded to non-Christian natives. During five months, Xavier preached to the colonists, tended the needy sick, visited prisoners, and taught religion to the children of Goa. He assembled the children by going through the streets and ringing a bell. Then, simply and lovingly, the great Jesuit instructed the little ones in the truths of the Faith and taught them how to pray.

Xavier was eager to go out among Asia's teeming pagans. His first mission was among the Paravas, poor pearl fishers on India's southern coast. He brought the whole lowly Parava caste into the Church. In 1545, Father Francis embarked for the Malay Peninsula. He evangelized Malacca, then the chief clearing station between India and the Far East. From Malacca, he set sail for the Spice Islands; and there he won dark-skinned converts on Amboina, Ceram, Ternate, and the Isles of the Moors, beyond Portuguese territory.

As Francis Xavier was returning to India, he met at Malacca a young Japanese by the name of Yajiro. The apostle made a thousand inquiries about the distant and mysterious Sunrise Islands. In 1549, with Yajiro as guide and with two Jesuits as fellow missioners, Xavier embarked to convert Japan. But he found conditions in the Empire very different from Yajiro's optimistic descriptions.

The proud Japanese scorned the poverty and the humility of the Jesuits. The missioners met with determined opposition from the Buddhist bonzes. And Xavier discovered that the "mighty Emperor" of whom Yajiro had spoken was a wraithlike prisoner in a ruined palace. Nevertheless, Francis Xavier soon stated that the Japanese were the delight of his soul; and he foretold that they would persevere in the Faith if ever they should embrace it.

The Jesuit newcomers noted that the most frequent Japanese objection to the Christian teaching was, "How is it that China knows nothing about this?" The saint concluded that Christianity must reach Japan and all the Far East through the evangelization of China, the fountainhead of Oriental culture.

Francis Xavier left Japan for India in 1551 in order to organize his last mission venture, the conversion of China. At Goa, he took measures to strengthen the seminary for the training of Asiatic priests, for the great Jesuit well understood the primary importance of an indigenous clergy. On Easter Day, 1552, the apostle said what was to be his final farewell to his confreres in Goa. He was never to reach the inhospitable mainland of China, then forbidden under pain of death to all foreigners.

The Apostle of the Orient died of fever on Sancian Island, off the coast of South China, on December 3, 1552. He was alone, except for a faithful Chinese servant. But death itself was powerless against the divine fire cast by St. Francis Xavier over immense distances of the Orient. Today the splendor of that glowing trail still draws Catholic missioners to high adventure for God and souls.

CHRISTLIKE COMPASSION

St. Francis Xavier shared the compassion of his divine Master for those who have not found the way to true peace. "I feel far more of compassion for those who fight against God, than of any desire to call down greater vengeance on their heads. They are already miserable enough in the mere fact that they do so fight," he wrote.

FATHER GONÇALO DA SILVEIRA, S.J. (*d. 1561*)

Gonçalo da Silveira belonged to one of Portugal's greatest families. He became a member of the young Society of Jesus; and very soon after his ordination to the priesthood, he was appointed to important positions in his homeland. He was everywhere in demand on account of his eloquent sermons. In his missionary journeys throughout Portugal, he usually slept in hospitals, where he tended the sick; and it was his custom to beg for his food from door to door. Shortly before the death of St. Ignatius Loyola, the founder of the Jesuits appointed Father Silveira to be Provincial of India.

The new Jesuit Provincial arrived at Goa in September, 1556; and during the next three years, he did much to relieve the native Christians of India from oppression by overbearing Portuguese settlers. Then the Society of Jesus received a call from a chieftain in southeastern Africa, asking for a Catholic missioner. Father Silveira was overjoyed when he, another Jesuit priest, and a Jesuit Brother were sent as pioneers to South Africa. It was known that a great Negro kingdom existed between the Limpopo and the

Zambezi Rivers, and that it was ruled over by the paramount chief of the Makaranga. Gamba, the ruler who had asked for a missioner, was a subject of the paramount chief. Consequently, Father Silveira had apostolic visions of converting all South Africa!

The Portuguese Jesuit was thirty-four years of age when he set out for his new mission. In the summer of 1560, after a most uncomfortable voyage down the African coast, the three apostles arrived at the kraal of Chief Gamba. Both Father Silveira and the Brother were ill with a high fever. Indeed, Brother André da Costa was so enfeebled that he was shortly afterward sent back to India; but the indomitable Father Silveira recovered.

Many converts were made in Gamba's kraal, and the chief even put away all his wives except the first. Father Silveira was eager to press on to the headquarters of the paramount chief. Leaving the other Jesuit priest at Gamba's kraal, he returned to Mozambique; and from there he sailed hundreds of miles up the Zambezi River, into the region now known as Rhodesia. After countless adventures, the lone missioner reached the primitive "court" of the paramount chief.

At first all went well. The chief, his mother, and many of his subjects were baptized. But Arabian traders in the kraal of the African potentate poisoned the suspicious ruler's mind against the Christian priest. They whispered that Father Gonçalo da Silveira was in reality a spy, sent by the Governor of India. In the dead of night, the chief sent assassins who seized the sleeping missioner and strangled him. So died, on March 16, 1561, the pioneer Apostle of South Africa.

NO COMPROMISE WITH EVIL

In matters that do not concern faith and morals, the Christian should avoid contentious condemnation of usages different from his own; but he may not compromise with evil. Eager as was Father Gonçalo da Silveira to convert African rulers to Christianity, he did not condone their polygamous customs.

BISHOP VASCO DE QUIROGA (*1470–1565*)

Don Vasco de Quiroga spent many years as a distinguished lawyer in Spain. He was already sixty years of age when, in 1530, he was appointed judge of the royal court in Mexico, or New Spain, as it was then called. The turbulent period of the conquest was drawing to a close in the New World colony, and many abuses had to be corrected. The ruler of Spain desired, in particular, that the conquerors and other Spanish colonists should be restrained in their oppression of the Indians.

Quiroga set to work in Mexico with great energy, and he soon reached a conclusion as to how the Indian problem should be solved. "The manner of living of the Indians is chaos and confusion; and there is no way of putting them in order or promoting good Christian life, eliminating drunkenness, idolatry, and other evils, unless they can be placed together in well-ordered communities," he informed the Council of the Indies in Spain.

Toward the close of 1531, the royal judge proceeded to put his ideas into practical effect, by founding an Indian community near Mexico City – at his own expense! The Indians came flocking to Don Vasco's foundation. Within a short while, more than thirty thousand red men had settled around the institution.

The Spanish Government soon became interested in the new Indian community, and subsidized Don Vasco de Quiroga's great work. The missionary lawyer proceeded to found similar communities in the neighboring region of Michoacán, where the plight of the Indians was especially pitiable. In Don Vasco's foundations, the Indians were shown how to live according to Christian morals. They learned how to read and write, and they were taught improved methods of agriculture, as well as various arts and crafts.

After the diocese of Michoacán had been created, the Spanish sovereign presented to the Pope the name of Don Vasco de Quiroga as a man pre-eminently qualified to head the new diocese. The learned and apostolic lawyer was ordained a priest and then consecrated a bishop in 1538. Thereafter, the great benefactor of the Indians ruled his diocese during twenty-six years.

Bishop Quiroga journeyed on muleback to every corner of his spiritual domain, and he dotted his whole territory with hospitals, schools, and churches for the Indians. He brought in a small army of missioners. At the age of ninety-five, Bishop Quiroga was engaged in a general visitation of his diocese, when death overtook the amazing old apostle suddenly — on March 14, 1565.

A Spanish biographer has written of Bishop Quiroga that the supreme enterprise of his life was "the material redemption of the native Mexicans, as a solid basis for the fruitful teaching of the Gospel."

MORE THAN MERE PHILANTHROPY

Like Bishop Quiroga, many Catholic apostles have been great social benefactors of their converts. But, again like him, they strove for a supernatural aim far above mere philanthropy. "The true conversion of the natives should be the principal intent of those in charge here," wrote Quiroga.

BISHOP BARTHOLOMEW DE LAS CASAS, O.P. (*1474–1566*)

In the sixteenth century, a priest who had labored in the New World stood before the throne of Emperor Charles V in Spain, and pleaded for the red men. The priest said: "Your Majesty, the lash and the stick are the only pay that the Spaniards give the Indians for their constant toil; and scarcely a word do the masters address to the red men, if it be not to call them 'dogs'!"

The speaker was the famous Dominican missioner, Father Bartholomew de Las Casas. By no means were all the Spanish conquistadors and colonizers in the New World guilty of the excesses depicted by Father Las Casas. But the need of laws for the protection of the Indians was proved by the fact that, soon after the arrival of the Spaniards in the West Indies, the native population of the islands passed away. The death of most of the red men resulted from the unaccustomed, forced labor in the mines and in the fields. Many other Indians died of diseases brought to their country by the white men.

Charles V appointed Father Las Casas "Protector of the Indians," and the Emperor issued laws to safeguard the native Americans. Seven times in all, the great Dominican sailed from the New World for Spain, to plead for the oppressed Indians. On one occasion, Father Las Casas submitted a scheme for colonizing and converting the mainland of South America. A long stretch of territory on the coast of Venezuela was assigned to the missioner for settlement; but the armed interference of Spanish soldiers aroused the fierce natives, and reprisals caused the apostolic experiment to fail.

Afterward, Father Bartholomew de Las Casas accomplished remarkable mission work in Haiti, Peru, Nicaragua, and Guatemala. He declined the rich diocese of Cuzco in Peru; but he accepted the poor missionary diocese of Chiapa in Mexico. There, with undiminished zeal, he continued to protect the Indians. When the noble missionary champion of the red men died, in the year 1566, he had obtained from both Pope and Emperor crucial decisions in favor of the Indians and their liberty.

FATHER OF HIS FLOCK

Because Bishop Bartholomew de Las Casas fearlessly protected the Mexican Indians, his life was actually threatened. Advised by some of his friends to go away, the brave apostle replied: "If the cause were mine, I should gladly leave. . . . But it is a question of my sheep, these miserable Indians, oppressed and worn out with an unjust servitude and insupportable taxes. Here I wish to stay."

PART VI

The Catholic Reformation

(1555–1648)

TODAY most estimates would couple in importance the Council of Trent (1545–1563) with the first Council of Nicaea. Pope Paul III hoped to convoke at Trent representatives of all Christendom, but the Protestants refused to attend. Twice adjourned for political reasons, the council nevertheless accomplished its crucial work. St. Charles Borromeo, nephew of Pope Pius IV and Cardinal Archbishop of Milan, worked untiringly for its success. Two Jesuits, Father James Laynez and Father Alphonsus Salmeron, were outstanding even among the distinguished theologians assembled at Trent.

Once the Tridentine plan of reforms had been translated into action, the Catholic Restoration made rapid strides. The heroic battle against heresy won back large areas of Europe to the Faith. The Council of Trent launched the whole modern movement for Catholic schools and seminaries. The Jesuits became the foremost educators of the period, raising up a generation of virile priests and lay Catholics to further the work of the Catholic Revival. At the close of the sixteenth century, the Papacy was stronger than it had been for generations.

Meanwhile, the sainted Pope Pius V had organized a naval victory over the Ottoman Turks, who had grown more menacing to

Christendom than ever before under Sultan Soliman the Magnificent. The Christian fleets of Spain, Venice, Genoa, Malta, and that of the Pope won a brilliant victory at Lepanto, on October 7, 1571.

In 1622, Pope Gregory XV founded the Sacred Congregation for the Propagation of the Faith. Through "Propaganda," as the congregation is briefly designated, the Holy See directed both the evangelization of non-Christian lands and the efforts to win back Protestant countries to the Faith. In spite of the numerous benefits resulting from the creation of "Propaganda," apostolic activity suffered in the seventeenth century from the rapid development of state absolutism in Europe.

All continental Europe was involved in the politico-religious struggle known as the Thirty Years' War (1618–1648). The Catholic armies won the earlier campaigns; but in his determined opposition to the Hapsburg power, Cardinal Richelieu, the strong minister of King Louis XIII of France, tipped the scale in favor of the Protestants. The Treaty of Westphalia (1648) barred the further spread of the Catholic Reformation, and endorsed the un-Christian principle of state supremacy.

The intense missionary movement of the Catholic Reformation brought more souls into the Church in the New World, in Asia, and in Africa, than had been lost to the Faith through the Protestant upheaval in Europe. The Philippine Islands, in particular, were thoroughly Christianized by Catholic Spain. Space permits here mention of only a representative few among the hundreds of zealous missioners of this splendid age.

FATHER MANOEL DE NÓBREGA, S.J.
(*c. 1517–1570*)

In the year 1549, the stanchly Catholic Thomé de Souza was sent to the Portuguese colony of Brazil as captain general. He was accompanied by six Jesuits, the leader of whom was Father Manoel de Nóbrega. Thomé de Souza founded the town of Bahia, and there the earliest Brazilian diocese was created. It had an unfortunate beginning, for its first bishop was captured and eaten by cannibalistic Indians!

Meanwhile, Father Nóbrega and his Jesuits had been living in a shack, and partaking of the same wild vegetables that the Indians ate. Father Nóbrega had an endless amount of zeal and patience, so he won the affection of the primitive, native Brazilians. The renowned apostle founded in northern Brazil flourishing Jesuit missions where the Indians were Christianized and civilized.

Father Nóbrega uprooted polygamy among his mission Indians, but at first he was less successful in weaning them from cannibalism. One day he heard that a group of Indians were about to make a meal of a captured prisoner. Father Nóbrega and some of his Jesuit companions hastened to the scene of the banquet. They arrived just as the prisoner's corpse was being placed on a fire – and they made off with the body. The Indians were so dumfounded by the missioners' courage that they remained as if glued to the spot. After the Jesuits had given decent burial to the dead prisoner, the capturers came meekly to Father Nóbrega and promised to eat no more human flesh. So it was by actions rather than by words that the great Jesuit put a stop to cannibalism among his Christianized red men.

Each of the three early governors of Brazil looked to Father Nóbrega for guidance in the religious and social organization of the colony. In southern Brazil, Father Nóbrega founded the College of São Paulo, later so wonderfully developed by Father José de Anchieta. When French intruders in southern Brazil won over the fierce Tamóios Indians, Father Nóbrega, at the imminent risk of being killed and eaten, successfully conducted peace negotiations with the Tamóios. His intrepid action made it possible for the Portuguese to drive away the French and to found the great city of Rio de Janeiro in 1565. There, five years later, the "father of the Christendoms of Brazil" gave his spirit to the Lord.

A UNIVERSAL FATHER

A confrere of Father Nóbrega wrote: "His death was deeply felt. . . . This great man was a universal father of the Christendoms of Brazil, which he saw abundantly founded and made into numerous villages of people brought from jungles, where they had lived like beasts."

ST. LOUIS BERTRAND, O.P. (*1526–1581*)

Nearly four centuries ago, a Dominican missioner was telling the gospel story to a group of attentive Indians in the mountains of northeastern Colombia in South America. The village chief suddenly hastened up to Father Louis Bertrand and said to him urgently: "Come quickly to the edge of the forest, Father! Fifteen hundred men of the distant tribe of Paluato are gathered there. We feared they had come to attack us, but they said that they have crossed the mountains only to find you!"

That was, indeed, good news to Father Bertrand. A short while previously, he had labored among the red men of Paluato; but they had refused to accept Christianity. Now God had miraculously changed their hearts.

The apostolate of Father Louis Bertrand in Spanish America lasted only seven and a half years; but he converted thousands of Indians in Colombia, Panama, and the West Indies. This great Dominican missioner was continually in poor health, yet he journeyed unceasingly through trackless tropical forests in his quest for souls. God granted to him the gift of tongues, so that his message was understood by Indians speaking widely different dialects. Father Bertrand won converts even among the Caribs – fierce cannibals who at first tried to poison the Spanish priest.

Louis Bertrand was a native of Valencia, Spain, and a relative of St. Vincent Ferrer. Before he went to America, he had won fame and veneration as a novice master and a preacher in his native land. After his return to Spain, Father Bertrand inspired many of his young countrymen to go as missioners to the New World. Soon after his death, St. Louis Bertrand was declared the patron of Colombia.

GOD LOVES THE HUMBLE OF HEART

Before going to the New World, St. Louis Bertrand gave special care to the instruction of lay Brothers. He often pointed out how well fitted they were for the contemplative phase of the Dominican ideal. "God is pleased to converse with the simple and humble of heart," he used to repeat.

BLESSED EDMUND CAMPION, S.J.
(*c. 1540–1581*)

"Take the traitor away!" cried Queen Elizabeth angrily. "I have offered him rich benefices if he would become a minister in the national Church of which I, his sovereign, am the head. But there is no English loyalty in the fellow. The time for mercy is past!"

Yet as Elizabeth watched the rough jailers drag the Jesuit priest away, the secret feeling of her heart was one of regretful remorse rather than of anger. She was thinking of the days when she had first befriended the handsome, brilliant Edmund Campion, then an outstanding scholar and orator at Oxford University. Later the royal Protestant had heard that the distinguished young humanist had undergone a deep spiritual experience, and had become an exile for conscience' sake. Well, Queen Elizabeth herself had once known the strong pull of the old Faith.

On the Continent, Edmund Campion had been received into the Society of Jesus; and he had been ordained to the priesthood at Prague. In the year 1579, Father Campion's superiors had sent him back as a missioner to his native land. In past centuries, England had been so devoutly Catholic that the fair island was known as "Our Lady's Dowry"; but at that time, heresy had done its deadly work.

For over a year, the fervent apostle had traversed the English countryside, ministering to the persecuted Catholics and bringing apostates back to the Faith. Early in 1581, hunters of priests had caught up with him. Now, in memory of past days, Father Campion had been granted an interview with his sovereign and had courteously refused her tempting offers.

Edmund Campion was then cruelly racked. When the Jesuit was brought to his trial, he had been so severely tortured that he was unable to lift his hand to take the oath. But just before he heard that he was condemned to be hanged, drawn, and quartered at Tyburn Cross, he found the strength to utter an immortal speech.

"In condemning us, you condemn all your own ancestors, all the ancient priests, bishops, and kings – all that was once the glory of England, the island of the saints and the most devoted child of the See of Peter!" cried Campion. "To be condemned with these old lights – not of England only, but of the world – by their degenerate descendants, is both glory and gladness to us."

After he had been dragged on a hurdle to Tyburn, five long miles from the Tower of London, Blessed Edmund Campion went joyously to his death; and he kissed the executioner's gory hands. A drop of the martyr's blood splashed on the fine clothes of Henry Walpole, a young elegant who stood close by the scaffold. Henry Walpole went away a changed man. Fourteen years later, he, too, died a Jesuit martyr at Tyburn Cross.

PROPHETIC TRUST

In these days, when the Catholic Faith is recording amazing advance in England, the following words of Blessed Edmund Campion have the ring of a prophetic trust in God: "This Church here shall never fail so long as priests and pastors shall be found for their sheep, rage man or devil never so much."

BLESSED RUDOLF AQUAVIVA, S.J. (*1550–1583*)

"An ambassador from the Great Mogul has arrived in Goa. He brings a message from Emperor Akbar, requesting that learned Jesuits be sent to Fatehpur Sikri at once!" the excited Portuguese colonists told one another, in the year 1579.

Akbar, the most illustrious of the Mogul rulers of northern India, had determined to found a new religion, so tolerant that it would gather into itself the many beliefs and peoples of his Empire. When Jesuits in Bengal had insisted that some Christian merchants pay their dues to the Emperor's treasury, Akbar was struck by a religion that would inspire such justice. Now he desired to know more about it.

The Jesuit superior in Goa decided to send to the splendid court of the Peacock Throne the young and gifted Father Rudolf Aquaviva, who came of an Italian family of proud lineage. After a long, eventful journey, Father Rudolf and his Jesuit companions reached Fatehpur Sikri, the "City of Victory," Akbar's magnificent new capital near Agra. The Jesuits were accorded every honor at court, but the Emperor did not openly proclaim to his subjects his toleration of Christianity. As a result, the Moguls did not dare to approach the missioners.

Akbar conceived a warm friendship for Father Rudolf, and he delighted in religious discussions with the Jesuits; but he showed no real intention of becoming a Christian. As a matter of fact, the Great Mogul felt that he could not afford to alienate his people by embracing a foreign religion, and by dismissing all the wives he had married for political reasons. At length, the Jesuits' superior determined to recall them to Goa.

Soon afterward, Father Aquaviva was sent to a region south of Goa, where the Hindus were fanatically devoted to their own religion. There, on July 25, 1583, the holy, young missioner and four Jesuit companions were martyred by a furious mob.

Emperor Akbar wept bitterly, when he heard of his loved Jesuit's death. "I should never have permitted my friend to leave my side," he mourned.

The Great Mogul often meditated on the teachings of Blessed Rudolf. Shortly before Akbar's own death, in 1605, he ordered to be inscribed on his splendid Gate of Victory, at Fatehpur Sikri, the following words: "Said Jesus, on whom be peace: 'This world is a bridge. Pass over it; but build no house there!' "

HE ASPIRED AFTER GOD

Blessed Rudolf Aquaviva aspired strongly after God from his youth. So on the day of his martyrdom, he merited to hear the Almighty say: "I have carried you upon wings of eagles, and have taken you to myself" (Exod. 19:4).

TWENTY-SIX MARTYRS OF JAPAN (*d. 1597*)

On February 5, of the year 1597, three altar boys in Japan were preparing to receive the Sacrament of Penance. Their confessions were to be their last, so the three boys examined their consciences very carefully, as they marched along the muddy road on their way to execution.

The three native altar boys were not the only Catholics who had been sentenced to die for the Faith on that day. Six Franciscan foreign missioners and three Japanese Jesuits were also to lay down their lives. Fourteen lay Christians, in addition to the altar boys, brought the number of the condemned up to twenty-six.

Twenty-six crosses lay ready on the ground, on a hill outside the city of Nagasaki. Soldiers were busy for a while, fastening each Christian to a cross with ropes and a heavy iron ring about his neck. Then strong hands lifted the crosses up, and set them in holes that had been dug about three feet apart. A great crowd had gathered to witness this scene, and the spectators noted with amazement the evident joy of the victims.

One pagan said to another, "Why, those Christians actually seem to expect some wonderful reward for their cruel sufferings!"

The commanding officer barked an order, and twenty-six soldiers stood in position, one in front of each cross. At a second order from the commander, each soldier raised his spear — but then halted at an unexpected sound. The voices of the condemned had suddenly arisen in the great chant of the *Benedictus:* "Blessed be the Lord God of Israel; because He hath visited and wrought the redemption of His people. . . . Through the mercy of our God, in which the Orient from on high hath visited us, to enlighten them that sit in darkness and the shadow of death."

As the swelling chorus died away, the sweet, reedy voices of the three altar boys began the *Laudate Pueri.* "Praise the Lord, O ye children!" they sang; and they fell silent only when the soldiers finally wielded the spears and pierced the hearts of all twenty-six sufferers. So died the first Christian martyrs of the young Church in Japan.

AS XAVIER FORETOLD

St. Francis Xavier foretold that Japanese converts would abide in their Faith. The saint's trust in the capacity of the Japanese for heroic sanctity was justified by the joyous constancy of hundreds of thousands of Japanese who died for Christ during the inhuman seventeenth-century mass persecutions in the islands.

ST. PETER CANISIUS, S.J. (*1521–1597*)

In the middle of the sixteenth century, a keen observer pointed out that, if a revival of Catholicism were to come about in Luther's land, it would have to be achieved through education and through literary activity. Those very weapons against Protestantism were employed by one of the great pioneer Jesuits, St. Peter Canisius. This Jesuit from Holland labored ceaselessly to promote the founding of Catholic colleges, and his eloquent pen was never idle.

St. Peter Canisius saw that many Catholics had no clear knowledge of their Faith, and that there existed no handy summary of Christian doctrine suitable to the times. So in the year 1555, he published at Vienna a best seller. Though Protestant critics wrote scathing reviews, the best seller went through more than two hundred editions in twelve languages even before its author died. The title of that remarkable book was *The Catechism.* It was of inestimable value to the heroic missioners of the Catholic Counter-Reformation.

His best seller was by no means Peter's only venture in the publishing business. He continued to write numerous books and articles on religious topics. He begged the Holy Father to send yearly subsidies to Catholic printers, and he induced more than one city council to establish a printing plant. St. Peter Canisius was a pioneer in promoting the idea of the Catholic Press.

During his long and fruitful apostolate, the gentle, charitable, and holy Dutch Jesuit led thousands to return to the Faith of their fathers. He continued to found Catholic colleges in Germany, Austria, and Bohemia. He acted as confidential agent of the Pope in matters of the greatest importance. Three times, the saint refused the see of Vienna. The illustrious and humble Doctor of the Church died in the year 1597. He had merited the titles popularly bestowed on him: "Second Boniface" and "Hammer of the Heretics."

GOD PROVIDES

The apostolate of St. Peter Canisius in sixteenth-century, German-speaking lands illustrates in a striking manner God's Providence. The Almighty raises up for His Church, in every age and land, the human instruments most fitted to preserve and propagate the Catholic Faith.

VENERABLE JOSÉ DE ANCHIETA, S.J. (*1533–1597*)

The most famous Jesuit of southern Brazil was Father José de Anchieta, often called "The St. Francis Xavier of the West." This Portuguese missioner arrived in the New World in 1553. He acquired a speaking knowledge of numerous Indian dialects and he composed the first Tupi-Guarani grammar. The primitive Indians of Brazil loved this eloquent, tireless white man.

On one occasion, Father Anchieta was held captive by an Indian tribe during six months. His fellow Jesuits feared that their confrere had been slain and roasted over a fire in the forest for a savage banquet. But the cannibalistic Indians did Father Anchieta no harm. On the contrary, the red men responded eagerly to the missioner's kindness; and they were amazed by his long prayers and his frequent miracles. Moreover, the captive priest had a fine voice and was always singing. How could the music-loving Indians kill a man who taught them such wonderful songs?

The English Protestant poet and man of letters, Robert Southey, described Father Anchieta as follows, in his *History of Brazil:* "Barefooted, with a crucifix, and a rosary around his neck, with staff and breviary in hand, his shoulders weighed down with the burden of the requirements for his altar, this missioner penetrated the forests, swam across streams, climbed the most rugged mountains, was lost in deserts, and faced the wild beasts; and he overcame all these dangers and labors, in order to win souls."

Father Anchieta ministered to the Brazilian Indians for forty-four years. He developed the College of São Paulo in a small building. "Our Lord Jesus Christ was in a far-straiter place, when it was His pleasure to be born among beasts in a manger," said the apostle cheerfully. Around Father Anchieta's college grew up what is today Brazil's great city of São Paulo.

THE USE OF TALENTS FOR GOD

Venerable José de Anchieta used to the utmost his considerable talents in the service of God and souls. Today, four centuries after Father Anchieta's labors for the aborigines of Brazil, modern philologists value for its scientific worth the grammar of the Tupi-Guarani tongue that he composed to aid his fellow missioners.

BROTHER ANTONIO, O.F.M. (*d. c. 1600*)

In a Franciscan monastery in Peru, Brother Antonio was washing pots and pans. He was not a man of much education, for he had quit school early to enlist as a soldier. But Brother Antonio had a keen intelligence, sharpened by experience; and at the moment, his mind was considering the islands newly named after King Philip II of Spain.

"The Augustinian Fathers are making many converts in the Philippines. How is it that we Franciscans have no missioners on those islands?" he asked himself. Suddenly an inspiration came to the former soldier.

"I know a lot about recruiting," he said to an astounded Brother who was paring vegetables nearby. "If I should go to Spain, I could surely find some Franciscans eager to enlist in this mission crusade!"

Brother Antonio washed his hands, took off his apron, and presented himself then and there before his superior. That worthy Father merely laughed at the Brother's proposal. "Go back to the kitchen, Brother Antonio," he said kindly.

Brother Antonio was not discouraged. He brought the matter up again and again. Finally, the superior began to see the possibilities in the persistent Brother's idea. He gave him permission to start on the long journey. Brother Antonio began his apostolic venture by walking all the way to Panama. There he begged passage on an eastward-bound vessel. Unfortunately, pirates overtook the ship just before it made port on the other side of the Atlantic. They beat Brother Antonio and threw him overboard.

After the Franciscan had kept afloat for about two hours, he was rescued by fishermen and taken ashore. At long last, he arrived in Spain. But it was a sorry-looking friar who found his way to the nearest Franciscan house and told his story to the superior. The Spanish Franciscans asked themselves if the bedraggled fellow was crazy. But there is no doubting that Brother Antonio had a way with him: he persuaded the Spanish superior to send him to Rome.

The Holy Father was enthusiastic about the Brother's idea. He sent the determined man back to Spain with warm letters of recommendation. Before long, the successful recruiter was on his return journey across the Atlantic, accompanied by seventeen Franciscan Fathers and Brothers. The voyage was so terrible that five of the new missioners died during the crossing. Finally the ship made port in Mexico. There Brother Antonio discovered five more Franciscan volunteers to take the place of the deceased missioners. The voyage was resumed, and the first band of Franciscans reached Manila in 1577.

Their tireless escort, Brother Antonio, returned to Spain for more volunteers. He led the second group of missioners safely two thirds of the way around the globe; then he settled down in a kitchen in the Philippines. Brother Antonio returned gladly to pots and pans, now that he knew his fellow Franciscans were ministering to the people of the Philippines.

PURITY OF MOTIVE

There was absolutely no self-seeking in Brother Antonio's desire to recruit Franciscan volunteers for mission work in the Philippines.

When God had rewarded with success his single-minded and tireless efforts, he returned to the kitchen as a matter of course. Of such is the kingdom of heaven.

ST. TORIBIO (*1538–1606*)

At Salamanca University, in Spain, Toribio Alfonso Mogrobejo was famed for his learning and for the good influence that his virtues had on his students. Toribio's sovereign, the deeply Catholic Philip II, was always in search of learned and holy men for key posts in his Spanish-American Empire; and he thought he had discovered such a leader in the distinguished professor at Salamanca.

As a beginning, Philip tested Toribio's mettle by appointing him Grand Inquisitor of Spain. Then the sovereign selected the gifted layman for the archbishopric of Peru. Toribio was ordained to the priesthood in 1578; and two years later, he received episcopal consecration. On May 24, 1581, the new prelate arrived at Payta, Peru.

The first thing that Archbishop Toribio did on landing was to walk to Lima, a distance of six hundred miles. That trek was only a start of the saint's apostolic journeyings in Peru. During his twenty-five-year apostolate in the New World, Archbishop Toribio covered on foot more than fifty thousand miles; and over most of those miles there were no roads, but only dizzy paths in the soaring Andes or faint trails in the jungles and across desert sands. Tropical heat, wild beasts, and savage tribes could not stop the great missionary archbishop in his ceaseless labors to lead the Peruvian Indians to Christ.

This missioner's favorite sermon to the Indians can be summed up in the sentence, "Time is not our own, and we must give a strict account of it."

Archbishop Toribio certainly could give a good account of the years he spent in Peru, for he baptized and confirmed almost 1,500,000 Peruvians. He also supervised the planning and construction of many roads. He built a great number of schools, chapels, hospitals, and convents. And to him belongs the distinction of having founded the very first seminary in the Americas.

After twenty-five years of journeying, preaching, administering the sacraments and building, Archbishop Toribio was tired. A journey that he made in March of the year 1606 proved to be his last. The apostle was stricken by fever on the road. He managed to drag himself to the church in the next village, and there he died soon after receiving Holy Viaticum.

"EVERYBODY DOES IT"

St. Toribio was no respecter of persons, and he did not hesitate to rebuke the evil committed by Spaniards in high position. Sometimes the offenders tried to offer the excuse, "Everybody does it." The missionary archbishop would then quote the following words of Tertullian: "Our Lord said, 'I am the truth.' He did not say, 'I am the custom.'"

ST. JOHN LEONARDI (*1543–1609*)

One day in the sixteenth century, two saints were in conversation in Rome. "I long to become a foreign missioner and to preach Christ to the pagans," said St. John Leonardi to his spiritual director.

"No, my son, that cannot be," replied St. Philip Neri. "It is God's will that you remain in Italy."

John Leonardi was born near Lucca, Italy, in 1543. He became a priest with a wonderful power of winning souls to Christ. His love for the poor and for the young was especially great. He founded for their instruction the Congregation of the Mother of God, a religious community that still carries on in Italy the vital work of its founder.

Father Leonardi spent the last twenty-five years of his life mostly in Rome. He was the counselor of several popes, who employed the saint in delicate work for the Apostolic See. After St. Philip Neri had told his holy penitent that it was the latter's duty to remain in Italy, the zeal of St. John Leonardi revealed to him a way in which he might still serve the missionary cause.

The apostolic saint founded in the Eternal City a seminary to train for the priesthood young men from all the mission lands.

This seminary was the germ that later developed into the Urban College of Propaganda. For more than three centuries, Propaganda College has sent forth thousands of priests of all nationalities, to carry the Gospel to their own peoples.

John Leonardi died in Rome in 1609. He went to plead in heaven for the millions who still "sit in darkness and in the shadow of death." He did it so well that, thirteen years after his death, Pope Gregory XV founded the Sacred Congregation for the Propagation of the Faith, to integrate the work of all Catholic missioners. St. John Leonardi was canonized in 1938, by Pius XI, "The Pope of the Missions."

VICTORIOUS OBEDIENCE

By his obedience to God's will, expressed to him through his spiritual director, St. John Leonardi finally accomplished incomparably more for the conversion of pagans to Christianity, than if he himself had gone to foreign lands. "An obedient man shall speak of victory" (Prov. 21:28).

FATHER MATTEO RICCI, S.J. (*1552–1610*)

Father Matteo Ricci, the Italian Jesuit who was the founder of modern missions in China, was described by a Chinese historian as the possessor of "a curly beard, blue eyes, and a voice like a great bell." When the illustrious pioneer arrived at Macao, in 1582, all trace of the medieval apostolate of Archbishop John of Montecorvino, at Peking, had vanished. Medieval Catholicism in China had shared the downfall of its protector, the Mongol dynasty; and the succeeding native Ming dynasty was harsh in the exclusion from the Empire of all European "barbarians."

The Portuguese had been permitted to found a trading post on the little island of Macao, off Kwangtung Province, South China. On the bare rock of Macao, Father Ricci began his nearly twenty-year-long advance to Peking. He gained permission to preach Christianity in Kwangtung Province, by presenting European watches and clocks to the enchanted Chinese officials. But all the while, the great capital to the north remained the Jesuit's final goal.

Seizing every opportunity of advancing northward, and surmounting countless dangers and hardships, the intrepid apostle founded Catholic missions in Nanchang and in Nanking. In this manner nearly twenty years passed. Then, at last, European gifts sent by Father Ricci to Emperor Wan Li won for the great Jesuit the permission to enter Peking. Wan Li was especially delighted with a marvelous clock that chimed the hours. He gave orders that the European priest must remain in the capital in order to wind the precious clock.

Emperor Wan Li lodged his clock winder and a number of Father Ricci's fellow Jesuits in Peking, and he allotted to their support a considerable sum from the imperial treasury. Officials and scholars flocked to gaze on the great "Sage of the West." After having excited the intellectual curiosity of his visitors by accounts of the scientific and mechanical wonders of Europe, Father Ricci would lead them on, bit by bit, to talk of the Christian religion.

Father Ricci devoted much time to the study of Confucianism, and he cited from the Chinese classics numerous passages that accord with Christian beliefs. He won to the Faith several near relatives of the Emperor and also a number of famous scholar-officials. During the twenty-eight years of his apostolate in China, Father Ricci appears to have made in all about twenty-five hundred converts.

The prestige of Father Ricci and his companions in Peking made it possible for other Jesuits to obtain new footholds in widely separated regions of the vast Empire. By the year 1605, steps had been taken for the training of a Chinese clergy. Father Ricci had to give time and thought not only to the mission work in the capital, but also to all the ventures of his confreres in the provinces.

Suddenly, the vitality of the brave pioneer gave way. To the Jesuits kneeling about his deathbed, he said: "I leave you facing an open door. But it will remain open only at the price of great merits, and not without much trouble and danger."

The Apostle of China died in May, 1610. All Peking mourned the passing of the illustrious teacher; and everywhere in the streets of the capital the people were saying, "The Saint of the West has saluted the world" – a Chinese idiom for expressing the fact of death. The Emperor decreed for Father Ricci a magnificent State funeral.

NOT COUNTING THE COST

In order to win the Chinese to Christ, Father Ricci perceived that he must strive to assimilate as much of their culture as possible. "Of Chinese letters, I have already, by the grace of God, a good foundation," he wrote to his General in Rome. "I have taken a very learned master, and in my old age I am going to become a schoolboy. It is not much, since it is done for love of Him, who, being God, became man for love of me."

ST. FRANCIS SOLANO, O.F.M. (*1549–1610*)

In the little Spanish town of Montilla, Francis Solano longed to become a missioner in Africa; but it so happened that the young Franciscan had musical ability that made him of great value to the friaries of his order in Spain. During twenty years of his religious life, Father Solano was in charge of the sacred music in various Spanish friaries. He served also as novice master and as Father Guardian. The townspeople venerated him for his holiness, and many of them said that he worked miracles.

In 1589, when Father Solano was forty years of age, he was at length assigned to the foreign missions – not to Africa, however, but to America. On the outward voyage, the sailing vessel was wrecked on a reef. Father Solano went down into the dark hold of the ship and freed eight hundred Negro slaves who had been imprisoned there. The slaves rushed up to the deck; but, of a sudden, the vessel broke in two.

Standing at the end of the section of the ship still caught on the reef, Father Solano spoke to the Negroes about God and about His wonderful heaven. In a strong chorus, the grateful slaves repeated after the priest fervent acts of faith and love. When the churning sea engulfed the eight hundred poor outcasts, God had granted them baptism of desire. Thus, on the way to the other side of the globe, Francis Solano had been a missioner to Africans.

Father Solano was among those rescued from the stricken vessel. He reached Lima; and from Peru, he journeyed on foot fourteen hundred miles to Tucumán, in northern Argentina. The Tucumán district is on the edge of the dread region known as the Gran Chaco, South America's "Green Hell." With wonderful success, the missioner-musician pioneered in the interior of South America. He entered the wild Gran Chaco and preached to the jungle Indians.

Father Solano founded more than fifty reductions for his numerous converts. God granted him the gift of tongues, and he was able to preach in all the local dialects, which he mastered with amazing speed. The Indians soon loved their new friend and teacher. They learned to sing psalms and hymns to the accompaniment of the Franciscan's violin; and sometimes, when the Spanish tunes grew gay, they danced.

The beloved Apostle of Green Hell died in Lima in 1610. But in the jungles, his converts still sang about the love of God for His Indian children.

A SAINT IS LIKE A CHALICE

St. Francis Solano said that a saint is like a chalice, because he has emptied his soul of earthly things so that it may hold Christ. The saint then has no other will but Christ's will; and in the chalice of his soul, the human will of God the Son is offered up in perpetual union with the will of God the Father.

FATHER PETER SKARGA, S.J. (*1536–1612*)

"Poland is my India!" cried the brilliant young Jesuit, Father Peter Skarga, as he returned from his studies in Rome in the year 1571. He found that, in his native land, the fate of the old religion hung in the balance. In spite of the fact that the majority of the common people maintained a devout loyalty to the Church, many of the powerful Polish gentry had embraced Protestant heresy. King Sigismund Augustus had remained a Catholic, but his weak character made it difficult for him to resist the Protestant factions.

In the saving of Poland for the ancient faith, the Jesuits acted as the Pope's shock troops; and Peter Skarga was their leading champion. He was such a magnificent orator that he has been called "The Polish Bossuet." His burning eloquence held spellbound foes as well as followers. King Sigismund Augustus cherished Father Skarga's friendship and leaned on the Jesuit's strength. Father Skarga wrote many Latin and Polish works in defense of the Faith. His books started numerous heretics on the road back to the Catholic Church.

In his dealings with the heretics, the great apostle was never unkind or violent. It was by his intense love for souls that he won his continual victories for Christ. Father Peter Skarga's death found him still fighting to save the soul of Poland. His eulogist, a Polish Dominican, hailed the ardent Jesuit champion of the Faith as "another Elias."

A TRIUMPH OF CATHOLIC EDUCATION

Father Peter Skarga strongly encouraged the educational activities of his confreres in Poland. Nowhere else in Europe did the Jesuit schools develop with comparable rapidity. Even Protestants sent their sons to the Jesuit colleges. The young men educated in these institutions played a vital role in saving Poland for Catholicism.

ST. LAWRENCE OF BRINDISI, O.F.M.CAP. (*1559–1619*)

There were many great Capuchin missioners of the Catholic Counter-Reformation; but even in such a glorious company of apostles, Lawrence of Brindisi was outstanding. Early in his religious career, Father Lawrence became widely known for his holiness, his mastery of Hebrew, and his extraordinary knowledge of the Bible.

Pope Clement VIII asked the young Capuchin to preach to the Jews in Italy. The Jews were delighted by Father Lawrence's amazing knowledge of Hebrew. They were drawn, also, by the missioner's unfailing courtesy and charity. He always addressed them as his "well-beloved brothers." In this extraordinarily difficult apostolate among the Jews, Lawrence of Brindisi had marked success.

In 1599, Pope Clement VIII sent Father Lawrence into central Europe, to found Capuchin monasteries in those regions where Protestantism was rife and to preach the Catholic Faith to heretics and apostates. St. Lawrence preached throughout central Europe, countering persecution by a simple dignity and by the strength of his zeal for souls. In Germany, he won many friends and vocations for his order by his courageous care of the sick during a plague.

In 1601, only thirty years after the great Christian victory at Lepanto, the Turks launched a new offensive against Hungary. Their sea power had been destroyed at Lepanto, but on land they were still able to send superior forces against the Christians. In this crisis, Lawrence of Brindisi was made head chaplain of the Christian armies.

On the eve of the encounter with the infidels, St. Lawrence delivered a rousing address to the troops. He told them that God was on their side and that, on the morrow, they would vanquish the enemies of the Cross. On the following day, the head chaplain, armed only with a crucifix, led the charge against the Moslems. The Turks suffered a crushing defeat. St. Lawrence of Brindisi died eighteen years later, at Lisbon, during one of his diplomatic missions.

ROCK-FIRM FIDELITY

When Pope Leo XIII canonized Lawrence of Brindisi, in 1881, he praised the illustrious Capuchin for "his stalwart love of the Catholic Faith, his horror of heresy and error, and his rock-firm fidelity to the See of Peter."

BLESSED LEONARD KIMURA, S.J. (*d. 1619*)

The Japanese authorities were well aware, in the early years of the seventeenth century, that the port of Nagasaki was a center from which the Christian religion, although proscribed, was widely propagated. So they became suspicious of a certain gentleman, who traveled about constantly for no reason that they could discover. They arrested this Mr. Kimura in the year 1616.

"Do you know any of the Jesuits?" a judge asked the prisoner.

"I certainly do," replied the suspect. "I can tell you where one of them is right now."

The magistrate jumped up in great excitement, calling for a detachment of soldiers. But he sat down again when Mr. Kimura announced quietly: "There is no need for soldiers. You already have your Jesuit; I am he."

The grandfather of Leonard Kimura had been baptized by St. Francis Xavier. The whole family had become fervent Catholics, so that they were glad to see Leonard teaching catechism to young children, while he himself was still a schoolboy. Later, the zealous young Japanese had assisted the Jesuit priests as a lay catechist. When he was almost thirty years of age, Leonard had asked to be admitted to the Society of Jesus. It was because of his unceasing quest for souls that Brother Kimura had been captured and taken before the magistrate.

The Japanese Jesuit was held in prison at Nagasaki for three years, and then the officials gave this decision: "That traitorous tool of the foreign priests must be executed! He is making Christians of all his fellow prisoners."

On a November morning in the year 1619, Brother Leonard Kimura was led out to die for his Faith. With him were four Catholic laymen. More than twenty thousand Japanese Christians had assembled on the hill of martyrdom and in little boats out in the harbor. In that great throng, there were many who owed their knowledge of Christ to the Jesuit Brother.

The five condemned Catholics were tied to stakes, and fires were kindled. The thousands of witnesses beheld the face of Blessed Leonard Kimura transfigured by joy. As they watched, the Jesuit gathered up firebrands with his blackened hands, and placed them on his head. So died, wearing a crown of flames, the heroic grandson of one of Xavier's Japanese converts.

A GIFT OF THE HOLY SPIRIT

The sublime courage shown by Blessed Leonard Kimura was more than the natural virtue of fortitude. It was that fortitude which is a gift of the Holy Spirit, a fortitude that supernaturalizes courage by strong patience and glad endurance.

ST. FRANCIS DE SALES (*1567–1622*)

One of the foremost missioners of the Catholic Counter-Reformation was St. Francis de Sales. This Frenchman belonged to an old, aristocratic family of Savoy, on the border of Switzerland. His father intended him for the magistracy, and the young man studied under distinguished Jesuit professors. When Francis felt the call to the priesthood, his father was bitterly disappointed. But the Catholic bishop of Geneva, who resided in Annecy, Savoy, encouraged Francis and took him under his special protection.

In the year 1594, after he had been ordained to the priesthood, Father Francis offered to evangelize the region of Le Chablais, in Savoy, which had become a stronghold of Calvinism. The bishop of Geneva accepted the young priest's apostolic offer. Father Francis journeyed through the mountainous district of Le Chablais, preaching everywhere he went. His sermons did not call down the wrath of God upon the heretics, for he believed that "a drop of honey catches more flies than a gallon of vinegar."

The kindness of Father Francis made him an easy man to approach. Many a poor mountaineer questioned him, as he stopped in the different villages. "What is so wrong about being a Protestant?" the peasants wanted to know.

The missioner explained why heresy is wrong in words that his simple questioners could understand. He did not send them away before he had shown them how much they were missing by not being members of the true Church.

For four years Francis worked in Le Chablais, and he led most of the people of that district back to the Catholic fold. At the request of Pope Clement VIII, the saint even went to Geneva to visit the Protestant leader, Theodore Beza. Beza lacked the courage to renounce his errors. However, St. Francis did convert a number of prominent Calvinists in France. Though he made use of "honey" to attract souls, St. Francis de Sales was very exacting in the direction of his converts.

After the death of the bishop of Geneva, in 1602, Francis was consecrated as his patron's successor. He became universally loved for his charitable zeal. Together with St. Jane Frances de Chantal, the bishop founded the Institute of the Visitation Sisters. He was the author of numerous works for the guidance of the Catholic laity, and he taught that "it is an error—it is even a heresy" to hold that piety is incompatible with any state of life.

This holy and gentle apostle, so attuned to the needs of the troubled period, died in 1622, when he was fifty-six years of age.

ON ILLNESS

St. Francis de Sales wrote to a nun afflicted by illness: "Do you not know that in one respect the very angels are jealous of us? And that for no other reason than that we can suffer for our Lord, while they have never suffered for Him. . . . Your cross has come to you: salute it and clasp it to you for love of Him who hath sent it."

ST. FIDELIS OF SIGMARINGEN, O.F.M.CAP. (*1577–1622*)

"It is bad enough when unscrupulous lawyers cheat the poor, but it is far worse when heretical leaders rob the people of the treasures of the Faith," said Mark Rey angrily to a friend.

Mark Rey, a native of Sigmaringen in South Germany, was himself a lawyer and a man of such noble integrity that he was known as "The Advocate of the Poor." He had just been reading an account of how, in the valley of the Grisons, in Switzerland, the Protestant leader, Zwingli, had robbed the poor peasants of their belief that Jesus is really present in the Blessed Sacrament. Mark Rey determined to help those deceived peasants.

In 1612, the German lawyer entered the Capuchin Order and received in religion the name of Fidelis. After his ordination to the priesthood, Father Fidelis was sent as a missioner to the Grisons. From the outset, he enjoyed great success in persuading the Protestant Swiss to return to the Catholic Church. He found his way to the hearts of those heretics by his love of the poor and his devoted care of the needy sick.

The ex-lawyer strove to convert the heretical leaders, too. He used against those prominent men the weapon of whole nights spent in prayer for their souls. His training as a lawyer was of no small aid to the Capuchin missioner, for it enabled him to detect immediately the weak spots in the arguments the heretics used against him. Father Fidelis welcomed many a Protestant minister back into the Catholic Church.

Finally the Protestant party determined to take action against the too successful missioner. They sent Father Fidelis threatening letters, and invented the story that the Capuchin was a political agent of the Austrian ruler. One day in April, 1622, when the apostle was preaching a sermon, an assassin made a vain attempt to murder him.

Father Fidelis set out calmly from the church to walk to the village of Gruch. On the way, an armed band stopped the priest. One of the ruffians felled the Capuchin with a savage blow. Father Fidelis struggled to his knees, and cried, "Lord, forgive my enemies!" Another of the band then stabbed the martyr.

THE MOST DEADLY ROBBER

St. Fidelis of Sigmaringen gave his life in defense of the treasures of the Faith that were being stolen from the Swiss. In these days, it is essential to recall that Marxian Communism is robbing millions of souls of their Christian beliefs. This in itself explains why the Holy Father has decreed that a Catholic who voluntarily becomes a Communist is *ipso facto* excommunicated.

BLESSED ROCH GONZALEZ, S.J. (*1576–1628*)

"The only way to civilize and make good Christians of the nomadic Indians of this region would be to gather them together into a settlement, under the constant supervision of Fathers of our Society," said Father Roch Gonzalez to his Jesuit superiors in Paraguay.

Unlike most of the Jesuit missioners in the New World in the seventeenth century, Father Gonzalez was a native of South America. He was born at Asunción, the capital of Paraguay; and ever since his ordination to the priesthood, he had been evangelizing the Indians dwelling along the mighty rivers of his native land. Time and again, the zealous missioner had seen epidemics and migrations destroy what he had been able to accomplish for the spiritual and material welfare of the red men.

The Jesuit superiors decided to make Father Gonzalez director of the Reduction of St. Ignatius on the Paraguay River. This was the first of one hundred Jesuit reductions that were established in Paraguay and parts of Uruguay, Brazil, and Argentina from 1609 to 1767. Father Gonzalez remained for four years at St. Ignatius, and his Indian charges made great advances in civilization and in their understanding of Christianity. Between 1614 and 1619, Father Gonzalez and his companions founded three new reductions along the Parana River.

"The consolation we receive from baptizing dying persons makes our trials bearable," wrote the pioneer organizer of reductions. "To keep alive, we eat roots, which must be boiled first, since they are poisonous. On many days we have nothing to eat until evening, and then we beg from door to door, for any food the Indians might care to give us."

Later, Father Gonzalez turned his attention to the dark forests and great swamps of Uruguay. There he met with fierce opposition from witch doctors, especially from a certain Nezú. Finally this Nezú persuaded some of his credulous followers to murder the missioners. The minions of Nezú slew Father Gonzalez with a stone hatchet and also slaughtered two of the martyr's Jesuit helpers, Father Alphonsus Rodriguez and Father John del Castillo.

Great were the sorrow and the anger of the majority of the Indians, when they discovered what had happened. They caught and hanged the murderers; but before the death of the guilty men, all save one were converted to the Faith.

"Father Gonzalez, the father of us all, and his two holy companions have been praying for their enemies in heaven," said the red men. "We know that they will not forget us, who were their loving friends."

WHAT HIS APOSTOLATE COST HIM

A seventeenth-century Spanish colonist, familiar with the territory in which Father Roch Gonzalez had labored, wrote of the Jesuit's hardships: "Hunger, exhaustion from traveling on foot, swimming across rivers, wading through bogs, not to mention plaguing insects and the discomforts which no man but a true apostle, who was as holy as this priest was, could have borne with such fortitude."

SAMUEL DE CHAMPLAIN (*1567–1635*)

"Of the pioneers of the North American forests, the name of Samuel de Champlain stands foremost on the list," wrote the American historian, Francis Parkman. "In the depths of Canada, while New England was a solitude, and the settlers of Virginia scarcely dared venture inland beyond the sound of cannon shot, Champlain was planting on shores and islands the emblems of his Faith."

Samuel de Champlain was born of a distinguished family of the French nobility. He served his country on many a battlefield and as captain in the French Navy. Later he became a great explorer and colonizer in the New World. He piloted settlers to Acadia (now Nova Scotia) in 1604. On that occasion he made a survey of the Atlantic coast from Nova Scotia to Cape Cod in Massachusetts.

Champlain founded Quebec, on the St. Lawrence River, in the year 1608. From then until his death, in 1635, the heroic pioneer stood firm in the face of famine, epidemics, attacks by the Iroquois, and temporary seizure by the English. It was due to Samuel de Champlain that New France succeeded in naturalizing itself under the rigorous sky of Canada.

But Champlain was more than a dauntless explorer, colonizer, and administrator. He was first and always a truly Christian man who longed to convert to his Saviour the poor savages whom he found living "like brute beasts, without faith, without law, without religion, without God." In 1615, Champlain brought three Franciscan priests and a Brother to Quebec. One of the Franciscan missioners, Father Joseph Le Caron, discovered Lake Huron and began the evangelization of the Huron Indians. Champlain went in person to Huronia, and gave Father Le Caron every possible aid. Later, Jesuits replaced the Franciscans among the Huron Indians.

Champlain presented the pioneer Jesuits to a party of Indian chiefs and warriors with the following words: "These are our Fathers. We love them more than we love ourselves. The whole French nation honors them. They do not go among you to trade in furs. They have left their friends and their country to show you the way to heaven. If you love the French, as you say you love them, then love and honor these our Fathers."

The gifted and beautiful wife of Champlain had been brought up a Huguenot; but under the instruction of her husband, she became a fervent Catholic. Madame de Champlain learned Algonquin and taught the Catechism to little savages. After Champlain's death – on Christmas Day, 1635 – she became an Ursuline nun.

HIS PRINCIPAL GOAL

In his *Memoirs,* Samuel de Champlain recorded that he had endured the toils of pioneering in Canada, in order "to plant in this country the standard of the Cross, and to teach the knowledge of God and the glory of His Holy Name. . . . The salvation of a single soul is worth more than the conquest of an empire."

PETER CARDINAL PÁZMÁNY, S.J.
(*1570–1637*)

"Peter Pázmány was born in Protestant Hungary, and he died in Catholic Hungary." So one writer has aptly summed up the apostolate of a great man who stemmed the progress of Calvinism in his native land.

Peter Pázmány was born of Protestant parents in the year 1570. At that time, the part of Hungary free from Turkish domination was virtually a Protestant country. Before the end of the third decade of the following century, Hungary was to be strongly Catholic again. The change came about largely through the labors of the Jesuits; and among the Jesuits, Father Peter Pázmány stood out in the Catholic Restoration in Hungary.

Peter became a Catholic because of the influence of his Catholic stepmother and his Jesuit professors. He entered the Society of Jesus, and was sent to Rome for his theological studies. There he had as professor that great Jesuit master of controversy, St. Robert Bellarmine. Well armed for warfare against the Calvinists, Father Pázmány returned to his native land where he labored in the pulpit and with his mighty pen. The Hungarian apostle won back to the Church more than thirty of the foremost families among the Magyar nobility.

After some years, Father Pázmány was made Primate of Hungary. In his new office, Archbishop Pázmány vigorously promoted the work of Jesuit colleges and seminaries. He so inspired the Catholics of Hungary that they were able to obtain a majority in the national assembly. With tireless energy, the apostolic prelate carried out in Hungary the reforms decreed by the Council of Trent.

On November 19, 1629, Pope Urban VIII made a cardinal of the restorer of the Faith in Hungary. No doubt, Cardinal Pázmány, in the seventeenth century, was an apostle very similar in character to Cardinal Mindszenty in our own age.

THE RECONVERSION OF A NATION

During the years of his apostolate in Hungary, Peter Pázmány sought the return of all classes of the population to the Catholic Faith. The Magyar nobles whom he converted spent their fortunes lavishly to promote Catholic education among the common people.

FATHER JOSEPH DU TREMBLAY, O.F.M.CAP. (*1577–1638*)

In plays that non-Catholics have written about the powerful French statesman, Cardinal Richelieu, there often appears, beside the imposing, scarlet-robed figure of the principal character, a sort of ecclesiastical Uriah Heep, ominously called "His Gray Eminence." That base caricature represents Richelieu's chief friend and adviser, the Capuchin priest, Joseph du Tremblay.

As a matter of fact, Father Joseph was a man of high distinction in the social, political, and ecclesiastical world of his time. That he was a servile hanger-on of Cardinal Richelieu was far from true; on the contrary, it was Father Joseph who assisted Richelieu to power. The Capuchin's advice to the Prime Minister of France was always prompted by an undeviating devotion to the Catholic Church.

But what concerns us here is that Father Joseph du Tremblay was one of the greatest missionary organizers of the Christian era. In France itself, Father Joseph and six Capuchin missioners went among the Huguenots. That little mission band converted thousands of heretics. Father Joseph and his Capuchins restored Catholicism in Languedoc, a region one sixth the size of France.

In the year 1625, the Sacred Congregation of Propaganda made Father Joseph prefect of the missions in England, the Near East, Morocco, and Canada. Capuchin missioners were sent to the Holy Land, Armenia, Egypt, and Abyssinia. At Beyrouth, the missioners of Father Joseph angered the Turkish authorities by the conversion of the Governor of the Holy Land. Five Capuchins were sent in chains to Constantinople, where they were beaten and left without food. Three of their number died of their sufferings. But the work in the Holy Land went on; conversions were made among Druses, Armenians, Greeks, and Mohammedans.

Father Joseph established in Lebanon a press for the printing of Catholic books in Arabic, Persian, Turkish, and Syriac. The Capuchins converted Jacobite and Nestorian heretics in Chaldea and Persia. In Abyssinia, two of Father Joseph's French Capuchins won the crown of martyrdom.

The genius of Father Joseph du Tremblay was much esteemed by Pope Urban VIII. Both friends and enemies expected the Capuchin to succeed Cardinal Richelieu; but before the drab habit of "His Gray Eminence" could be replaced by scarlet robes, Father Joseph died. As the great organizer of missions in the Near East lay on his deathbed, he asked to have read to him the history of the conquest of the Holy Land by the Christian warriors of the First Crusade.

THE EVIL OF THE TONGUE

"If any man offend not in word, the same is a perfect man" (Jas. 3:2). Calumnies against Father Joseph du Tremblay were rife during his lifetime and they persisted up to the present century. During the past fifty years, the study of authoritative documents has revealed the base mendacity of these calumnies.

FATHER LUIS DE VALDIVIA, S.J. (*1560–1642*)

In the sixteenth century, Spanish conquistadors marched southward from Peru into Chile. But in Chile, the adventurers encountered a formidable obstacle in the presence of the brave and hardy Araucanian Indians. The war between the white men and the Araucanians was to last for three hundred and forty years.

Meanwhile a great Spanish Jesuit, Father Louis de Valdivia, had been pioneering among the Indians of Peru. He had seen that the chief obstacle to the conversion of the red men was the slavery to which they were subjected, coupled with the immorality of their

Spanish masters. Father Valdivia became interested in the stubborn Araucanians, and he journeyed southward to visit them. Those fierce warriors soon gave their guest their friendship, and they consented to a truce with the Spaniards.

"If all white men were like you, we would become Christians," the Araucanians told the Jesuit. "But nothing will make us give up our freedom!"

Thereupon, Father Valdivia sailed to the Old World, for the purpose of obtaining from the King of Spain stringent laws against the abuses of the colonists. On his return to South America, the fearless apostle established in Peru four central Indian missions, which soon were flourishing.

He hoped to accomplish similar work among the Araucanians, but the Spaniards in Chile had other ideas. They were a long way from Spain, and they proceeded to ignore their sovereign's orders. Finally, they made it impossible for Father Valdivia to remain among the Araucanians. The Jesuit pioneer of Peru and Chile died in 1642, at the age of eighty-two years.

Long afterward, the white rulers of Chile saw the wisdom of Father Valdivia's policy. In 1881, they recognized the independence of the Araucanians. Those brave Indians still reverence the memory of the Blackrobe who loved and defended their people.

RESPECT FOR FREEDOM

The true Christian respects the legitimate liberties of other men. It is useless to expect pagans to be attracted to the religion of those who seek to take unfair advantage of superiority in technical progress.

ST. JOHN DE BRÉBEUF, S.J. (*1593–1649*)

"*Echon! Echon* has come back to us!" cried the red men of a Huron village, as they recognized the tall figure of their missioner and ran to meet him. The Huron Indians had chosen a good name for the heroic, selfless Father John de Brébeuf, for in their tongue *Echon* meant "He Who Drags the Loads."

Father Brébeuf, a Norman of noble lineage, was the pioneer Jesuit among the Huron Indians in Canada. He arrived in Huronia in 1628, after a nine-hundred-mile journey in an Indian canoe up the Ottawa River. On the way, the travelers encountered about forty waterfalls, around which long portages of the canoes and the baggage had to be made. Usually the only food was a little corn, coarsely broken between two stones.

During three years, the young Jesuit labored alone in the wilderness. One summer the land of the Hurons was parched by a terrible drought. The Indians decided in council that the cause of the curse was the red cross over the missioner's wigwam. In their mythology, thunder was a celestial turkey flapping its wings – and what turkey takes kindly to red? But the Jesuit explained once more to the Hurons the meaning of the symbol of the cross, and he gathered them around to honor the cross in the Christian fashion. Truly, thought the awe-stricken Indians, the God of the white men is great, for rain immediately poured down in torrents!

After other Jesuits had arrived on the shores of Lake Huron, Father Brébeuf was the leader of his brave co-workers. He built mission residences in various Huron villages, and established his fellow priests as pastors. He journeyed to evangelize neighboring Indian tribes in the dead of winter, and during a cold so intense that it was splitting the trees. None of the other Jesuits was equal to the immense and ceaseless labors that *Echon* so quietly performed.

As time passed, the Hurons listened more readily to Father Brébeuf's explanations of Christianity, and they clung to his strength. They were in great trouble, for the fierce Iroquois had begun to make ghastly inroads into their territory. The Jesuit realized that the Hurons were a doomed nation, but he merely labored the harder to gather in his eleventh-hour harvest of souls.

On March 16, 1649, the Iroquois seized Father Brébeuf and Father Gabriel Lalemant in the midst of their Christians. The two Jesuits were barbarously martyred. Father Brébeuf was tied to a stake and burned in every part of his body. The savages cut off strips of his flesh, roasted them, and devoured them before his eyes. They mutilated the priest in various horrible ways; but through the three hours of hideous agony, the Jesuit stood like a rock. Finally an Iroquois warrior split open the martyr's skull with a tomahawk.

The Protestant historian, Francis Parkman, wrote: "Thus died at the age of fifty-six years, John de Brébeuf, the founder of the Huron mission, its truest hero, and its greatest martyr. He came of a noble race – the same, it is said, from which sprang the English Earls of Arundel. But never had the mailed barons of his line confronted a fate so appalling with so prodigious a constancy. To the last he refused to flinch, and his death was the astonishment of his murderers."

THE COMPLETE OBLATION

After the terrible and glorious martyrdom of Father John de Brébeuf, the following passage was found in the book of his spiritual memoirs: "Grant that I may so live, that You may wish me at length to die for You. Thus, my Lord, I shall accept Your chalice, and I shall call upon Your Name, Jesus, Jesus, Jesus!"

ST. ISAAC JOGUES, S.J. (*1607–1646*)

While Father Isaac Jogues was a co-worker of Father Brébeuf in Huronia, a party of visiting Ojibways came down from Lake Superior. They asked for a Jesuit mission in their own country. Father Jogues and Father Raymbault were chosen for the pioneer venture. They were the first white men ever to stand on the shores of Lake Superior. But Father Raymbault fell critically ill, and the mission among the Ojibways had to be abandoned for the time being.

In 1642, Father Jogues was sent to Quebec to secure sorely needed supplies for the Huron missions. On the return journey up the St. Lawrence River, his party was attacked by seventy Mohawk warriors. The priest and two courageous young lay helpers, René Goupil and William Couture, were among the prisoners whom the Mohawks took down to their settlement of Ossernenon (the present Auriesville, in New York State). All along the way, the white men were cruelly tortured and were made to carry heavy burdens. The savages bit off several of Father Jogues's fingers.

At Ossernenon, William Couture was adopted into the tribe; but René Goupil was soon slain, for having made the sign of the cross on the forehead of an Indian child. Father Jogues endured a terrible captivity for more than a year's duration. He baptized some seventy Indians: dying babies and Huron captives about to be burned at the stake. It was New York's first baptismal record. At length, the merciful Protestant Dutch in New York succeeded in ransoming the Jesuit slave of the Mohawks; and they soon gave Father Jogues passage to Europe.

Christian Europe was deeply stirred by the presence of the heroic missioner. The Holy Father granted Father Jogues special permission to offer the Holy Sacrifice of the Mass with his mutilated hands. The dauntless priest returned to Quebec in 1644; and two years later, he was sent as an envoy to the Mohawks. When that assignment was successfully completed, Father Jogues secured the reluctant permission of his superior to found a mission among his former torturers.

The Jesuit then wrote to a friend, "I go – but I shall not return."

Accompanied by a saintly layman, John de La Lande, Isaac Jogues started on his last mission. At Ossernenon he and his companion were tomahawked by the treacherous Mohawks in October, 1646. The murderers hacked off the heads of their victims and flung their mangled bodies into the Mohawk River. At the time of his immolation for the souls of the Iroquois, Father Jogues was thirty-nine years of age.

"IT IS ALL TRUE!"

In France, the Queen Regent, Anne of Austria, kissed Father Jogues's mutilated hands, saying, "People write romances for us – but was there ever a romance like this? And it is all true!" Catholics should cultivate a taste for reading about the true adventures of the saints, invariably illumined by the romance of the love of God.

JOSEPH CHIWATENWA (*d. 1640*)

A sermon by Father John de Brébeuf led the Huron brave, Chiwatenwa, to desire baptism. But the seventeenth-century Jesuit missioners in Canada were very exacting. They kept Chiwatenwa long under instruction, though the talented Indian never forgot a word he was taught and, with burning eloquence, preached Christ to his fellow red men. In the midst of widespread polygamy, Chiwatenwa remained faithful to one wife. He never fell into the common Indian vices of gambling and drunkenness.

In 1638, when Chiwatenwa was about thirty-five years of age, he was attacked by an illness that brought him to the threshold of death. A Jesuit Father suggested baptism to the sufferer. "Baptism!" exclaimed the ardent neophyte. "I have asked you for it a hundred times. Whenever you came to my cabin, I wondered if you were going to baptize me!"

Chiwatenwa received the baptismal name of Joseph. Two days after his baptism, the new Catholic was well again. He invited his friends to a great banquet, at which he made eloquent speeches about the Christian religion. Then he went to the chapel to make a public offer of his services to the Jesuits. After that, apostolic Joseph Chiwatenwa gloried in the title the Hurons gave him – "The Believer." On every occasion, he preached the Faith with power.

"Our ancestors were excusable, for they never heard what you have heard," the zealous convert would tell the fascinated Indians. "But as for you, you will suffer grievous punishment if you remain in the degradation from which the missioners wish to raise you."

In 1640, the Jesuits asked "The Believer" to carry a message to Quebec. The Indian apostle never arrived in that distant city, because, as he was making ready for the journey, he was surprised and slain in the forest by Iroquois warriors. The European missioners mourned him as one of themselves. There is reason to believe that the Huron Indian, Joseph Chiwatenwa, may be one of America's uncanonized saints.

THE GIFT BEYOND COMPARE

Joseph Chiwatenwa long desired baptism and made countless sacrifices to merit the grace of this saving sacrament. After his baptism, the remainder of his life was an ardent thanksgiving to the Blessed Trinity. Have Catholics who receive the Sacrament of Baptism in infancy a like appreciation of what they owe God for this gift beyond compare?

ST. PETER CLAVER, S.J. (*1581–1654*)

In the seventeenth century, Cartagena, in Colombia, was the central slave mart of Spanish America. In those days, a thousand African slaves were landed at Cartagena each month for distribution over the tropical regions of the Spanish-American colonies. One day, as a slave ship was being tied to its moorings, a Jesuit priest approached one of the dealers.

"What part of Guinea are these Negroes from?" Father Peter Claver asked the dealer. The missioner wished to know which interpreter to take with him when he should board the ship, for the Africans of Guinea spoke some thirty dialects.

As soon as the gangplank had been lowered, Father Claver and his interpreter went down into the stifling heat of the ship's hold. There the stench was almost unbearable. Closely packed together, row on row of Negroes lay chained to the floor. During the long voyage from West Africa to Cartagena, many of the unfortunate blacks had already perished. With the aid of the interpreter, the Spanish Jesuit spoke lovingly to the slaves who were near death. He told them that soon all their sufferings would be changed into joy; then he baptized his Negro "thieves of heaven."

Meanwhile the dealers were driving ashore the blacks who could still walk. Once on land, the slaves were herded into fenced enclosures. After his work on board ship had been done, Peter Claver followed the slaves into the pens. He soothed the poor, half-crazed creatures, fed them, gave them medicine, and cleansed their festering wounds. While the Negroes were awaiting purchase at Cartagena, Father Claver visited them constantly, instructing them in the Faith.

The Apostle of the Negroes found time to instruct the masters of the slaves also. First he reminded the owners that, from an earthly viewpoint, reasonable care of their slaves would protect their investments. Then as to what concerned the eternal welfare of the masters themselves, Father Claver pointed out that the Son of God had died to save the soul of each unhappy black.

St. Peter Claver arrived in Cartagena in 1610, and he labored there among the slaves until his death in 1654. The fruit of his forty-four-year apostolate was the baptism of three hundred thousand black children of God. On July 7, 1896, the Church declared that the heroic apostle of the slaves should be invoked as the special patron of all Catholic missioners among the Negroes.

THE FIRE OF CHARITY

As St. Augustine expressed it, "One loving heart sets another on fire." After Father Claver had visited a man condemned to die and spoken fervently with him about the love of God, the prisoner wrote in a prayer book found after his execution: "This book belongs to the happiest man in the world."

FATHER ROBERT DE NOBILI, S.J. (*d. 1656*)

Father de Nobili, a brilliant Italian Jesuit of noble birth, arrived in southern India in 1605. He was sent to the Madura mission, somewhat in the interior, where a Portuguese Jesuit had already labored for fourteen years.

"How many converts have you baptized?" the young Father de Nobili asked Father Fernandez.

"Almost none," the Portuguese Jesuit answered sadly. "I have found it impossible to make contacts with the influential people of the country; and without the favor of the powerful, members of the lower castes fear to embrace Christianity."

Evidently something was wrong. Father de Nobili talked with the Indians themselves. He found that the Hindus despised Father

Fernandez, because the Portuguese priest ate meat and drank wine. Therefore Father de Nobili resolved that, insofar as no compromise with pagan superstition was involved, he would adopt the dress and the manner of life of the Brahmans; he would abstain from wine and meat, and live on rice.

The young Jesuit withdrew to a secluded hut, where he practiced great austerity. He made it his business to outdo the Brahmans in knowledge of their own language, literature, and religion. The people soon heard of the European holy man and flocked to visit him. They were deeply impressed when they heard the foreigner sing the songs of the ancient Hindu poets. They enjoyed discussing with him some of the fundamental truths of Christian theology; and they were amazed when he proved that those truths had been actually set down long ago in their own sacred books, the Vedas.

Father de Nobili labored for forty-two years among the upper classes in India. He made thousands of converts, but at length he was forced to rest. The eyes that had pored over so many Indian manuscripts were worn out, and he was almost completely blind. The grand old Apostle of the Brahmans died at Mylapore in 1656.

IN THE FOOTSTEPS OF CHRIST

The Son of God, in order to redeem men, became like unto them in all things except sin. In the spirit of his Master, Robert de Nobili embraced the way of life of a Hindu ascetic in all except pagan practices. By his superhuman generosity, the Italian Jesuit won for Christ numbers of hitherto unapproachable Brahmans.

FATHER ANDREW WHITE, S.J. (*1579–1656*)

On March 25, 1634, red men on the shores of Chesapeake Bay saw sailing on its waters "canoes as big as islands, with as many men on them as there are trees in the forest." The "canoes" dropped anchor near an island, and one of the first passengers to be rowed ashore was a Catholic priest. With the aid of his two Jesuit companions, Father Andrew White at once set up a rude altar and offered the Holy Sacrifice of the Mass. As it was the feast of the Annunciation, the colonists dedicated the new country to the Queen of Heaven and called it "Maryland."

Father White had known frequent persecution before his arrival in the New World. He had been educated for the priesthood in Spain. When he had returned to serve the hunted Catholics of his native England, the young priest had been arrested and sentenced to perpetual banishment. Father White had then crossed over to France and entered the Society of Jesus. After he had pronounced his vows, he had been sent on perilous missions to England.

There he had met old Lord Baltimore who had asked him to join as chaplain a proposed expedition to a land where there was hope for religious liberty. Shortly afterward, the old man had died; but his son, Cecil Calvert, the second Lord Baltimore, had taken charge of the expedition which sailed as planned.

In Maryland, Father White immediately began missionary work among the Indians. He mastered their language and prepared a catechism for their use. In times of famine, he and the other Jesuits sacrificed a large share of their own rations to help feed the Indians; and they induced many of the colonists to do likewise. Because of this friendship with the red men, the settlers of Maryland were the only colonists in North America free from the danger of Indian attacks.

Among Father White's converts was Chitomachon, chief of the Pascatoways. After his baptism, Chitomachon assembled his warriors and told them: "There is but one God worthy of the homage of brave men. The herbs and stones we have until now adored are but the humble work of this Great Creator's hands." The warriors applauded this brave speech, and thereafter Christianity made a rapid conquest of Chitomachon's people.

The apostolate of Father White among the Indians of the New World lasted for ten fruitful years. Then persecution caught up with the heroic Jesuit. White marauders from Virginia plundered the Jesuit establishments in Maryland. The aging Father White was captured and was sent back to England in chains. He was condemned to death, but the sentence was never carried out. Father White died in London in the year 1656.

HOLINESS HAS UNIVERSAL APPEAL

A Protestant writer paid Father Andrew White and his Jesuit companions the following heartfelt tribute: "The history of Maryland presents no better, no purer, no more sublime lesson than the story of the toils, sacrifices, and successes of her early missionaries."

ST. ANDREW BOBOLA, S.J. (*1591–1657*)

Andrew Bobola's family was wealthy, and his uncle was a chamberlain at the Polish court. The high-spirited, talented, and quick-tempered young man could have led a life of vivid adventure among his tumultuous countrymen. But when Andrew was twenty years of age he entered the novitiate of the Society of Jesus at Vilna in Lithuania.

Thirteen years later, his long training completed, Father Bobola began his missionary work in Lithuania and eastern Poland. His territory was rife with schism, so that Father Bobola's success in leading converts back to the Catholic fold aroused bitter enmity. The angry schismatics bestowed on him the title, "Robber of Souls."

Meanwhile, in the course of his hard ministry, the young Jesuit overcame his hasty temper and achieved sanctity. The years passed in preaching, hearing confessions, giving missions, and bringing entire villages into reunion with Rome. Then came the days of the Cossack raids. Those fierce horsemen of southern Lithuania and Transylvania were enraged by the Polish ruler's attempts to reunite the schismatics with Rome.

In 1657, a band of Cossacks captured Father Bobola and tortured him with unspeakable cruelty. The saint spoke only to pray for his murderers and to urge them to become Catholics. As the tortures were multiplied, the bleeding victim became scarcely recognizable as a human being. At last, a soldier plunged his sword into Father Andrew Bobola's side. Christ's glorious "Robber of Souls" was martyred in the month of May, 1657.

CORRESPONDENCE WITH GRACE

In his youth, St. Andrew Bobola was criticized by his Jesuit companions for his hasty temper and his insistence on his own opinions. As the years passed, the saint burned out the dross of his imperfections by the fiery zeal of his correspondence with divine grace.

FATHER ALEXANDER DE RHODES, S.J. (*1591–1660*)

"This monopoly of the Portuguese in mission work in the Orient is harmful to the Church!" declared Father Alexander de Rhodes. "Things have come to such a pass that no missioner may sail for the Far East without the approval of the Portuguese Government. The native peoples associate Christianity with the corrupt lives of some Portuguese colonists. Moreover, the traders from other countries, jealous of the Portuguese commercial monopoly in the Far East, tell the natives that all the missioners are Portuguese spies. I will journey overland, if it is necessary, to inform Rome of this state of affairs."

Alexander de Rhodes was born in Avignon, in 1591. He entered the Society of Jesus in 1612, and was assigned to the East Indies when he was only twenty-six years of age. On his way to Cochin-China, the young apostle made numerous converts at Goa, Tuticorin, and Malacca. In Cochin-China, and later in Tonkin, Father Alexander de Rhodes was a great fisher of souls. When he was persecuted and thrown into jail, as he often was, the irresistible missioner converted his jailers and many of the prisoners. On one occasion, Father Rhodes was put aboard a ship, to be carried into exile. He instructed and baptized the captain and the crew, and persuaded them to put him ashore in an isolated place, where he could begin a new apostolate.

When Father Rhodes determined to inform the Pope of the evil effects of the Portuguese ecclesiastical monopoly in the Orient, he tramped overland from the East Indies to Rome, a stupendous trek of three and one half years. On the island of Java, the Dutch threw the Jesuit into jail; but as usual, the missioner converted his keepers. After Father Rhodes had regained his freedom, he resumed his journey through India, Persia, and the Near East.

Rome was impressed by the report of Father Alexander de Rhodes. Plans were then made for the creation in the Orient of vicars apostolic, that is, missionary bishops responsible directly to the Holy See. The Pope sent Father Rhodes to France to select candidates for the new and difficult missionary vicariates. While he was in France, the great Jesuit inspired the foundation of the Paris Foreign Missions Society.

Portuguese officials learned the reason for Father Rhodes's journey to Rome, so it was no longer possible for the apostle to return to Tonkin. Though he was then over sixty years of age, he was sent to undertake mission work in Persia. Father Rhodes set to with a will to master the language. When death came to the selfless Jesuit, in the year 1660, he was planning new missionary activity in Georgia and in Tartary.

The Persians had great esteem for the old apostle, and they buried him with pomp in the city of Ispahan. The contemporaries of Father Alexander de Rhodes called him by the glorious title, "The Francis Xavier of Cochin-China and Tonkin."

NO ROOM FOR NATIONALISM

Father Alexander de Rhodes was intrepid in condemning narrow nationalism in Catholic missionary endeavor. True Christianity is supranational; and the Catholic apostle should labor solely to promote the coming of God's Kingdom on earth.

ST. VINCENT DE PAUL, C.M. (*c. 1580–1660*)

"I cannot understand why you have given up your religion," said the Moslem wife of an apostate Frenchman in the service of the Sultan of Barbary. "Your Christian slave," she said to her French husband, "has been telling me of your Faith, and my heart was so full of joy while he spoke that I do not believe I shall be so happy even in the paradise of my fathers."

The Christian slave of whom the Moslem woman spoke was Vincent de Paul, the son of a Gascon peasant. He had been ordained to the priesthood at the early age of twenty and subsequently captured by Moslem pirates during a voyage between French ports. Now the conscience of Vincent de Paul's apostate master was stirred by his wife's words. He escaped to France, taking the young priest with him.

In France, Father Vincent won the friendship of Father, afterward Cardinal, de Bérulle, who placed the young cleric in the house of a great nobleman, Count de Gondi, as tutor for the latter's sons. The count and his wife soon fell under the influence of Father Vincent's holiness. Thenceforth the Gondi fortune was at the service of the saint's multiple works of charity.

He established among the great ladies of France confraternities of charity to minister to the poor and the sick. Count de Gondi was General of the King's Galleys, which in those days were rowed by convicts. Horrified by the sufferings of these poor wretches, Father Vincent organized hospitals for their care. Louis XIII made the saint Almoner to the King's Galleys.

In 1625, Father Vincent de Paul founded a new religious institute, for the preaching of missions and retreats, to rich and poor, to laymen and to members of the clergy. The institute was recognized in 1652 by Pope Urban VIII under the name of the Congregation of the Mission. Before their founder's death, the Vincentian priests labored in Africa, Madagascar, Poland, Ireland, and the Hebrides, as well as in France.

In 1633, with the aid of a devout widow, St. Louise de Marillac, Father Vincent organized the congregation of the Sisters of Charity, who have ever since been a world-wide, glorious feature of Catholic life. The religious daughters of Father Vincent went out among the poor, tended the sick, nursed wounded soldiers, cared for foundlings, and taught Christian doctrine to little ones.

While St. Vincent de Paul was organizing his amazing works of charity, the Jansenists were spreading their dangerous heresies. Father Vincent was fearless in opposing them. The Jansenists saw in this humble priest the most formidable of their enemies.

In his last illness, King Louis XIII sent for Father Vincent and died in the saint's arms. The Regent, Anne of Austria, also recognized Father Vincent's holiness; but she was too much under the influence of Cardinal Mazarin to persevere in following the advice of the apostle of charity. Father Vincent de Paul labored for his divine Master to the very close of his long life. He died murmuring, "*Confido*" – "I trust in You."

SIMPLICITY AND HOLINESS

St. Vincent de Paul desired his priests to preach through the example of their own holiness, rather than by means of fine flights of oratory. "The Fathers of the Mission will speak to convert and not to be esteemed," he declared. "If men are to be converted, they must understand what is said."

PART VII

Secularization, "Enlightenment," Revolution

(1648–1801)

IN THE second half of the seventeenth and in the eighteenth centuries, the secularization of Europe continued at an accelerated pace, inevitably accompanied by a general lowering of religious vitality and zeal. Because of increasing State absolutism and sharp rivalry among the contending nations, shifty diplomacy became a prevalent bane. The Catholic States were losing power, while the Protestant countries of England, Holland, and Prussia were strongly on the ascendant. Even in Catholic countries, anti-Papal feeling was often rife.

There was a flash of the old crusading spirit when the Catholic king of Poland, John Sobieski, defeated the invading Turks at Vienna, in 1683, thus crushing the last serious Turkish threat to Europe. New religious apostolic institutes were founded, among which were the Passionists (1720) and the Redemptorists (1732). But on the other hand, the anti-Catholic forces grouped themselves in the first half of the eighteenth century into a powerful secret association, known as Freemasonry.

As the eighteenth century advanced, the trend toward unbridled religious speculation led to crass materialism and outright atheism.

The "philosophers" of France took the lead in considering religion as an outmoded popular superstition. They undermined stable government by evolving the political principle that the right to govern is derived, not from God, but solely from the people.

Not unnaturally, all the enemies of the Church perceived in the Jesuits, the shop troops of the Pope, specially hated adversaries. The powerful Bourbon courts of Europe leagued themselves together for the destruction of the Society. St. Alphonsus Liguori, the founder of the Redemptorists, said of the attacks on the Jesuits: "It is a plot hatched by the Jansenists and the 'philosophers.' Their fondest wish will be gratified if they succeed in destroying the Company of Jesus."

Pope Clement XIII resisted all the pressure of the Bourbon courts; but his successor, Clement XIV, gave in. He issued the brief of suppression in 1773, in an effort to avert schism in the Church. In the providence of God, Catherine II of Russia would not publish the brief of suppression in her Empire. Pope Pius VI acknowledged this situation; and finally Pope Pius VII declared the Society of Jesus to be rehabilitated for the whole of Russia. Thus the Society was never totally suppressed.

During this period, the Catholics of Ireland and Scotland were cruelly oppressed. The Partitions of Poland (the final one took place in 1795), by Russia, Prussia, and Austria, exposed millions of Catholics to subsequent Czarist persecution.

Meanwhile the mocking blasphemies and the inflammatory political ideas of the "philosophers" had descended from the French intellectuals to the lower classes. Parisian mobs did not listen passively to such sentiments as the coarse wish of Diderot that "the last king might be strangled with the entrails of the last priest." In 1789, the terrible storm of the French Revolution broke.

Ten years later, a *coup d'état* made Napoleon Bonaparte ruler of France. Napoleon negotiated a concordat with the Holy See in 1801, but he intended to make the Church the handmaid of his own imperial power.

The American Revolution of 1776 had developed very differently. The new nation across the Atlantic proclaimed the principle of religious freedom; and this principle was to prove of inestimable value to the Catholic Church in the United States.

Though the Holy See continued its centralizing organization of apostolic endeavor during this age, the missions declined. They suffered from disputes among the various religious institutes, from national rivalries in the colonies, and from the disastrous repercussions of the French Revolution. In Africa, the Faith made relatively small gains. North Africa was predominantly under Moslem control, and the evangelization of Negro Africa was hampered by Portugal's effort to maintain an ecclesiastical monopoly on the great continent.

The severest single blow to the missions in this age was the expulsion of the Jesuits from the far-flung fields of their great apostolate. In some of the regions evangelized by the early Jesuits, no adequate compensation for their loss was ever found. In our century the writer Julian Duguid visited the lonely ruins of a Jesuit mission in eastern Bolivia. "A gigantic crucifix, stretching its arms against the dark blue sky, seemed to mourn the glory that had departed," he recorded.

FATHER ADAM SCHALL VON BELL, S.J. (*1591–1666*)

In the year 1644, China was in the bloody throes of a change of dynasty. The native Mings had been driven out, and Manchu "barbarians" from above the Chinese Empire's northeastern boundaries had arrived to sit upon the Dragon Throne. During the fierce fighting in Peking, a Jesuit priest, Father Schall, had protected numerous Christian converts at the Catholic mission. When a band of looters battered down the front door of the mission residence, they were confronted by the tall, bearded figure of the German priest, armed with a gleaming sword. The looters wisely withdrew.

Father Adam Schall von Bell was a native of Cologne. Because of his outstanding knowledge of astronomy, he had been appointed director of the Imperial Board of Astronomy in Peking. That was a position of much influence because, since the earliest centuries, the imperial calendar had served as the time schedule of the entire Chinese people. The Manchus retained Father Schall and his Jesuit companions on the Board of Astronomy.

The first Manchu ruler, a mere boy, conceived a lively affection for Father Schall. Emperor Shun Chih helped the Jesuits to erect a church, the first Christian church to be built in the capital of China since the days of the thirteenth-century Archbishop John of Montecorvino. The young Emperor consulted Father Schall on important affairs of state, and made him a mandarin of the first class. Father Schall had high hopes that the first Manchu Emperor in China would become a Catholic; but Shun Chih died of a fever in the year 1661.

The Chinese scholars whom the Jesuits had displaced in the Board of Astronomy had long been awaiting an opportunity for revenge. During the minority of the new ruler, they launched a violent attack on the Christian religion, on the Jesuits, and on foreign astronomy. The displaced astronomers were eagerly supported in the assault by the Buddhist bonzes and by envious court eunuchs. The Jesuits were arrested and thrown into a cold, foul jail, where they were chained like wild beasts.

The trial of the foreign priests dragged on for nearly two years. Then, in the month of May, 1666, Peking was shaken by repeated earthquakes, and the sun was darkened by a great dust storm. The terrified regents freed the Christian prisoners – but Father Schall did not long survive his protracted sufferings. The noble old missioner died in the following August. Father Adam Schall von Bell had been for many years the chief support of Christianity in China. During his apostolate, the number of Catholics in the Chinese Empire had increased from thirteen thousand to over two hundred and fifty thousand.

HUMILITY IN GREATNESS

Father Adam Schall was always tender to the poor and to the weak, and he had an especial love for children. There was, indeed, something childlike in the simple fervor of the faith of this great apostle.

MOTHER MARY OF THE INCARNATION (*1599–1672*)

Early in her religious life, Mother Mary of the Incarnation was inspired by God with an intense desire to labor for the conversion of pagans; but it did not seem likely that her longing would ever be satisfied. In the seventeenth century, people thought that nuns should remain in their European cloisters. It happened, however, that a wealthy French widow, Madame de la Peltrie, had made a vow to found a convent in Canada. A Jesuit Father told the widow about Mother Mary of the Incarnation.

Madame de la Peltrie and three Ursuline nuns embarked for the New World in 1639. For three years, Mother Mary of the Incarnation and her two companions carried on their work in a cold, crowded shack. So small was their dwelling that they had to fasten their narrow bunks to the walls in tiers. The hardships of the close quarters were increased not a little by the fact that the Sisters' Indian pupils had at first no conception of cleanliness.

"We daily find strange objects in our soup," wrote Mother Mary of the Incarnation in a matter-of-fact way.

In their primitive shack, the pioneer Ursulines nursed the Indian children through a terrible epidemic of smallpox, a disease against which the red race had no immunity. There was great rejoicing when, after their first venture in building, the Ursulines and their charges were able to move into a real convent. They had lived in the new home less than a decade when it was utterly destroyed by a midnight fire.

Mother Mary of the Incarnation became a resolute beggar for Christ. It was her energy that secured from France the donations for another building. She and her Sisters labored with the workmen on the foundations of a second convent. The living space was all the more urgently needed because the Ursulines had recently harbored fugitive Huron girls. The fierce Iroquois had driven the girls' kinsmen out of Huronia, and the pitiful remnant of the hunted tribe had followed their Jesuit missioners down the St. Lawrence River to Quebec.

When Mother Mary of the Incarnation died, in 1672, she had been for thirty-three years an intrepid missioner and a source of unfailing strength to the young Church in Canada. The great seventeenth-century orator, Bossuet, did not hesitate to call her "The Saint Teresa of the New World."

SHE CALLED THEM TO GOD

Two centuries after the death of Mother Mary of the Incarnation, the chiefs and braves of the then almost extinct Huron nation wrote to Pope Pius IX. They asked him to receive, "with the last breath of the Huron tribe," the testimony of their gratitude to her "who called us from the depths of our forests to teach us to know and worship the true Lord of life."

FATHER JACQUES MARQUETTE, S.J. (*1637–1675*)

Father Jacques Marquette came to the New World from Laon, France. He did not look like an explorer; in fact, he gave the impression of being a rather frail man. But the young Jesuit was possessed of a courage that more than compensated for his delicate health. Moreover, Father Marquette had fallen in love with the Illinois Indians. So he was very happy when, on December 8, 1672, the able and adventurous young fur trader, Louis Joliet, brought him a message from the Governor of Canada. The Count de Frontenac had commissioned Father Marquette and Louis Joliet to rediscover the Mississippi River.

Father Marquette had met a number of Illinois Indians at La Pointe mission on Lake Superior, at that time considered the extreme Far West. The Illinois had told the Jesuit that many of their tribe dwelt along the shores of the mysterious "Father of Waters" on which no white man had looked since its discovery in the previous century by the Spaniard, Hernando de Soto. Now Father Marquette would be able to visit and evangelize his dear Illinois!

Missioner and fur trader set out on their great adventure on May 17, 1673. They skirted the northern shores of Lake Michigan and embarked on the Wisconsin River. In June, they entered a vast expanse of wind-blown waters. They had found the Mississippi! They went down the mighty stream, encountering on its banks various Indian tribes. Needless to say, Father Marquette was especially drawn to his Illinois. At length, the approach of cold weather forced the young explorers to turn their canoes northward.

Exhausted by the hardships of the wilderness, the uncomplaining Jesuit came near to death on the return voyage. In the autumn of 1674, Father Marquette's health was thought to be restored, and he was given the welcome order to found a mission on the upper waters of the Illinois River. The apostle set out with two French boatmen. It was late in the season for such a journey, and soon the freezing of the river blocked further advance. Father Marquette passed the severe winter in a rude log hut in the forest. He was again dangerously ill.

In April the missioner pushed on to his Illinois village, but he knew that his time was short. He said Mass in the open air for his Indians; spoke to them of the Faith; told them that he loved them; and asked them to receive kindly his successor. Then he left the Illinois; to their great sorrow. On May 18, 1675, Father Jacques Marquette died in the wilderness, and he was buried in a lonely grave on the shores of Lake Michigan. The Jesuit who had loved the Illinois tribe so well was then thirty-eight years of age.

PERSEVERANCE IN PRAYER

During a number of years, Father Marquette prayed that he might become the apostle of the Illinois Indians. In the end God permitted him to be with them only long enough to make these red men feel his love for their souls. But once the Illinois were converted, they never fell back into paganism nor did they forget Father Marquette. "We are Indians of the prayer," said their renowned chief, Chikagou.

KATERI TEKAKWITHA (*1656–1680*)

This Indian girl, whom many in the United States hope to see raised to the altars of the Church, was born of a Mohawk father and an Algonquin Christian mother at Ossernenon (Auriesville, New York) ten years after St. Isaac Jogues was martyred there. At the time of the child's birth, no missioner was in the village; but Christian Indian captives comprised about a fifth of the population.

The little girl lost her parents at an early age and was adopted by an uncle, who was a respected Mohawk chieftain. She was a thoughtful, industrious child, naturally modest and reserved. The barbarous tortures inflicted on captives by her tribesmen filled her with horror. Jesuit missioners came again among the Mohawks in 1667, and the Christians in the village could once more practice their religion. Tekakwitha learned about the Catholic Faith from these friends. Much to her uncle's displeasure, she refused marriage with a young Indian brave.

Tekakwitha longed with increasing ardor for baptism. A Jesuit missioner, Father James de Lamberville, baptized her on Easter Sunday, 1676. She received the Christian name of Kateri (the Indian for Catherine). From then on, Kateri heroically suffered the persecution of the pagan Indians in the village and of her own uncle. Finally, with the consent of Father Lamberville, she escaped to the Christian Indian settlement which the Jesuits had founded in Canada, in sight of Montreal.

Kateri was lodged with a devout Catholic family. She spent most of her time thenceforth in prayer and works of charity. In 1679, her pastor permitted her to make a vow of virginity. Kateri inspired those about her to a more perfect following of Christ, and she hoped to undertake educational work for Indian children. God called her to Himself, however, in April, 1680. Kateri's last words were, "Jesus, I love You!"

THE FLOWER OF SANCTITY

Kateri's tomb was considered a holy place by her tribesmen. They had inscribed upon it the words: "Fairest flower that ever bloomed among true men."

FATHER JOHN LE VACHER, C.M. (*d. 1683*)

A young French student sought the advice of St. Vincent de Paul in the year 1643. John Le Vacher was not sure if it would be well for him to ask the hand of a certain young lady in marriage.

The saint looked at the young man, and spoke as the Holy Ghost inspired him to do: "You should not ask any young lady in marriage, my son. God is calling you to the priesthood and to a missionary life."

Now, it was very exceptional for St. Vincent de Paul to speak in this fashion. He made it a rule never to urge anyone to become a Vincentian missioner. John Le Vacher did not disappoint the saint. He responded generously to the call of God, and gave no further thought to a worldly career. Two years later, St. Vincent de Paul sent Father Le Vacher to minister to the Christian slaves of the Moslems at Tunis.

Then began for the zealous missioner a long and arduous apostolate among the miserable galley slaves. There were priests among the captives, and Father Le Vacher did everything possible to obtain from their Moslem masters permission for the priest-prisoners to say Mass. He begged funds for all his pitiful charges; and he gave them the consolations of their Faith as abundantly and as frequently as the outpouring of his energies permitted. When Christians were tempted to become renegades, he pleaded with them and made sacrifices for their perseverance.

Father Le Vacher helped numerous slaves to make good their escape. Occasionally the Bey of Tunis became angry with the French missioner and cast him into prison for a few days. But the Moslem official always repented of having imprisoned a man "who did evil to no one; but, on the contrary, did good to all." When Father Le Vacher later labored for some years at Algiers, the Moslems of that city were likewise attracted by his all-embracing charity.

So time passed, until Father Le Vacher was sixty-four years of age. In 1683, there was trouble between the French and the Moslems. French warships bombarded Algiers, and feeling ran high against the Europeans. A change of government took place at Algiers, in consequence of which a certain Mezzomorto became bey. Mezzomorto hated Father Le Vacher for having saved a Christian slave from his harem.

The new bey decreed that, if the French missioner did not become a Moslem, he would be shot from the mouth of a cannon. No Moslem or Jew would fasten the old apostle to the cannon; it was a renegade Christian who performed the deed. Father Le Vacher begged the European slaves who stood near him to abide firmly in Christ. Then the signal was given — and the cannon hurled the shattered body of the missioner upon the French warships. So died the first Vincentian martyr.

THE SPIRIT OF LUCIFER

The renegade Christian who co-operated in martyring Father Le Vacher was possessed by Satan. He had fallen from grace, and instead of repenting, he was filled with black hatred against the representative of the Love and Truth he had shut out of his heart.

FATHER YURY KRIJANITCH (*1610–1683*)

"They call me a wanderer. This is not true! I have come to the Czar of my race, to my own people, to the only country where my works can be utilized and do some good," wrote the Croatian Father Krijanitch, in the year 1659, when he thought that he had at last acquired a firm footing in Moscow. But, as has since happened to many others who have fallen in love with Moscow, Father Krijanitch was doomed to bitter disappointment.

Yury Krijanitch was born in Zagreb, Croatia, in territory now within the boundaries of Yugoslavia. He became passionately interested in Muscovy, the mysterious power that had arisen amid the vast forests of the Russian plains. He believed that all the Slavs should unite under the leadership of Moscow.

From his extensive study of religion in Muscovy, Krijanitch concluded that the Russians had followed Constantinople into separation from Rome merely through ignorance of the truth. The young

Croat felt that it was his vocation to undertake the Russians' enlightenment. He studied theology in Vienna, in Bologna, and in Rome. In the latter city, he was admitted to the college that the Sacred Congregation of Propaganda had established to train missioners for Slavic lands.

Soon after his ordination to the priesthood, Father Krijanitch joined a foreign embassy en route for Moscow, but it was not possible for him to remain in that inhospitable capital. Undaunted, the Croatian missioner succeeded a second time in reaching Moscow. He had concealed his priestly character, and, as a scholar, he offered his services to the Czar. The Russian potentate granted the Croat a small subsidy and ordered him to prepare a grammar and a lexicon. Yury Krijanitch was filled with joy.

Soon, however, Moscow authorities began to suspect that the learned Croatian scholar was in reality a Catholic priest. In the year 1660, Father Krijanitch was banished to faraway Tobolsk, in Siberia, where he spent the following fifteen years in exile. He was not harshly treated, but no opportunity was afforded for the apostolate he so ardently desired. During those years, the Croatian priest wrote a complete survey of seventeenth-century Muscovy.

At length he was permitted to return to western Europe. On his way to report to the Sacred Congregation of Propaganda in Rome, Father Krijanitch halted in Vienna, which at that time was besieged by the Turks. There he died while tending the sick and the wounded.

FRUSTRATION COULD NOT DULL HIS ZEAL

Muscovy grievously disappointed the generous heart of Father Yury Krijanitch; but the information he gathered was of great value to the Holy See, and also to later apostles in the heartbreaking mission field of Russia.

BISHOP FRANCIS PALLU, P.F.M. (*d. 1684*)

A number of persons had a hand in the founding of the great Paris Foreign Missions Society; but, among them, Francis Pallu played a leading part. As a young priest in the middle of the seventeenth century, Father Pallu belonged to a group of fervent Frenchmen directed by an apostolic Jesuit, Father Bagot. One day Father Bagot presented to his young followers a famous confrere, Father Alexander de Rhodes.

Father Rhodes had made thousands of converts in Indo-China, but the new Catholics were without priests. The Jesuit apostle feared that the suspicion of local authorities would be aroused if any considerable number of European missioners should seek to enter Indo-China. Finally Father Rhodes said to himself: "Why not ask Rome to send two or three missionary bishops to the Orient, with power to ordain worthy, indigenous priests? Is it not the essential task of foreign missioners to found indigenous churches?"

Father Rhodes submitted his ideas to Rome, and the Pope told him to seek men worthy of becoming missionary bishops, depending directly upon the Holy See — the first vicars apostolic. Father Bagot believed that he had men of such strong caliber among his young followers. Father Francis Pallu, for one, was fairly on fire with zeal for the conversion of the Orient.

But Rome moved slowly. Portugal claimed the ancient privileges of the royal patronage in the Orient, without being still capable of fulfilling the entailed missionary obligations. Rome knew that the Portuguese would be bitterly offended by the establishment of vicars apostolic. In 1657, Father Pallu was among several young Frenchmen who made a pilgrimage to Rome to implore the Holy Father to appoint vicars apostolic for the Orient. Their request was strongly supported by St. Vincent de Paul. A year later, Father Pallu was consecrated a bishop and appointed one of the first vicars apostolic.

In order to stabilize the new institution, the special purpose of which was the creation of indigenous churches in mission lands, Rome called for the foundation of a missionary seminary in Paris. Bishop Pallu was detained in Europe until 1662 by his inspired labors for the foundation of the wonderful Paris Foreign Missions Society. Through the remainder of his life he continued, even from a distance, to kindle and guide his society's deep inner piety and intense outward activity for the conversion of souls.

In the Orient, Bishop Francis Pallu worked mostly in Indo-China. He ordained Asiatic priests and founded seminaries. The ardent pioneer died in China in 1684. Some years before the death of its principal founder, the Paris Foreign Missions Seminary had been specially recommended to King Louis XIV by Pope Clement X. In praising the new society, the Holy Father said that it had already supplied "many good and valiant laborers for the Lord's Vineyard."

HE FOUGHT THE GOOD FIGHT

An inspired pioneer in the movement to make Catholic foreign mission activity dependent directly on the Holy See, and not on any one individual nation, Bishop Francis Pallu prevailed in the face of determined opposition. He was worthy to be a principal founder of the Paris Foreign Missions Seminary, one of the greatest nurseries of apostles and martyrs that the world has ever known.

FATHER FERDINAND VERBIEST, S.J.
(*1623–1688*)

Father Ferdinand Verbiest was the last of the great missionary triumvirate – Father Matteo Ricci, Father Adam Schall, and then he himself – who gave great prestige at court to the early Jesuit missions in China. He became the most influential Jesuit in the Empire in 1666, after the death of Father Schall. The young Emperor K'ang Hsi made Father Verbiest his tutor.

K'ang Hsi had a passion for learning, and, needless to say, Father Verbiest seized every opportunity of introducing the subject of religion. This Emperor appears to have been interested in religion chiefly from an academic viewpoint. But his friendship for his tutor led him to issue an edict putting an end to the persecution of Christianity throughout the Chinese Empire.

Father Verbiest was K'ang Hsi's chief astronomer. The Emperor grew so fond of the Jesuit that he liked to have his European friend always by his side, even on the imperial hunting expeditions into Tartary. In the intervals between the hunts, K'ang Hsi would discourse with Father Verbiest on matters of science and philosophy.

During more than two decades, the gifted Belgian Jesuit made use of his great influence to spread and benefit Christianity in China. He wrote learned books about the stars, in which he spoke also of the Creator of the celestial bodies. His highly esteemed books were a means of imparting the gospel message to Chinese scholars, whom no ordinary missioner could reach.

Father Verbiest died in 1688 after a short illness. Emperor K'ang Hsi mourned his friend's passing sincerely. With great official pomp, Father Verbiest was laid to rest by the side of Father Ricci and Father Schall, in the cemetery outside the Western Gate of Peking.

FIDELITY TO PENITENTIAL PRACTICES

In his later years, Father Verbiest held a position at the Chinese court which must have been the envy of native officials. But in the midst of so much power and splendor, the Belgian missioner was assiduous in private personal practices of severe Christian austerity.

BISHOP GREGORY LO, O.P. (*1616–1691*)

"In view of the fact that persecution is expelling the foreign missioners from the Far East, and that the Chinese priest, Father Gregory Lo, has shown himself to be a faithful son of the Church and full of zeal for the conversion of pagans, we beg that he may be raised to the dignity of a bishop." Such was the petition received in Rome, in 1673, from the European bishops of Siam, Cochin-China, and Tonkin.

Father Gregory Lo was the first Chinese to be ordained to the Catholic priesthood. He was born of pagan parents in a village of Fukien Province. At the age of seventeen, the Chinese boy heard a sermon by a Franciscan missioner, Father di Santa Maria. The boy asked to be received among the European priest's catechumens and was baptized in the year 1634. Already young Gregory was an apostle. He brought his elder brother and other members of his family into the Church.

Gregory Lo offered his services to Father di Santa Maria as catechist. When persecution exiled the Franciscan to Peking and then to Macao, the faithful Gregory followed the missioner. From Macao, the young Chinese was sent to Manila, where he became a houseboy at the Dominican College of St. Thomas. Gregory wished to join the Dominican Order; but for a time he was sent back to Fukien, to aid the European missioners during a period of persecution. Then he became a Dominican, in January, 1650. Four years later he was ordained to the priesthood by the Spanish Archbishop of Manila.

Soon Father Lo was sent back to China to begin his priestly apostolate among his countrymen. In 1665, when persecution drove European missioners from the Chinese Empire, Father Lo remained alone at his post during several years. He journeyed through ten provinces of China, ministering to the faithful with unwearying zeal, winning back apostates and making new converts to Christianity. In spite of persecution, he alone baptized over five thousand adults.

It is not surprising that Rome considered Father Lo a very worthy condidate for the episcopate, and heeded the plea of the European missionary prelates. Father Lo was consecrated a bishop in Canton on April 8, 1685. After his consecration, the new prelate continued his former simple and hard-working missionary life.

Bishop Gregory Lo died in 1691, and after him no other Chinese was raised to the episcopate for over two hundred and thirty years. Then, on October 28, 1926 – a historic date – Pope Pius XI, "The Pope of the Missions," consecrated at St. Peter's, in Rome, six Chinese prelates.

HEROIC ARCHETYPE

In mission lands, the Church is not firmly founded until it has indigenous priests and prelates. Bishop Gregory Lo was the heroic archetype of the Chinese prelates who in our age have stood firm against every device of Red persecution.

ST. JOHN DE BRITO, S.J. (*1647–1693*)

"Do you think that it is wise to see your mother?" his superior asked Father Brito, who was about to sail for India.

"Yes, I am confident that our Lord will show me how to console her," answered the young Jesuit.

Dona Beatrice Pereyra de Brito, the widow of a former Viceroy of Brazil, had recently lost her eldest son in battle. Now she could not bear the thought of parting from her beloved John. But Father Brito spoke to his mother in such an inspired manner of the mission vocation that her own deeply Catholic heart took fire and she made the great sacrifice gladly.

Father Brito was assigned to the Madura mission field, where Father Robert de Nobili had labored. He followed the mission methods of his famous Jesuit precursor. As Father Robert de Nobili had done, Father Brito adopted the dress, the rigorous diet, and the ascetic practices of Hindu holy men. But he worked among the lower castes, rather than among the Brahmans. The apostolate of the young Jesuit was amazingly successful, and he was venerated by the Pariahs as a very angel of mercy.

In the year 1686, the missioner was captured by hostile pagans and cruelly tortured. Soon after his release, Father Brito was summoned to Portugal, to represent the Madura mission field at an important meeting of the Society of Jesus. Dona Beatrice found it difficult to recognize her once-handsome son in the emaciated, wounded apostle; but she rejoiced that he had won so many souls for Christ.

Two years after his return to India, Father Brito was again captured by pagans. After a brief imprisonment, the Apostle of the Pariahs was beheaded. It was on Ash Wednesday, February 4, 1693, that St. John de Brito consummated his passion.

When the news of the missioner's martyrdom reached Portugal, King Pedro II invited Dona Beatrice to the court. The mother of the martyr put on a white robe and a scarlet cape. Then she went to attend at court a Solemn Mass of Thanksgiving. Dona Beatrice received from Catholic Portugal the homage usually reserved for queens.

A MISSIONER'S PATRIOTISM

On one occasion a European nobleman remarked to Father Brito that in India the Jesuit was far from Portugal, his native country.

The missioner replied: "You are mistaken. My country is the one which will give me birth in heaven. I shall shed my blood for Christ in the Madura Mission."

FATHER JOSEPH VAZ (*1651–1711*)

Joseph Vaz, who was of Brahman stock, was born in Portuguese territory in India. He was ordained to the priesthood at Goa; and in that city he became the head of a community of native priests who followed the rule of the Oratory of St. Philip Neri. Father Joseph's Oratorian community would later assure the continuity of the Indian apostle's work on the island of Ceylon.

The heart of Father Vaz burned within him, when he heard of the terrible distress of the Christians of Ceylon, since the Dutch conquest of that southern island. The Protestant conquerors had expelled the Catholic priests, profaned or pulled down the churches, and destroyed the holy images.

With the permission of his archbishop, Father Vaz disguised himself as a barefoot, migratory laborer and embarked for Ceylon in March, 1686. After a storm-buffeted voyage, the Indian priest arrived at Jaffna, in the south of the island. There, Father Vaz carried on for four years his secret ministry among the hunted Catholics. As he was celebrating Midnight Mass in the year 1690, Dutch soldiers surrounded the house. The apostle barely made his escape. Three hundred native Catholics were arrested and sentenced to crushing fines, one leader of the Jaffna Catholics was whipped to death by the Dutch, and seven others died of starvation in prison.

Father Vaz made his way to the little independent kingdom of Kandy, in the center of the island. The Indian apostle won the favor of the native ruler by saving the local rice crop. The country was devastated by drought, and the petitions of the pagan priests had been of no avail. Then the ruler asked the Catholic priest to obtain rain from his God. Father Vaz prayed, and at once the monsoon rains began to fill the irrigation ditches.

Father Vaz reorganized the Catholic community in Kandy, and

built a church dedicated to Our Lady of the Conversion of Pagans. Using Kandy as his safe mission base, the Indian apostle proceeded to journey in disguise over the whole island. He then summoned from Goa nine of his Brahman Oratorians and placed them in strategical posts. Despite the Dutch, the Catholic harvest of souls flourished everywhere in the fields of the Indian Oratorians.

Father Vaz was approaching the close of his great apostolate, when the Holy See offered him the bishopric of Ceylon. The Indian missioner begged to remain a simple priest. During the twenty-five years that Father Joseph Vaz had labored on the island, he had converted thousands of Buddhists, and had organized a Catholic community of seventy thousand faithful. Thanks to his Oratorians, his work would go on. When the Apostle of Ceylon died, at the age of sixty, the ardent desire of his young manhood had been fulfilled: he had saved the Church of Ceylon.

A MAN OF MILDNESS

A gifted modern French Jesuit, Father Pierre Charles, wrote of Father Joseph Vaz: "In the frequently atrocious circumstances in which life placed him, in the midst of the most unjust persecutions and the most tragic conflicts, never did he hurt any man. He always preferred the role of the anvil to that of the hammer."

FATHER EUSEBIO FRANCISCO KINO, S.J. (*1645–1711*)

Father Eusebio Kino was the sort of optimist that God loves. When Eusebio was a boy on his father's farm, in the Tyrolese village of Segno, he longed to become a missioner in China. But in 1680, as a young Jesuit, Father Kino was sent to Mexico, instead. The man from Segno was far from being crushed by this disappointment. He was thrilled when he was assigned to pioneer on the barren peninsula of Lower California. In fact, he at once became one of the earliest boosters for the "Great Kingdom of the Californias."

To his indulgent eyes, the timorous, half-starved natives of the peninsula seemed to be "the most docile, laughing, and jovial of all those in all America." But in the end, after a series of disasters, the conversion of Lower California had to be suspended. It was a terrible blow, yet Father Kino did not for a moment lose hope. He had been transferred to the frontier in northwestern Mexico. There he would be able to pioneer, even beyond the rim of Christendom. And he planned to make the fertile sections of the mainland a source of supplies for the missions of arid Lower California.

Father Kino founded Mission Dolores among the Pima Indians, in the year 1687; and during nearly a quarter of a century, the thrifty Blackrobe from the Tyrol made Dolores the mother of missions in Pima Land. From thence he sallied forth time and again, leading a cavalcade of livestock to some new outpost of Christianity. The stock-raising industry of nearly twenty localities in northern Mexico and southern Arizona owes its beginnings to Father Kino.

In the year 1689, Father Juan Maria de Salvatierra, an apostle after Kino's own heart, was appointed visitor of Pima Land. The two Jesuits became lifelong friends, and Father Kino planted in Father Salvatierra's heart his own Christlike enthusiasm for the conversion of Lower California. Father Salvatierra later became the founder of permanent missions on the barren peninsula; and until his death, Father Kino nourished the needy missions in the territory of his first apostolate.

In the evangelization of his Indians, Padre Eusebio explored the whole of northwestern Mexico and much of southern Arizona. The Spanish authorities could depend on him to pacify the Indians; to the red men, Father Kino's word was law. They loved his understanding smile, his courage, and the shelter of his sturdy protection. As for Father Kino, he looked on all his Indians as his "children, great and small."

Until he was sixty-six years of age, Father Kino continued to push farther north the frontiers of Christianity and of civilization. In 1711, "The Padre on Horseback" fell ill, during his last ride; and he died "with great peace." In the regions where Eusebio Francisco Kino had labored, Indian folklore surrounded his memory with an ever brighter glory.

HIS ONE BURNING AMBITION

In his fine biography of Father Kino, Herbert Eugene Bolton wrote: "Kino was in the fullest sense a pioneer of civilization. But to him all this was incidental. His one burning ambition was to save souls and push outward the rim of Christendom."

FATHER JOHN BAPTIST SIDOTTI, S.J. (*d. 1715*)

In the year 1709, the distinguished Japanese writer, scholar, and judge, Arai Hakuseki, had before him a singular prisoner. He did not know what to make of Father John Baptist Sidotti, an Italian Jesuit who declared that the Pope had sent him to Japan.

At that time, Christianity had apparently been stamped out in the Sunrise Islands by the fearful persecutions of the past century. The Italian missioner had landed alone in the province of Satsuma, and had been at once arrested. Now the lonely, emaciated foreign priest stood before the great scholar.

Arai Hakuseki had a stern sense of duty, so he could not but admire the prisoner's devotion to the Italian's religious chief, the Pope. Moreover, the scholar in Hakuseki appreciated Father Sidotti's scientific knowledge. But the Japanese judge was a thinker of the positive type; and to him, the story of the Redemption of mankind was pure folly.

"When this man begins to speak of religion, his talk is shallow and scarcely a word is intelligible. All of a sudden, folly takes the place of wisdom. It is like listening to the talk of two different men," marveled the perplexed judge.

According to his lights, Hakuseki was an upright man. He therefore recommended that the brave foreign fanatic be sent back to Italy. That merciful counsel was not followed. Father Sidotti was walled up in a small cell, where he died in the year 1715.

Seeing the inexplicable joy and the patience of the young priest in the midst of such horrible suffering, two untutored jailers of Father Sidotti showed greater understanding than had the learned Arai Hakuseki. At a time when discovery of their conversion would mean death under unspeakable tortures, they dared to embrace their prisoner's Faith.

Something over thirty years later, three other Jesuits landed in Japan. In order to reach that country of almost certain martyrdom, one of these missioners had been obliged to serve ten years as a cook on a Dutch vessel. No record exists of the fate of those intrepid sons of St. Ignatius.

THE STUMBLING BLOCK OF PRIDE

Though the renowned scholar, Arai Hakuseki, was naturally virtuous, he could not lay aside pride in his own human learning. Thus, the wisdom of God that Father Sidotti sought to reveal to his compassionate judge, was to the worldly Japanese merely unintelligible folly.

FATHER SEBASTIAN RASLE, S.J.
(*1658–1724*)

Father Sebastian Rasle came to Quebec from France in the year 1689. He was sent to an Abnaki Indian mission village that had been formed nearby. Even at the beginning of his apostolate, Father Rasle was sufficiently Christlike to accept with profit a rebuke he received from his outspoken flock. One day, when eating with his Indian hosts, the young priest was unable to conceal his dislike for their food.

"You must overcome your distaste!" admonished the Abnakis. "Is this so hard for a Father who understands the prayer (religion) so perfectly? We, on our part, have great difficulties to surmount in order to have faith in what we cannot see."

"Then I could hesitate no longer," wrote Father Rasle. "It became necessary to accommodate myself to their manners and usages, in order that I might win their confidence and gather them into the fold of Christ."

In 1691, Father Rasle was sent westward to work among the Illinois Indians, but the Abnakis had won his first love. He was glad when he was recalled to spend the remainder of his life among them. From the year 1695 until his martyrdom, Father Rasle made his headquarters on the Kennebec River, near the present town of Norridgewock, Maine. When the crops had been sown, the Jesuit and his Indians journeyed to the seacoast to fish. The winters were spent in hunting, either on the coast or in the mountains. During these expeditions in search of food, Father Rasle offered the Holy Sacrifice in a tent which the travelers carried with them and set up at their successive bases.

In the early years of the eighteenth century, the war between France and England spread to the colonies. Faithful to their missioner, the Abnakis sided with the French. The government of Massachusetts set a price on Father Rasle's head. Several times the aged Jesuit and his mission were attacked by soldiers from New England. Finally, in 1724, a party of English soldiers and Mohawk warriors suddenly surrounded the mission.

In the hope of saving the lives of his Indians, Father Rasle advanced calmly toward the enemy. The attackers shot him down immediately, and the Jesuit fell near the cross that he had planted in the middle of the village. Then the enemy withdrew, after having fired the little mission church. So died the beloved missioner-martyr of the Abnakis.

THE TRUTH WILL OUT

The Puritans of New England accused Father Rasle of being a bloody inciter of Indian war. But after the political murder of the aged missioner, the Abnakis fought with such ferocity that a governor of Maine was forced to admit the restraining influence of the French apostle on his Indian flock.

FATHER SAMUEL FRITZ, S.J. (*1654–1724*)

The Maynas missions were a long way from Bohemia where, in the latter half of the seventeenth century, a redheaded boy who was to be named Samuel Fritz was born. But Samuel Fritz grew up, became a Jesuit, and crossed the Atlantic to South America, to evangelize the Indians of the Maynas missions. The Maynas country lay in Ecuador, Peru, and western Brazil, on the eastern slope of the Andes Mountains and in the tropical lowlands beyond.

The sturdy Father Samuel Fritz crossed the Andes from the west coast in the year 1685. That pioneer missioner was to explore and evangelize a vast area in the Amazon country. Father Fritz later drew a map of the Amazon River, and he wrote on the margin: "Made with no little toil and exertion, after having navigated the river in the greater part of its course as far as it is navigable."

But map making was not the primary purpose of the Bohemian Jesuit as he journeyed along the swollen river through dense, dark forests. In his canoe, he carried a wooden cross and a portable altar. He summoned the Indians to the riverbanks by ringing a bell, and they came in crowds to hear the tall white man tell about Christ.

The lonely dwellers in the forest saw that the visiting stranger loved them. They believed everything that the missioner told them about a God who wanted men to call Him by the wondrous title of "Our Father." Their hearts lifted in a new freedom from the fear of evil spirits. Under the guidance of Father Fritz, the red men settled down in villages.

The great Jesuit traveled from one to another of his Christian settlements. He cared for the sick, and instructed the children. He did most of the work in the building of forest churches. At one time, the apostolic pioneer fell ill of a high fever, and the Indians were terrified at the thought of losing their priest.

"You must not die!" they implored Father Fritz. "If you should die, who would be our father, lover, and protector?"

The apostle of the Amazon Indians did not die of that illness. He labored in the Maynas missions for nearly forty years. Once he journeyed to Lima to obtain financial and military aid for his missions. In that fine city, he appeared clad in a cassock made of palm fiber. He wore hemp sandals and carried a rude wooden cross. The people of the City of the Kings were awed by this tall, thin, bearded jungle apostle.

POLITICS HARM THE MISSIONS

Father Samuel Fritz and his Jesuit confreres were prominent among the colonial missioners of Latin America. In the eighteenth century, the Blackrobes were expelled, for political reasons having their origin in Europe. The expulsion of the Jesuits was a main cause of the subsequent decline of Latin America's Catholic missions.

FATHER GABRIEL DE MALAGRIDA, S.J. (*d. 1761*)

In the eighteenth century, a Jesuit missioner was tried and condemned with infamous injustice that recalls the contemporary treatment of Cardinal Mindszenty by the Hungarian Communists. But the persecutor of Father Gabriel de Malagrida was not a Communist. He was Pombal, the nominally Catholic minister of Portugal. Pombal had determined to undermine the influence of the Church in official circles. He was especially hostile to the Society of Jesus.

At that time the most venerated of the Jesuit preachers in Portugal was the aged Father Gabriel de Malagrida, an Italian who had spent thirty years laboring among the Brazilian Indians. All classes of society considered the holy old apostle a saint, and King Joseph I expressed a wish to make a retreat under Father Malagrida's direction. The furiously jealous Pombal singled out the aged missioner for his chief victim.

In the year 1758, a mysterious nocturnal attack was made, in the course of which King Joseph was slightly wounded. Pombal immediately proclaimed that the Jesuits were conspirators in an alleged plot against their sovereign's life. He said that Father

Malagrida was the ringleader of the traitorous culprits. Pombal's accusation was so manifestly absurd that the ordinary judges refused to consider it. So the honest judges were removed, and Pombal set up a tribunal of which his own brother was made president. But even that despicable court could not convict Father Malagrida as a would-be murderer.

Then, after the old missioner had been ill-treated for two and a half years in a filthy dungeon, Pombal's "court of justice" produced heretical documents which it attributed to the Jesuit's authorship. The extravagances of those documents were so wild that no one believed the Italian Jesuit had written them – unless, indeed, the aged apostle had lost his reason from the horrors of his imprisonment. Nevertheless, Father Malagrida was condemned as a heretic. The saintly missioner was publicly strangled to death, and his body was burned at Lisbon on September 21, 1761.

BRAZIL'S DEBT TO THE JESUITS

Of Father Malagrida and the other early Jesuits in Brazil, a distinguished Brazilian statesman has said: "One cannot fail to recognize that they rendered the greatest service to the land of Brazil. As missioners they imparted civilization to many thousands of Indians, and thanks to their self-sacrificing work, the native race has taken a considerable part in the development of the Brazilian people."

FATHER JUNIPERO SERRA, O.F.M. (*1713–1784*)

Junipero Serra, the Franciscan apostle who laid the foundations of Christianity in the territory of the present state of California, was born of a peasant family on the lovely island of Majorca, east of Spain. After his ordination to the priesthood, Father Serra acquired renown as a professor of philosophy, and as an eloquent preacher; but his heart was in the mission fields of the New World. He and his friend, Father Palou, volunteered for America. They sailed from Spain in the year 1749.

In Mexico, the two Franciscans from Majorca volunteered for the difficult missions among the Pames Indians in the craggy regions of the Sierra Gordas. Father Serra was less happy during a period of seven years that he spent as preacher in Mexico City. His ire was especially roused by a custom of the fair ladies of the capital. They had cups of hot chocolate brought to them in church, and they sipped their favorite beverage during the celebration of the Mass!

Father Serra rejoiced when he was transferred to the missions in lower California. He did not remain long on that barren peninsula, for at that time, Spain was greatly afraid that Russians would descend from Alaska and seize upon Upper California. An expedition was sent, therefore, by way of Lower California, to "occupy and fortify San Diego and Monterey for God and the King of Spain." Father Serra was chosen as the superior of the missions to be founded in Upper California.

When the expedition started, in 1769, Junipero Serra was fifty-six years old and lame. But he set out on foot, with all the ardor of youth. As he tramped northward, he rejoiced to see the land grow "smiling and gladsome"; and he fell in love at once with the Indians encountered along the way. His enthusiasm was not dampened by the discovery that those same red men were shameless beggars and thieves. They even tried to pilfer the Padre's spectacles! At San Diego, Father Serra founded the first mission in the new country. Shortly afterward, when dire misfortune had overtaken the expedition, the unshakable faith of Junipero Serra alone prevented the Spaniards from abandoning California. The second mission was founded at Monterey on the Carmel River. For the remainder of Father Serra's life, Monterey was to be his headquarters and the place he loved best on earth.

Together with his faithful Franciscan helpers, Father Serra Christianized and civilized his lazy Indians. His great plan for his beloved California was a chain of missions, along the coast from San Diego to San Francisco; and during the founder's lifetime, nine of those missions did grow up beside "The King's Highway." Up and down the coast, the lame old apostle journeyed ceaselessly until, in the year 1784, he made the final round of his California missions.

Then Father Junipero Serra returned to Monterey and said with a contented smile, "I have come home to die."

Today, it is difficult to discover a full-blooded Indian in California. But the ruins of the old missions along the coastal highway — *El Camino Real* — still stir Christian hearts with the memory of Father Serra's immense love of the red men's souls.

NEVER TO TURN BACK

Father Junipero Serra resolved "to go forward and never to turn back" in his work of winning souls for Christ. On the journey to San Diego he became dangerously ill, but he would not alter his resolution. "If it be God's will that I die on the road," he said, "then bury me there and I will remain contentedly among the Gentiles."

PETER RI (*Baptized 1784*)

On the Korean peninsula, Christianity had unique beginnings. Before any foreign missioner was able to slip secretly into the sealed-off "Hermit Kingdom," over four thousand Catholics had been baptized in Korea. This strange development came about in the following way.

Korea had been for centuries a vassal of China, and every year an embassy journeyed to Peking to pay tribute to the Chinese Emperor. Some of the Korean envoys had taken back to their peninsula doctrinal writings of the Jesuit missioners in Peking. In the year 1777, those writings fell into the hands of a group of Korean scholars, who had withdrawn to a mountain solitude "to seek the truth about human nature, heaven, and the world."

Those men of good will recognized the true doctrine in the Christian books. But how were they to learn more about this true religion? Fortunately, one of the scholars had an intimate friend who was to journey to China with the annual embassy in the year 1783. This scholar persuaded his friend to seek from the missioners in Peking further information about Catholic teachings. The friend was converted and baptized in China under the name of Peter.

On his return to Korea, Peter Ri baptized two of the Korean scholars. Those new converts, fired with the zeal of apostles, baptized numerous followers. Persecution came almost at once, but the greater part of the converts stood firm.

In spite of martyrdoms and some apostasies, the number of Korean Catholics rose to over four thousand in the year 1794. This glorious first page in the history of the Church in Korea was being entered in the Book of Life while George Washington was President of the infant United States of America.

CHRIST CALLED THEM BLESSED

Without direct evangelization, the first Korean Catholics came into the Faith because of their ardent desire for divine truth: "Blessed are they that hunger and thirst after justice, for they shall have their fill" (Mt. 5:6). Almost immediately those Oriental converts underwent persecution: "Blessed are they that suffer persecution for justice' sake, for theirs is the kingdom of heaven" (Mt. 5:10).

PART VIII

Unprecedented Missionary Expansion

(1801–1914)

IN THE years between 1801 and 1914, the West made such remarkable progress in general literacy, political freedom, material well-being, scientific discovery, and world-wide expansion of influence and domination that a mood of complacent optimism was engendered. But outside the Catholic Church, there was a general undermining of Christian faith and principles, destined to produce the global catastrophes of the present age.

In spite of the rise of extremists in rationalism, liberalism, nationalism, and communism, the Church gained new strength. Pope Pius IX proclaimed the dogmas of the Immaculate Conception of the Blessed Virgin and of Papal Infallibility. In 1858, our Lady appeared to Bernadette Soubirous at Lourdes. Pope Leo XIII, a stanch friend of the laboring classes, was eminent in diplomacy, scholarship, and holiness. The saintly Pius X was fearless in condemning the errors of the movement known as Modernism. The nations on both sides of the global conflict sought the great services of Benedict XV in succoring the victims of World War I.

The upsurge of faith among members of the Catholic Church produced the most world-wide expansion of Christianity until then witnessed. As a consequence of the marked expansion of English-speaking peoples, Protestantism at this time also entered mission countries in force. Largely because of the central direction furnished with increased efficacy by the Sacred Congregation of Propaganda, Catholic mission activities were better organized than before. France took a strong lead in the inspiring outburst of apostolic zeal; but the Catholic missionary revival manifested itself likewise in Italy, England, Germany, Belgium, Holland, and various other European countries. In the year 1911, the Catholic Church of the United States gave birth to Maryknoll, the Catholic Foreign Mission Society of America.

Pope Pius VII restored the Society of Jesus for the whole world in 1814, and the Jesuits began to return to the fields where they had formerly labored. The years between the French Revolution and World War I witnessed the founding of more than forty societies of priests, twelve societies of Brothers, and one hundred and fifty societies of Sisters for the express purpose of Catholic mission work. A vital feature of the age was the entry of thousands of Catholic Sisters into foreign mission fields, where they were remarkably successful in fostering the religious vocations of native young women.

A rich missionary literature began to rouse the Catholic laity to a realization of their obligations in the work of spreading the Faith. Many lay associations were formed to aid the missions by prayers and by money contributions. Pauline Jaricot founded the Society for the Propagation of the Faith at Lyons in 1822. The Association of the Holy Childhood owed its birth to a French prelate, Bishop Charles de Forbin-Janson. Two French women, Madame Bigard-Collin and her daughter, founded the Association of St. Peter the Apostle for the aid of indigenous seminarians in all of the mission fields.

In this age many missioners and thousands of native Catholics died for Christ, during outbreaks of persecution in mission countries. It became evident that a fundamental cause of the persecutions was distrust of the missioners as the supposed agents of rapacious Western nations. This distrust of foreign apostles emphasized anew the crucial obligation of developing everywhere a strong indigenous clergy.

On the eve of World War I, the Holy Father could survey the far-flung mission fields of the Catholic Church with justifiably strong hope of an increasingly abundant harvest of souls.

In Latin America, new sees had been created and missions were being reopened. Selfless apostles had evangelized the Indians and the Eskimos of Alaska and the Arctic regions of Canada. On Pacific Islands and in Australia, Catholicism had waxed strong. Christianity was on a rising tide in almost every country of Asia. The situation in Africa was so spiritually bright that the total conversion of that great continent seemed a not too remote possibility.

IGNATIUS, *Apostle of the Flatheads (d. 1837)*

"Let us go west with the traders of the Hudson's Bay Company," said the Indian, Ignatius, to three of his friends in the Canadian colony for Catholic Iroquois. "We have the Faith. But what about those Indians out there, who still believe in witch doctors? Now is our chance to tell our brother red men about Christ."

Ignatius was a member of the Wolf family that had voted to spare the life of Father Isaac Jogues at Ossernenon (Auriesville, New York). He was a born leader, and his friends did as he suggested. In the year 1820, the four Catholic Iroquois journeyed hundreds of miles until they reached the Rocky Mountains. There they came upon the Flathead Indians and were adopted into that tribe. Before long, the handsome and strong Ignatius was elected a chief of the Flatheads.

The new chief was a powerful orator, and his speeches were all about the Catholic religion. The Flatheads listened to him eagerly. They felt such a burning desire to become Catholics that they resolved to send four of their tribe all the way to St. Louis to ask for a missioner. The four Flatheads did reach St. Louis; but there two of the exhausted envoys died after having received baptism. The two remaining Flatheads perished or were slain during the return journey.

Ignatius was not discouraged. He decided that he himself would go in search of a priest for the eager Flatheads. After a journey of frightful privations and sufferings, Chief Ignatius and his two sons arrived at St. Louis. But at that time, the bishop had no missioner to spare for the distant tribe in the Rocky Mountains. On his way back to his expectant brethren, Ignatius was killed by hostile Sioux.

The Flatheads sorrowed long over the loss of their brave apostle, but they were all the more determined to seek the religion that he had preached to them. In 1840, another deputation of Flatheads trekked across the wilderness to St. Louis. That time, the bishop had a missioner available. It was because of Ignatius, Apostle of the Flathead Indians, that the great Jesuit, Father Peter De Smet, became the pioneer priest of the Rockies.

THE BLOOD OF MARTYRS

Jesuit martyrs died for the conversion of the Iroquois. Later, an Iroquois apostle labored and laid down his life for the conversion of the Flathead Indians. So the sacred flame of apostolic zeal passes from race to race, and from generation to generation. In no century of the Christian era has the blood of martyrs failed to nourish its Catholic seed.

BLESSED LAWRENCE IMBERT, P.F.M.
(*1797–1839*)

From his childhood, Lawrence Imbert had desired to become a missioner, so he entered the Paris Foreign Missions Seminary. In 1821, Father Imbert was assigned to Szechwan Province, China. The new missioner mastered Chinese quickly; and during twelve years, he proved himself an outstanding apostle in Szechwan.

Like all other missioners in the Orient, Father Imbert had been thrilled by the story of the unique beginnings of Christianity in Korea. In 1836, he heard with joy that the Holy See had entrusted the spiritual care of Korea to his own society. He volunteered at once for that land of martyrs.

On the recommendation of his superiors, Father Imbert was consecrated a bishop and became the first Vicar Apostolic of Korea. He set out immediately on the long journey through the Chinese Empire. In Manchuria, the new bishop found two priests of his society who had been assigned to be his helpers: Father Maubant and Father Chastan. After repeated attempts, the two priests succeeded in crossing the frozen Yalu River and in entering Korea; they wore as disguise the voluminous native mourning costume. At the end of 1837, Bishop Imbert, also, secretly crossed the Yalu over the ice.

The suffering Church in Korea awoke to a new life, but gains were made only at the cost of great hardships and privations on the part of the French missioners. They were obliged to minister to the Christians in secret, moving constantly from house to house to avoid detection. In January, 1839, there came into power a prime minister who was a bitter enemy of the Christians. He at once began a fierce persecution. For months an unrelenting search for the foreign priests continued, and finally Bishop Imbert was discovered and arrested in Seoul, the capital city.

Hoping that the Christians might be spared torture if his confreres gave themselves up, Bishop Imbert wrote to his priests, "The good shepherd giveth his life for his sheep."

The heroic French prelate and his two fellow missioners were cruelly tortured and then beheaded on September 22, 1839. Those of the Korean faithful who escaped death were scattered and reduced to misery. But the very dispersion of the Christians spread the teachings of the Church far and wide throughout the peninsula.

A NOBLE CHARACTER

When Bishop Imbert was about to leave China for the arduous journey to Korea, his former religious superior wrote of him: "Bishop Imbert is loved by all. He is a noble character, kind, cheerful, accommodating, and enterprising."

BLESSED JOHN GABRIEL PERBOYRE, C.M. (*1802–1840*)

"Please God that I may replace my brother in China!" said Father John Gabriel Perboyre, when he learned that his younger brother, also a Vincentian priest, had died during the long voyage to the Orient.

John Gabriel Perboyre was born on a farm in southern France. His fervent Catholic parents gave six of their eight children to the service of God in religion. John Gabriel was attracted to the missionary life of the Vincentian Fathers. After ordination to the priesthood, Father Perboyre hoped to be assigned to the missions, but his superiors needed him in France. During a decade, Father Perboyre served as a professor and as novice master.

At last, in 1835, an assignment to China came. Soon afterward, Father Perboyre left France forever. On reaching China, the new missioner remained for several months at the Portuguese colony on the island of Macao. While there, he mastered Chinese quickly by dint of unremitting application.

In that period, Father Perboyre wrote to his superior in Paris: "Just now Christianity is enjoying great peace in the interior of China. Our missions are progressing, but the priests – all too few in number – are being literally worked to death. They are but half nourished, living on rice and herbs. The Christians to whom they minister are the poorest of the poor and can do little for them."

After Father Perboyre had journeyed into the interior of China, he led for about three years the life of hardship that he had previously described to his superior. Then violent persecution broke out anew. Father Perboyre was arrested in Hupeh Province. A renegade Christian had betrayed the priest's hiding place for thirty pieces of silver. During the following year, the French missioner was horribly tortured, yet he remained calm and even joyous.

Father Perboyre was condemned to death by strangulation. Like his divine Master, John Gabriel Perboyre was led out to be executed between criminals, and he was put to death on a cross on a Friday in September, 1840.

THE MOTHER OF A MARTYR

In France, on receiving the news of her son's death, the mother of the martyr said: "Why should I shrink from sacrificing my son to God? Did not the Blessed Virgin generously sacrifice hers, for my salvation? I love my son far too dearly not to rejoice that he is now perfectly happy."

ST. PETER CHANEL, S.M. (*1803–1841*)

"The devil ate him!" Thus the inhabitants of Futuna, a small island in the South Pacific, were accustomed to describe death. In the year 1836, a young French priest came to tell the people of Futuna that death need not deliver the soul of man into the power of the evil one.

Father Peter Chanel, the son of hard-working French peasants, was one of the pioneer Marist missioners in Oceania. He endeared himself to his cannibalistic Polynesian flock by his gentle charity and invariable cheerfulness. At first the ruler of Futuna was friendly to Father Chanel, but suddenly the Polynesian king turned against Christianity and the French priest. He sent his henchman, a certain Musumusu, to murder the European missioner.

Early in the morning of April 28, 1841, Musumusu assembled some natives who, like himself, were of the pagan party. They went to Father Chanel's hut and asked him to dress some wounds that Musumusu had received in battle with the Christians. While the priest was preparing a lotion to apply to the wounds, Musumusu's followers attacked him with their clubs. Father Chanel sank to the ground, repeating the words of oblation, "It is well; it is well." Musumusu himself seized a hatchet in the hut and struck Father Chanel so violently that the blade entered the martyr's skull.

The king of Futuna had calculated wrongly when he concluded that he could drive Christ out of his island by killing the European missioner. Other Marists arrived, and converts to Christianity continued to multiply. One of the most fervent of those new converts was Musumusu, the murderer. Today, everyone on the island of Father Chanel's martyrdom is a Catholic.

GOD'S WORK CANNOT FAIL

"Whether they kill me or not, the Faith has been planted on the island. It would lose nothing by my death because it is not the work of men, but of God." – *St. Peter Chanel*

BLESSED ANDREW KIM (*1820–1846*)

"Poor young man! In what terrible labors he has lived since childhood!" exclaimed the pagan judges of Father Andrew Kim.

The young captive, the first Korean to be ordained a Catholic priest, had just told a court of Korean judges the story of his short life. Andrew Kim was born of a well-to-do family that had already given several martyrs and confessors to the Church. Father Maubant, one of the pioneer French missioners in Korea, had sent the young Andrew to the Catholic seminary in Macao, South China. Father Maubant was martyred in 1839; but Andrew continued his education in Macao, where he learned with facility Chinese, Latin, and French. He was ordained to the priesthood in China.

Father Kim had told the judges of his ceaseless attempts to introduce European missioners into tightly sealed Korea. After having journeyed through Manchuria's great forests and having suffered shipwreck, hunger, and exposure, the heroic young Korean had succeeded in smuggling a French bishop and a French priest into his native land. Then he had tried to arrange for the arrival of still other missioners. But on that attempt, he had been detected and arrested, so he was on trial and under the shadow of almost certain death.

Father Kim's fearless and noble bearing touched the hearts of his judges. They decided to appeal to the highest authority in the land, and asked the king of Korea to spare the captive's life. But such clemency would have been contrary to the harsh laws of the country. The young apostle was finally condemned to death as a traitor.

"If I have communicated with foreigners, it was for my religion, for my God. It is for Him that I die!" stated Father Kim with calm courage. He was beheaded on September 16, 1846, when he was twenty-six years of age.

A MAN OF LIVING FAITH

Blessed Andrew Kim's bishop wrote of the young martyr: "Father Andrew Kim was a man of living faith, of sincere piety, and of astonishing facility of speech. In his priestly administrations, he surpassed all our hopes."

BLESSED ANNE MARIE JAVOUHEY
(*1788–1851*)

A remarkable Frenchwoman, Anne Marie Javouhey, founded a religious community when she was but nineteen years of age. In those days it was thought that Sisters should lead the cloistered type of life in their homeland convents, but Mother Javouhey was determined that her Sisters of St. Joseph of Cluny should do foreign-mission work. In the year 1819, the foundress sent some of her Sisters to Senegal, in West Africa; and she soon followed them there. Mother Javouhey almost died of fever in Senegal, but she wrote, "How I love Africa!"

It was, however, in French Guiana, a colony on the northeastern coast of South America, that Mother Javouhey was to accomplish her greatest mission work. The French Government gave her a very difficult task in Guiana. Over five hundred Negro slaves in the colony were to be liberated. But before the Negroes were freed, the Government decreed that they should be Christianized, civilized, and trained to earn their own living. Mother Javouhey embarked on this work with such energy, and achieved such amazing success, that King Louis Philippe said of her, "Mother Javouhey is a great man!"

Colonial officials savagely opposed Mother Javouhey's plans for the betterment of the Negroes, but they found themselves bravely outfaced. Under the fostering care of this "Mother of the Blacks," the slaves were ready for their freedom when the time came. While she was carrying on her heavy task, Mother Javouhey found means to establish a leper colony. In addition, she and her Sisters did mission work among the Indians, instructing whole tribes in the Faith.

The spiritual daughters of this foundress, whose courage earned for her the title of "great man," have labored for Christ throughout the French colonies. Their work has extended to the island of Ceylon and to India. But it is especially in West Africa, the region of their mission pioneering, that their activities have expanded most widely. There the Sisters of St. Joseph of Cluny have rescued many an African woman from the cruelties of polygamy, and they have trained generations of Christian brides.

DISREGARD OF HUMAN RESPECT

Mother Javouhey encountered widespread criticism when she decided that her Sisters should undertake foreign-mission work; but in her love of God and souls, she did not heed human opinion. God is never outdone in generosity, and now Mother Javouhey is recognized as an outstanding pioneer in the modern participation of women in active foreign missionary endeavor.

VENERABLE FRANCIS LIBERMANN, C.S.Sp. (*1804–1852*)

The foremost organizer of mission work in West Africa, the Venerable Francis Libermann, never saw an African village. Libermann was a native of Alsace in France. Like St. Paul, he was a convert from Judaism. His conversion was a great blow to his father, a fervid rabbi. But Francis persevered in his determination to study for the priesthood.

On the eve of being ordained subdeacon, the young convert was suddenly stricken with epilepsy. He accepted the heavy cross with ready resignation. During thirteen years, Libermann's disease made it impossible for him to be ordained to the priesthood. He had meanwhile become ardently interested in mission work among the Negroes. The converted Jew sought and obtained the permission of the Holy Father for a new society, dedicated to the conversion of the Negroes.

Libermann founded his community in the year 1841. His own health had by then so much improved that he was finally ordained priest. At the suggestion of the Pope, Father Libermann's community was united with an older society, the Holy Ghost Fathers, who had been organized for the evangelization of Negroes in the French colonies. Father Libermann became the Superior-General of the united societies.

Meanwhile, the United States was sponsoring in West Africa the development of the present Republic of Liberia, begun as a colony for liberated American slaves. Father Edward Barron of Philadelphia was raised to the episcopate and appointed Vicar Apostolic of Upper and Lower Guinea; but fever made it impossible for him to remain in Africa. Before Bishop Barron returned to the United States, however, he went to France to recruit missioners for his vicariate, and during that visit he had a providential meeting with Father Libermann.

Father Libermann sent seven priests to West Africa in the year 1843. Within a few months, six of those missionary trail blazers died from fever; but the great work of the Holy Ghost Fathers on the Dark Continent was not abandoned. It later spread to East Africa, where the missioners of Father Libermann were again the real pioneers. Today, there are more than three thousand Fathers and Brothers of the Holy Ghost Society. They are at work among the Negroes in the two Americas, as well as in many missions of Africa.

GOD'S CHOICE

The story of Father Libermann's life and apostolate is best summed up in the words of an earlier Jewish convert and missioner to the Gentiles: "The weak things of the world hath God chosen, that he may confound the strong . . . that no flesh should glory in his sight" (1 Cor. 1:27–29).

BLESSED PHILIPPINE DUCHESNE (*1769–1852*)

"Where are you going so fast?" an Indian mother called to her little boy and girl, as they were running out of the tent.

"To the church, to watch the praying white woman," said the children.

"Be sure that you do not talk and disturb the holy woman!" warned the squaw.

"No, no! We never talk, for the white woman does not understand our language," the children protested.

The little Indians' "praying woman" was Mother Philippine Duchesne, a Madame of the Sacred Heart. In the year 1817, Bishop Dubourg of Louisiana had asked Mother Sophie Barat, foundress of the Religious of the Sacred Heart, for the aid of her daughters. Mother Barat sent Mother Philippine Duchesne and four other religious to North America.

Mother Duchesne hoped to work among the Indians, but the needs of the white settlers in the vast New World were so pressing that her desire remained unfulfilled. At last, in 1842, when Mother Duchesne was over seventy years of age, the great Jesuit, Father De Smet, was strongly impressed by the old nun's undiminished ardor for the conversion of the red men. Father De Smet took Mother Duchesne in an oxcart to one of his Indian missions.

It was too late for the old religious to master the Indian language, but she could pray for the people she loved so much. Seeing the venerable nun in long hours of conversation with God, the red men came to speak lovingly of her as "The Woman Who Prays Always." Mother Duchesne had shown the way. Her community later pioneered among the Indians in Kansas.

THE SUCCESS OF FAILURE

The foundations of the remarkable accomplishments of the Religious of the Sacred Heart in the United States were laid on the sufferings and apparent failures of their first superior in this country. Through it all, Blessed Philippine Duchesne had and held God Himself.

PAULINE JARICOT (*1799–1862*)

In her youth, Pauline Jaricot was the beautiful and much-sought-after daughter of a wealthy merchant of Lyons, France. But in the midst of gay social activities, Pauline felt that God was calling her to serve Him alone.

One of Pauline's brothers belonged to a missionary congregation, and he spoke often of how the missioners in pagan lands were hampered by lack of funds. In 1819, an idea for helping the missioners came suddenly to Pauline. She asked ten of her friends to give a penny each week for the missions. Each one of those friends was to persuade ten more people to contribute a penny a week; and thus the work was to go on, expanding indefinitely. In this humble manner, the future Society for the Propagation of the Faith was born.

During the first year, Pauline and her friends collected about one hundred and fourteen dollars, which they gave to the Paris Foreign Missions Seminary. The plan gradually spread to many villages and cities. Priests and lay folk, rich and poor, became interested. Then, in 1822, a group of men perceived the world-wide possibilities of Pauline's idea. They formed the Society for the Propagation of the Faith, and before long Pauline was pushed into the background.

"Are you going to let them treat you like that?" a friend of the foundress asked.

"Well," answered Pauline, "I merely served as the match to light the fire. Why should a match expect to be talked about?"

Pauline Jaricot later established the Society of the Living Rosary, as a means of reparation for the spread of unbelief in France. She also founded an enterprise for workingmen. In this last undertaking, she was betrayed by businessmen in whom she had trusted. The remainder of her life was spent in dire poverty and the vain effort to repay her debts. She died in want and obscurity in the year 1862.

In our own day, Pauline Jaricot has been universally recognized and venerated as the actual foundress of the Society for the Propagation of the Faith. As a contemporary Church leader has said,

"This organization has galvanized and reorganized all forms of missionary charity, and has distributed on behalf of the missions immense sums of money."

LOVING ACCEPTANCE OF THE CROSS

The Curé of Ars said of Pauline Jaricot: "She knew how to accept the heaviest cross with love."

BLESSED THEOPHANE VENARD, P.F.M. (*1829–1861*)

One day in the third decade of the past century, two children sat in a meadow of Poitiers in southern France. As they tended their father's goats, Theophane and his loved sister, Melanie, were reading about Father Charles Cornay, missioner and martyr in Tonkin, Indo-China.

Suddenly Theophane exclaimed, "I, too, will go to Tonkin, and I, too, will be a martyr!"

Later, it cost Theophane dear to leave his family, to whom he was intensely devoted. Especially hard was the parting from Melanie. But grief did not lead to melancholy; at the Paris Foreign Missions Seminary, Theophane was a favorite on account of his bright and sunny nature. The seminarian once wrote to his younger brother: "True devotion is natural, gay, and bright, according to the words of St. Paul, 'Rejoice in the Lord always; again I say, rejoice.'"

Father Theophane Venard's brief and heroic apostolate in Tonkin lasted only five years. During most of that time, persecution forced him to carry on his ministry in hiding—in boats, caverns, and mountain fastnesses. Arrested in November, 1860, Theophane was placed in a bamboo cage. In that cramped confinement the young missioner remained until he was beheaded on February 2, 1861.

A few days before his execution, Blessed Theophane wrote to Melanie: "Now, as my last hour is approaching, I want to send you, my darling sister and friend, a special word of love and farewell; for our hearts have been one from childhood. You have never had a secret from me, nor I from you. . . . At this news [of his execution], you will shed tears – but they should be tears of joy! Think of your brother wearing the aureole of the martyrs, and bearing in his hand the palm of victory!"

Bishop James Anthony Walsh, the cofounder of Maryknoll, wrote a biography of Blessed Theophane Venard. The story of this young French missioner and martyr has inspired numerous mission vocations in the United States. So it is that the flame of missionary zeal circles the earth.

HOW DO WE KNOW?

"'Piety,' some say, 'is only good for priests and nuns. God does not expect so much of us.' How do you know?" – *Blessed Theophane Venard*

FATHER THEOPHILE VERBIST, I.H.M.
(*1823–1868*)

One bitter night in February, 1868, the heads of the ten Catholic families in Tiger Valley, Mongolia, stood helplessly around the brick bed in a mud hut. On the bed, the foreign Spiritual Father stirred restlessly, his body shaken by painful spasms of the dread typhus. The chief catechist looked sorrowfully at his companions – then shook his head.

Only three days earlier, Father Theophile Verbist had arrived in their village to preach, offer Mass, and administer the sacraments, especially Confirmation. For Father Verbist was provicar of the vast, new mission territory of Siwantzu, and he had the faculties of a bishop. He had been tall and stately, and there he was, prostrated, writhing in agony. The Christians could do nothing to halt the progress of the dread malady.

Father Verbist regained consciousness long enough to scribble a few words of farewell to his fellow missioners; then he fainted again. A message had been sent to the nearest priest, Father Chang, in a village two hundred and fifty miles from Tiger Valley. A week later, when the Chinese priest arrived at top speed, the dying missioner was unconscious, but still breathing.

On February 23, 1868, Father Verbist succumbed to the same Mongolian typhus that, in succeeding years, was to take the lives of hundreds of his spiritual sons. For Father Verbist was the founder of a new religious family, the Missionary Congregation of the Immaculate Heart of Mary. He had been inspired to found a missionary society, while he was serving as national director of the Holy Childhood Association in Belgium. He had established his mission headquarters at Scheut in 1862 and, three years later, had led his pioneer missioners into the four hundred thousand square miles of Mongolian territory that had been entrusted to their care.

"Don't be in such a hurry!" a Roman cardinal had advised the founder. But Father Verbist was impelled to hurry because his time was short.

The founder did not lay down his life in vain in that forlorn Mongolian valley. Today, over a thousand spiritual sons of Father Verbist are caring for 1,300,000 Christians in the Far East and the Congo, and they are reaching out for 15,000,000 pagans. They have also begun missionary work among the Negroes in the United States of America.

IMPELLED BY THE HOLY SPIRIT

Human advisers thought that Father Theophile Verbist had acted with too great haste in taking over the Siwantzu mission territory in Mongolia; but his missionary congregation survived and flourished because its founder had faithfully obeyed the inspirations of the Holy Ghost.

BISHOP FREDERIC BARAGA (*1797–1868*)

In Yugoslavia, the bishop was looking with sharp inquiry at a young priest. "Are you sure, Father, that this desire to become a missioner among the North American Indians is not some ill-considered impulse?" the prelate asked. "We have great need of zealous priests here in eastern Europe to promote reunion of the Orthodox Church with Rome. Have you never thought of that work?"

Father Frederic Baraga shook his head. "No, I have never felt myself called to that work," he answered. "But I am convinced that my vocation is to be a missioner in North America."

"Then go where the Holy Spirit bids you," said the bishop. "And may your missionary life be fruitful!"

So Father Baraga left his homeland and sailed for the Western Hemisphere. One cold day in January, 1831, he knocked on Bishop Fenwick's door in Cincinnati, Ohio. During the next three months, the young priest from Yugoslavia burned the midnight oil studying Indian dialects. Then he was assigned to a little village in Michigan, where he began a thirty-seven-year apostolate among the red men of that state and of northern Wisconsin.

From the outset, Father Baraga loved the Indians. He journeyed ceaselessly to visit his scattered flock. In winter, he traveled on snowshoes or in a sleigh drawn by dogs; in summer, he crossed the choppy waters of the lakes in a birchbark canoe. Wherever it was suitable, the missioner built a little church and school. He busied himself, also, in compiling a grammar and dictionary of the Chippewa language and in composing prayer books and catechisms.

Twenty-two years went by in this way. By that time, northern Michigan needed a prelate. Bishop Baraga was consecrated in the cathedral at Cincinnati. He then acquired many additional cares, but his consecration did not alter his missionary activities. Until his death, on January 19, 1868, the first Bishop of Marquette continued to win Indian souls for Christ. Slovenian Catholics of the United States have formed an association to promote the canonization of this holy missioner from Yugoslavia.

FIDELITY TO HIS VOCATION

Father Frederic Baraga knew well the crying need of zealous Catholic priests in his native Yugoslavia, but he was convinced that the Holy Spirit was calling him to the foreign-mission apostolate. His faithful correspondence to his God-given vocation resulted in a rich harvest of Indian souls in North America.

FATHER PETER JOHN DE SMET, S.J. (*1801–1873*)

In the summer of 1868, a Jesuit sixty-eight years of age was riding westward from St. Louis across the wilderness. His long, arduous journey ended in an almost inaccessible valley in the heart of the Rockies, the hiding place of the fierce chief of the Sioux Indians, Sitting Bull. The Government of the United States needed safe-conduct guarantees for the settlers going into Oregon. But no white man had ever seen Sitting Bull and returned alive. So the authorities had asked Father De Smet, whom the Indians called "Big Blackrobe," to find Sitting Bull and arrange a treaty with him.

The redoubtable chief received Father De Smet kindly, saying that the "Big Blackrobe" was like a brother to the red men. "If you say that the Great Father in Washington will keep his promises, then we will sign a treaty of peace," agreed Sitting Bull.

Father De Smet was happy. He had secured safety for the white settlers; and in addition, he had also performed a great service to his loved Indians. He knew that, if the Sioux persisted in keeping on the warpath, the government troops would eventually destroy them. In the words of a prominent American statesman of that day, Father De Smet had done "more for the welfare of the Indians in keeping them at peace and friendship with the United States than an army with banners."

Peter John De Smet was born in Belgium. In his boyhood, he read about the Jesuit missions in Paraguay; and later he resolved to accomplish similar work for the Indians of North America. He journeyed to the United States in 1821, and entered the Jesuit novitiate in Maryland. Before long the young Belgian was transferred to St. Louis. His first mission work was among the Potawatomi, who were suffering morally and physically from the white man's "firewater."

In 1840, Flathead Indians from the Bitter Root River, in what is now Montana, traveled all the way to St. Louis to ask for missioners. They had heard about Christianity from some Iroquois, whose ancestors had been converted by seventeenth-century Jesuits in Canada. Father De Smet led a band of apostles into the territory of the Flatheads; and among those wonderful Indians, he reproduced the intense Christian life and the material prosperity of the Paraguay reductions. But before his death, he was to see his work among the Flatheads ruined by the inroads of white settlers and the advent of the degrading "firewater."

The fame of the Big Blackrobe spread over the plains, and Indians of many tribes sent delegates to ask him to teach them about "The Man on the Cross." Father De Smet crossed the Atlantic nineteen times to seek funds for his Indian missions. He had interviews with popes and presidents and kings and ambassadors and archbishops and great statesmen and Mormon leaders – always in the interests of his red men. The tireless Apostle of the North American Indians died on May 23, 1873.

EVERYONE TRUSTED HIM

All types of white and of red men had faith in the "Big Blackrobe." In every human soul, Father De Smet saw the likeness of its Creator, and thus he had a buoyant belief in its essential goodness. Christlike trust inevitably awakens in its recipient a return of confidence.

FATHERS THEODORE AND MARY ALPHONSUS RATISBONNE, N.D.S. (*d. 1884*)

Among the many distinguished Jewish converts of the nineteenth century, two brothers, Theodore and Mary Alphonsus Ratisbonne, founded permanent works for the conversion of their own people. Theodore, the elder of the brothers, studied for the priesthood after he had become a Catholic. His ordination took place in 1830. Alphonsus resented Theodore's conversion bitterly; and it seemed to the younger brother an unbearable outrage that Father Ratisbonne should exercise the priestly ministry in Strasbourg, his native city.

In 1842, Alphonsus visited Rome. To please a Catholic friend, he consented to wear a Miraculous Medal. The Blessed Virgin appeared to the young Jew in a church where he was waiting for this friend. Alphonsus Ratisbonne took the name of Mary at his baptism. The joy of Father Theodore Ratisbonne can be imagined.

The Blessed Virgin had revealed to Alphonsus that the brothers should devote their lives to the conversion of Jews. Pope Gregory XVI gave his special blessing to their undertakings. Mary Alphonsus Ratisbonne was ordained to the priesthood in September, 1843; and during that same month, Father Theodore founded the Congregation of the Sisters of Our Lady of Sion, to labor for the conversion of the Jews. Later he founded the Fathers of Our Lady of Sion for the same purpose.

Thereafter, the elder convert continued to work in France for the firm establishment and development of his religious congregations. Father Mary Alphonsus went to the Holy Land where he aided the Sisters of Our Lady of Sion to open a convent in Jerusalem itself. Thenceforth he devoted himself to the Jews in the land of his ancestors, returning to Europe only to beg funds for his establishments.

Fathers Theodore and Mary Alphonsus Ratisbonne both died in 1884, within a few months of each other. Today there are centers of Our Lady of Sion in Palestine, France, England, Austria, Belgium, Italy, Australia, Brazil, Costa Rica, Canada, the United States, and Africa. From all those centers rises the prayer of missioners consecrated to the conversion of the Jews: "Father, forgive them, for they know not what they do" (Lk. 23:34).

THE LOST SHEEP OF ISRAEL

Our Christian religion has ancient roots in the Old Testament. Filial piety should impel us to pray often that the Jews may come to know the Redeemer whom they ardently expected through thousands of years.

BISHOP BERNARD PETITJEAN, P.F.M. (*d. 1884*)

On a spring day in 1865, Father Petitjean, a missioner from Paris, was kneeling before the main altar of the Church of the Twenty-Six Martyrs in Nagasaki, Japan. Except for the foreign priest, the church was empty. A recent treaty that Japan had signed with France permitted the erection of Catholic buildings in the ports of Hakodate, Yokohama, and Nagasaki. But those churches were to be for the exclusive use of foreign worshipers. For the Japanese themselves, the edicts of persecution had not been abolished.

Suddenly the lonely missioner felt a hand on his shoulder. He turned and was amazed to see a Japanese looking at him earnestly. Now the man was whispering hurried questions.

"Are you married?"

"No, I am not," replied Father Petitjean.

"Do you give allegiance to the Holy Father in Rome?"

"Yes. It was the Holy Father who sent me to Japan."

"Do you revere Mary as the Mother of God?"

"Most assuredly I do!"

"Then I know that our long wait is over!" exclaimed the questioner joyously. He motioned toward the back of the church, and the missioner saw that a little group of Japanese were standing timidly near the doorway.

"We are Catholics like you yourself!" continued the daring Japanese Christian. "There are thousands like us back in the hills and on the nearby Goto Islands. We are the descendants of Catholics who hid from the persecutors over two hundred years ago. During all the years since then, there have been secret Christians in Japan."

Though Father Petitjean and his fellow missioners exercised every caution in their visit to the members of the heroic Japanese Christian underground, the Japanese Government became aware of the latters' existence and hunted them down. This fresh outburst of persecution did not cease until 1873. Meanwhile, Father Petitjean had been consecrated a bishop. He had secretly trained some young Japanese for the priesthood; and before his death, Bishop Petitjean was able to ordain three Japanese priests.

THE SUPRANATIONAL CHURCH

Because of their amazing perseverance in the Faith during more than two centuries of savage persecution, Japanese Catholics have been called the Irish of the East. The true Church knows no national boundaries, as befits the creation of a Founder who died for the salvation of all mankind.

ARCHBISHOP CHARLES JOHN SEGHERS (*1839–1886*)

The founder of permanent Catholic missions in Alaska was a Belgian apostle, Charles John Seghers. Father Seghers began his work in America among the white settlers and the Indians of Vancouver Island. In 1873, he was appointed bishop of Vancouver Island (today Victoria). The United States had purchased Alaska only a few years previously, and Rome made the great northern territory a part of Bishop Seghers' diocese.

The thought of that vast expanse of tundra and snowy wilderness, where no permanent missioners ministered to the scattered Indians and Eskimos, gave the new prelate no rest. He made several exploratory trips to Alaska, and lost his heart to the country. In the course of his missionary journeys, Bishop Seghers evangelized various villages along the Yukon River. He learned the native languages easily and found them beautiful.

In 1878, Bishop Seghers was made coadjutor to the Archbishop of Oregon City, and two years later he became the head of the archdiocese. It cost the apostolic prelate much to abandon his plans for Alaska. A few years later, the see of Victoria was left vacant by the transfer of its bishop to Montana. Archbishop Seghers immediately volunteered to return to the smaller diocese. Pope Leo XIII was deeply touched by this sacrifice made for the sake of taking Christ to Alaska.

Archbishop Seghers obtained two Jesuit missioners for Alaska, and he himself made the journey to install them in their posts. Frank Fuller, a Jack-of-all-trades, accompanied the apostles. The unfortunate man's mind became unhinged by the wilderness. He imagined that Archbishop Seghers was abusing him; and on November 27, 1886, Fuller murdered the Apostle of Alaska.

The sacrifice of Archbishop Seghers' life was not in vain. His pioneering for Christ in Alaska was magnificently continued by the Society of Jesus. Before long, three Sisters of St. Ann arrived on the Yukon River; and since then, Sisters of Providence, Ursulines, and Sisters of St. Joseph have also volunteered for service among the Eskimos and the Indians in Alaska. Following the example of Archbishop Seghers, all these priests and Sisters make light of Alaska's bitter winters, unpalatable food, and grueling poverty.

ACCEPTANCE OF GOD'S WILL

Archbishop Seghers looked forward to years of apostolic endeavor on behalf of Alaska. Instead, God asked him to give his life immediately in a quick and stark oblation. On seeing the murderer's gun leveled at him, the heroic missioner crossed his arms on his breast and bowed his head in total acceptance of his divine Master's will.

VENERABLE PETER DONDERS, C.SS.R. (*1809–1887*)

In Holland, Peter Donders was attracted to the priesthood from his earliest years; but his parents were very poor, and he was frail and not especially talented. At length an opportunity came to work his way through a preparatory seminary, as a servant-student. After six years of exhausting struggle, the persistent candidate was admitted into the major seminary. Peter Donders was thirty-one when he said his first Mass.

Shortly afterward, a missioner from Dutch Guiana arrived in Holland, seeking volunteers for that tropical colony in northern South America. Owing to its fever-laden air, its clouds of stinging mosquitoes, and its polyglot population of Negroes, Indians, Jews, Mohammedans, and Oriental coolies, Dutch Guiana was not, humanly speaking, an attractive field. But Father Donders volunteered to go to it.

The selfless priest arrived at Paramaribo, capital of the colony, in 1842. Father Donders ministered tirelessly to the four thousand Catholics scattered throughout the region, and he gave special care to the religious instruction of the young. In 1856, he became pastor of the government colony of lepers at Batavia. Thereafter, there was no sacrifice that he was not willing to make, in order to win all his poor lepers to Christ.

When the care of Dutch Guiana was given to the Redemptorists, Father Donders joined their congregation. At one time he went out into the forest to preach Christ to the Indians. He made almost seven hundred converts; but after a few months, he returned to his beloved lepers. The Dutch apostle was received by his charges with an immense outpouring of joy. Father Peter Donders never left his lepers again. He died among them, in 1887, at the age of seventy-seven years.

HE SAW CHRIST IN THEM

Father Donders never found it difficult to see Christ in his lepers. Burned into his apostolic heart were the words spoken of the Saviour by the Prophet Isaias: "He hath borne our infirmities and carried our sorrows. And we have thought him as it were a leper, and as one struck by God and afflicted" (Isa. 53:4).

FATHER DAMIEN (*d. 1889*)

Father Damien, the son of a sturdy Flemish farmer, was a missioner of the Congregation of the Sacred Hearts of Jesus and Mary, which is commonly known as "The Picpus Fathers" because the congregation's headquarters are on Picpus Street in Paris. The young priest had already labored for nine years in the Hawaiian Islands when he volunteered for service among the lepers of Molokai. Bishop Maigret, the Vicar Apostolic of the Islands, had had totally different plans for the talented Fleming. But he realized that, of all his priests, the energetic, strong-willed, former farmer was the best equipped for life among the lepers. So the apostolic bishop made the sacrifice, and Father Damien landed on "Gray Molokai" in 1873.

The leper colony then contained about eight hundred outcasts. The tumble-down, dirty huts of the lepers were on a shelf of a great, dark, rock wall rising up out of the Pacific. Vegetation was sparse, and the water supply was very scanty. The lepers, sunk in apathy and vice, waited in sullen despair for death.

Into that desolation came a healthy man who showed that he loved the afflicted ones. He dressed the lepers' wounds and ministered to their souls. He prevailed upon the civic officials to send pipes, so that water might be brought to the leper settlements. Then he persuaded the people to clean their foul huts and to start a building campaign. Under the missioner's stimulating care, the lepers built their own church and decorated it with crude, bright colors. A children's choir, trained by Father Damien, sang with shrill voices that their teacher found beautiful. The missioner formed burial associations among the members of his flock, so that the funerals of the lepers might be dignified and solemn occasions.

During his twelfth year at Molokai, Father Damien noticed that his strength was failing. One evening as he was bathing his feet after a long missionary journey, he accidentally spilled boiling water over them – but he felt no pain. On the following Sunday, when the missioner was preaching to his flock, the startled people heard their pastor say, "we lepers."

As the dread disease worked in Father Damien's body, the leper priest labored with feverish energy. There was still so much to accomplish for his people! But God was about to send aid to His heroic servant. Joseph Dutton, a convert and a former Vermont farmer, arrived to spend the rest of his life in the service of the lepers. The government assigned a doctor to Molokai. Two zealous priests were sent to take over Father Damien's spiritual ministry. Three Franciscan Sisters from Syracuse, New York, came to care especially for the women and young girls.

Father Damien de Veuster died on April 15, 1889. His weeping people followed the leprous body of their friend and spiritual father to the grave. Yet they were not wholly desolate, for they knew that forever after they would have in heaven a protector who, of all the blessed, could best understand the slow agonies of their living death.

LIKE MOTHER, LIKE SON

Father Damien dreaded to inform his aged mother that he had become a leper. In her last illness the mother saw an article in a Belgian newspaper, describing the appalling fate of her beloved son. With gentle calm, Madame de Veuster said only: "Well then, we shall go to heaven together."

WILLIAM CARDINAL MASSAIA (*1809–1889*)

Ethiopia (Abyssinia) received the Faith from St. Frumentius, in the fourth century. Three centuries later, Ethiopia was cut off from Rome by encircling Islam, and then its Christians followed the Patriarchate of Alexandria into the Coptic heresy. In the seventeenth century, Jesuit missioners achieved in Ethiopia brilliant, but transitory, success. Among the Friars Minor and Capuchins who followed the Jesuits in that African country, there were several martyrs. Then, in 1846, Bishop Massaia began his great apostolate among the Gallas in Ethiopia.

Bishop Massaia, an Italian, was a member of the Capuchin Order. He had been confessor to Prince Victor Emmanuel, afterward king of Italy. The royal family of Piedmont desired to nominate the gifted Capuchin to an episcopal see in his homeland, but Father Massaia begged to be assigned to the foreign missions of his order. In 1846, the Congregation of Propaganda entrusted to the Capuchins the vicariate apostolic for the Gallas in Ethiopia. Father Massaia received episcopal consecration and was placed over the new mission territory in Africa.

At that time, there was a movement among the Copts toward union with Rome. Bishop Massaia won the friendship of the Ethiopian ruler, founded many missions, and labored incessantly to train native boys for the Catholic priesthood. But political agitations constantly hampered the Italian prelate's great work. He nevertheless baptized, in all, some thirty-six thousand Ethiopians.

During his thirty-five years as a missioner in Ethiopia, Bishop Massaia was seven times exiled; and seven times he returned, with undaunted courage, to resume his labors. The last time that the Italian apostle was banished, he knew that his failing health would prevent him from returning. He looked long on the Ethiopian mountains in the distance, and his camel driver saw that the old missioner was weeping.

Pope Leo XIII made Bishop Massaia an archbishop and then a cardinal. Cardinal Massaia died in Italy in 1889. He was one of the greatest missioners of the nineteenth century and, indeed, of all the Christian ages.

GODLIKE LOVE

The beautiful love of Cardinal Massaia for both his friends and his enemies among the Ethiopians made him see them all alike as his dear children. This charity was a faithful image of God's love for all mankind, both for His obedient children and for the ungrateful sinners who flee the shelter of His arms.

CHARLES CARDINAL LAVIGERIE, W.F. (*1825–1892*)

The future founder of the White Fathers was born in the Basque country of France. After his ordination to the priesthood, the brilliant Father Charles Lavigerie studied for doctorates at the Sorbonne; and soon became a professor there. In the year 1860, terrible massacres of Christians occurred in Lebanon. Father Lavigerie collected more than a million francs to aid the survivors of the massacres; and he himself left for Syria in order to supervise the distribution of relief.

For the first time, the ardent Father Lavigerie found himself in a Moslem land and beheld the havoc wrought by the fanaticism born of Islam. There grew in his soul an immense desire to labor as a missioner in Islam-ridden countries. But on his return to Europe, the young priest was appointed as an auditor of the Rota Tribunal in Rome. Then he was made bishop of Nancy. After a few years, Bishop Lavigerie was asked if he would consider a transfer to the archbishopric of Algiers. He saw in the offer the long-awaited opportunity to enter on his missionary apostolate.

Archbishop Lavigerie arrived in Algiers in 1867. From the outset, his apostolic endeavors met with heartbreaking opposition from the French officials; but he never faltered in the good fight. Soon after his arrival, the archbishop took under his protection nearly two thousand starving Moslem orphans, victims of a terrible famine and cholera epidemic. In course of time, the apostle built two villages for his grown-up Arabs and Berbers, established them as farmers, and arranged marriages among his charges. Thus a Christian oasis was formed in the heart of Islam.

In 1868, Archbishop Lavigerie founded the Society of the White Fathers; and a few years later, he established the White Sisters, destined especially for school and hospital activities. The founder desired that his missioners should devote themselves exclusively to the conversion of Africa, searching out its peoples in desert and jungle. Before Cardinal Lavigerie's death, his spiritual sons had given martyrs to the Sahara, and they had sent mission bands into "darkest" Central Africa.

Archbishop Lavigerie himself evangelized the villages of the Kabyle Berbers. He often reminded them that their entire nation had once been Christian, and that the Arabs had forced their ancestors to become Moslems. After his own visits, Archbishop Lavigerie sent three of his White Fathers to open schools for the children of the Kabyles.

Pope Leo XIII gave Lavigerie the red hat of a cardinal. In the year 1888, the Holy Father officially charged Cardinal Lavigerie to preach a crusade against the Moslem traffic in Negro slaves. The great missioner journeyed through France, England, Belgium, and Italy; and Christian Europe responded to his voice. The principal nations began to take official, concerted, and energetic action against the terrible traffic in human beings in Africa.

Death came to Cardinal Lavigerie in 1892. For a quarter of a century, he had been for the world a symbol of Africa, and he had stirred hearts with the challenge of an immense, mysterious continent yet to be won for Christ. Pope Leo XIII placed Charles Cardinal Lavigerie "among those men who have merited the most of Catholicism and of civilization."

GREATNESS OF SOUL

In the closing years of Cardinal Lavigerie's life, while he was rousing Christian Europe against the Moslem traffic in Negro slaves, Pope Leo XIII said to the founder of the White Fathers and Sisters: "What greatness of soul you manifest, when the salvation of human beings is at stake!"

FATHER SIMEON LOURDEL, W.F. (*d. 1890*)

The few members of the first band of White Fathers to reach the heart of Africa were holding a council on the southern shore of Lake Victoria Nyanza in the year 1878. It was only four years after Henry M. Stanley—friend of the great Protestant missionary, David Livingston—had discovered the highly intelligent Baganda Negroes in Uganda.

"Father Lourdel, the votes of the council have elected you for the task of establishing friendly relations with King Mutesa of Uganda," the secretary of the meeting announced.

Father Simeon Lourdel, the great Catholic pioneer of Uganda, was a man of powerful frame and unflinching will. He sailed northward up Lake Victoria Nyanza in a frail native canoe. King Mutesa immediately took a liking to Father Lourdel, and gave the French priest land for a Catholic mission. But both Protestants and Moslems did their utmost to turn the Negro ruler against the Catholic apostle.

Because of his enemies' attacks, Father Lourdel was forced to withdraw to the southern rim of the lake. Two years later, however, Mutesa died; and his son, Mwanga, asked the French missioner to return to Uganda. Father Lourdel found that his catechumens had persevered. Soon many new converts were made, and all conditions seemed to promise well for the spread of the Faith among the Baganda. But King Mwanga was a man of evil morals, and the restraints of Christianity irked him.

"The people who pray must all be put to death," decreed the tyrant in the year 1885.

Mwanga condemned to death his royal chamberlain and fifteen of his pages, because they had fearlessly proclaimed their Catholic Faith. The youngest of the condemned pages was only thirteen years of age. Father Lourdel was not allowed to speak to his converts. He could merely look into their eyes over the shoulders of the guards.

The condemned Christians were shackled and marched to a place of execution forty miles distant from the capital. One of the boys was burned alive on the way. Material was gathered for an immense pyre, and the martyrs were rolled in reed mats, to become living faggots. Repeated efforts had been made to induce the pages to apostatize, but not one of them faltered. The tom-toms sounded; the sorcerers leaped and danced; and the flames began to crackle. After the pyre had burned for more than a day, only the ashes of the victims were left.

In the following months, Father Lourdel saw many more of his African converts suffer death rather than deny Christ. Then, on May 12, 1890, the pioneer Catholic missioner of Uganda went to join the Negro martyrs in heaven.

VICTORIOUS FAITH

At one time, King Mutesa determined to force all his subjects to become Mohammedans. Inspired by God, Father Lourdel offered to walk through a fierce fire with the Bible in his hand, while a Moslem teacher did the same, carrying the Koran. The faith of Father Lourdel was rewarded by the Moslems' refusal to accept the challenge. Mutesa then proclaimed that his subjects might pray as they wished.

BISHOP HENRY FARAUD, O.M.I.
(*1823–1890*)

Father Faraud, a pioneer Oblate priest in Canada, was a combination of an Arctic explorer and a St. Paul. In 1851, he established the mission of Lake Athabasca; and during the following year, he journeyed northward to Great Slave Lake, where no missioner had ever been. Along the Peace River, Father Faraud ministered to a number of Indian tribes, but especially to the Beavers.

In the early days of Father Faraud's apostolate, an Indian came to him from the far north. "At the present time, you can only speak my language like an infant," said the frank savage. "I will come again to ask you questions, when you will be able to talk like a man."

Three years later, the Indian did return and began to take instructions. He had a marvelous memory and soon mastered the catechism. Father Faraud proposed baptism. "No!" answered the convert, "I have done nothing as yet for Almighty God. Next year, you'll see me here again, and then I shall be ready for baptism."

The Indian returned the following spring. In the meantime, he had taught the catechism to the greater portion of his tribe on the shores of the Arctic Ocean. Again it seemed to the missioner that baptism was in order.

"Not yet!" insisted the neophyte. "I want to be called 'Peter.' St. Peter is the one who holds the keys to heaven. He will be more likely to open the gate for me if I bear his name and am baptized on his feast. And that's not all! I want to fast for forty days and forty nights before my baptism, as our Lord did." Thus it was that the Indian Peter became a Christian.

Father Faraud lived so far from civilization that the news of his appointment as first Vicar Apostolic of Athabasca-Mackenzie did not reach him until the following year. He was consecrated a bishop in 1864. The purple did not prevent Bishop Henry Faraud from setting out as before on his long missionary journeys. He died in 1890, after having pioneered for forty-three years in the snowy Canadian wilderness.

THE MEASURE OF LOVE

In his later years, when he was suffering acutely from sciatica, Bishop Faraud wrote: "Nature cries out, 'Enough; lay down your burden!' But grace says, 'The measure of love is to love without measure.'"

FATHER CONSTANT LIEVENS, S.J. (*1856–1895*)

One day Father Constant Lievens, a missioner in India, heard that pagan villagers were threatening one of his native catechists. The Belgian missioner rode at once to the village where the catechist was stationed. He arrived just as the mob of screaming pagans were dragging their victim to a river with the intention of drowning him. Father Lievens spurred his horse into the crowd, seized the catechist in his arms, and vanished from sight before the amazed pagans had recovered their breath.

It was on his father's farm in Flanders that Constant Lievens acquired the fearless horsemanship that was later to make him known far and wide in western Bengal as "The Great Riding Sahib." In Constant's childhood the village priest noted the boy's unusual talents and made it possible for him to enter a preparatory seminary. As the young seminarian advanced in his studies, he was strongly attracted to the foreign missions. He entered the Society of Jesus; and while still a scholastic, he was assigned to the Jesuit mission field in western Bengal.

Father Lievens was ordained to the priesthood in Calcutta in 1883. Two years later he began work in Chota Nagpur, a hilly district some three hundred miles west of Calcutta. On Father Lievens' arrival, there were only two aged missioners and a handful of Catholics in the entire district. The simple, aboriginal tribes of Chota Nagpur were cruelly oppressed by their rapacious Indian landlords.

Father Lievens learned with astounding rapidity the language of the aborigines, and then he set himself to master the complicated judicial system of the district. He was soon able to champion in the British courts the cause of the downtrodden, aboriginal tenants. The English judges eventually came to seek the Belgian missioner's advice in difficult cases of litigation between landlords and tenants. Thousands of aborigines had recourse to the aid of Father Lievens, and his charity led them to ask for instruction in the Catholic Faith.

The apostle drove himself without mercy, but it was impossible for one man to minister to so many thousands. He trained native catechists and pleaded urgently for more priestly helpers from his Society. In the evenings his arm often ached from administering the Sacrament of Baptism to such numbers. But even Father Lievens' strong constitution and iron will could not indefinitely withstand the ceaseless toil. Tuberculosis set in; and in 1892, after only nine years in the priesthood, the Apostle of Chota Nagpur wept as he gave his Christians his last blessing.

During his brief missionary career, this priest had won eighty thousand converts. Father Lievens has been called "The greatest missioner since the time of St. Francis Xavier." Today, Chota Nagpur, in India, is still one of the Church's most fertile mission fields.

TOTAL OFFERING OF SELF

Soon after the start of his apostolate in India, Father Lievens wrote: "I only desire to work and die here for Christ. At times I feel the task is too heavy, and that I shall not last for long; but where it is a matter of saving souls, who would not even leap into a fire?"

FATHER FELIX WESTERWOUDT
(*1861–1898*)

The thoroughly Catholic Westerwoudt family in Amsterdam was large, closely knit, and well to do. When Felix felt that God was calling him to the foreign missions, he encountered no opposition at home. At that time there were no missionary institutions for secular priests in Holland, so the Westerwoudts saw their loved Felix leave for the Mill Hill Foreign Mission Seminary in England. The next leave-taking was even more difficult. Father Westerwoudt sailed for Borneo in the autumn of 1885. That parting was to be final for this world.

On his arrival in North Borneo, the young priest was sent to work among five thousand Dyaks who lived on an almost inaccessible plateau, halfway up a solitary and steep mountain. Those Dyaks existed in indescribable filth and moral corruption. They received the white man with cold indifference and rewarded his Christlike services with callous ingratitude.

Father Westerwoudt was of an affectionate disposition, and it is easy to imagine what it must have cost him to live alone among such people. Yet when his superior spoke of transferring him, the young priest begged to remain with his Dyaks. He brought two heroic English Sisters to the mountain plateau to care for the native women and girls. He continued to educate wild Dyak boys, and to minister to the loathsome diseases of their elders. He journeyed to neighboring tribes, in burning sunshine and drenching rain. Festering sores broke out on his legs.

After thirteen years of grueling labor in Borneo, Father Westerwoudt had baptized only twenty, half-savage adult converts. Suddenly he was attacked by a combination of malaria and pneumonia. The Dyaks wept bitterly when their missioner died, for Father Westerwoudt had won his way to their cold hearts at last. They received their first priest's successor with touching eagerness; and, a few years later, they constituted what the Prefect Apostolic called "Borneo's most promising mission."

ASK NOTHING, REFUSE NOTHING

The life of Father Felix Westerwoudt among the Dyaks was the realization of the maxim of St. Francis de Sales: "Ask nothing, refuse nothing." The missioner asked nothing of his seemingly indifferent flock, and he was always smilingly at their disposal.

FATHER SIX (*1825–1899*)

Peter Triem, an Indo-Chinese Christian, had just been ordained deacon when persecution swept over Tonkin. The young man dressed up in his bishop's robes in order to give the real prelate – a French missioner – time to flee and hide in the hills. The persecutors arrived and gleefully threw the sham bishop into jail.

His fellow prisoners called Peter Triem Mr. Six, because a deacon has six orders. Mr. Six had a wonderful personality, and he used it on his jailers. They looked the other way while Mr. Six stole out of jail one night and went to be ordained a priest by his fugitive bishop. Naturally, the young man kept his word and returned to jail after his ordination.

Two years after the persecution had ended, Father Six was made a pastor. His flock was very poor, and there was no Catholic church in Phat-Diem. But up in the surrounding hills, there was plenty of marble. Father Six got his Catholic men to volunteer to make trips to the stone quarries. After the daily Mass offered by the pastor in his temporary shack, the women of the congregation spent two or three hours polishing the marble. Many decorative details for the church-to-be were worked on by entire families in their own homes.

Gradually, on the church site, huge blocks of marble were raised and set in place with primitive tools. The final result was breathtaking. Until the Communists took over northern Vietnam, the beautiful church at Phat-Diem was in use, and its three daily Masses were crowded. At each Mass, two priests gave out Holy Communion to thousands of parishioners.

Father Six, who built so well for God in marble and in the souls of men, went to his reward on July 6, 1899, at the age of seventy-four. Surely, in heaven the robes of Peter Triem must far outshine in glory those of any earthly bishop.

HIS WORKS FOLLOW HIM

Vietnamese Catholic priests of today have been inspired since boyhood by the heroic tradition of Father Six. Imitating this great exemplar, they have stood firm against relentless Communist persecution.

SISTER HELEN DE JAURIAS (*1824–1900*)

At her parents' chateau, in the diocese of Perigueux, France, Helen de Jaurias gave devoted care to the poor. No one was surprised when, at the age of twenty, the young heiress became a Sister of Charity. In 1855, she was assigned to China, as superior of one of the houses of her congregation in Ningpo, about seventy-five miles south of Shanghai.

Sister Helen de Jaurias had organized flourishing works for the Christian education of her orphans in Ningpo, when the antiforeign Taiping Uprising swept up from southern China. It was eight months before European troops relieved Ningpo. In the meantime, the Sisters and their charges had been exposed to incessant danger, hunger, and disease. After the rescue, Sister Helen de Jaurias was preparing to extend her mission activities; but in 1862, she was ordered to found the International Hospital of Shanghai.

Thanks to the activity and organizing skill of the French Sister, the new hospital was soon ready to receive numerous patients. When it was known that the selfless religious longed to build an extension to the hospital, so that Chinese could be cared for, funds were raised to realize the apostolic desire. But before the hospital for the Chinese was finished, Sister Helen de Jaurias was assigned to Peking.

There she was to labor in the Catholic establishment known as the "*Pe-tang,*" close to the walls of the Forbidden Imperial City and the foreign legations. The *Pe-Tang* comprised the cathedral, the bishop's residence, and the works of the Sisters of Charity. Sister Helen de Jaurias improved the *Pe-Tang* orphanage and built a hospital for destitute Chinese. Then she established a normal school for Chinese girls and a catechumenate for the older women.

The turn of the century saw the outbreak of the bitterly anti-foreign and anti-Christian Boxer Uprising. For over two months, the *Pe-Tang* endured a terrible siege. Had it not been for the supplies that Sister Helen de Jaurias had stored up for her orphans and patients, the three thousand people hemmed in by the Boxers would have starved. The old French Sister gave hope to all by her calm courage.

Deliverance came on August 16, 1900, when the Allied troops marched into Peking. Sister Helen de Jaurias directed the provision of food and shelter for her charges with her usual courageous vigor; but she was unutterably weary. The grand old religious suffered a paralytic stroke and died five days after the rescue.

SELF IS FORGOTTEN

Sister Helen de Jaurias wrote to a loved friend: "You complain that I do not speak about myself. What am I to say? I have so little time to think about myself that I sometimes forget I am on earth."

BISHOP ROSENDO SALVADO, O.S.B. (*1814–1900*)

Two apostolic Spanish Benedictines, Dom Rosendo Salvado and Dom Joseph Serra, offered their services as missioners to the Sacred Congregation of Propaganda, which assigned them to assist the first bishop of Perth in western Australia. The Spanish Benedictines arrived at Fremantle in 1846. Their bishop asked them to found a mission for the black aborigines in the wild bush about a hundred miles north of Perth. A pioneer Irish settler, Captain Scully, sent some of his employees with a bullock cart to drive the missioners into the bush.

One day the travelers could discover no water, and it seemed as if they must all die of thirst. Dom Salvado went alone into the scrub and chanted the prayer *Salve Regina.* A native boy was attracted by the singing and still more by the Benedictine's smiling face. He led Dom Salvado to a large brook of clear water. That black lad was Dom Salvado's first convert.

Captain Scully's men returned to their master's farm, leaving the missioners alone in the wilderness. During two months the

Benedictines went hunting with the blacks, contenting themselves with a fare of kangaroo flesh, lizards, grubs, and whatever edible roots they could find. Having mastered much of the language during their two months with the aborigines, the missioners determined to found a center, where they could teach the blacks to till the soil.

Funds were utterly lacking, so Dom Salvado made the terrible journey on foot, back to Perth. There he found that his bishop had nothing to give him. Undaunted, the Spanish missioner advertised a piano recital to take place in the courthouse. No one could resist the courageous zeal of the ragged, weatherbeaten apostle, and so his concert was a great financial success.

The Spanish Benedictines named their mission New Norcia — after the birthplace of St. Benedict, in Italy. The priests plowed and planted, teaching the aborigines agriculture. Craftsmen from Perth gave their services free and erected a stone building at New Norcia. The mission was stocked with sheep and cattle.

In 1848, Dom Serra was called away from New Norcia. For fifty-two more years, Dom Salvado continued to be the apostle of western Australia's aborigines. He built homes for his people, so that his mission became a flourishing Christian center in the wilderness. In the course of time, forty-seven other Benedictines arrived to aid the great pioneer. Orphanages and schools were founded.

Dom Salvado was raised to the episcopate in 1849. His new dignity did not make him less approachable to his dear native Australians. Toward the close of his long life, the missionary bishop journeyed to Europe to seek a successor. He died in Rome on December 29, 1900. His childlike aborigines would not be comforted. For fifty-four years their father in Christ had been with them. They could not understand why he did not return when they needed him so greatly.

CHARITY GRAPPLES WITH CRUDE REALITY

Bishop Salvado quickly understood that he must find means of feeding his starving Australian aborigines before he could teach them the Christian religion. "Hard experience has taught me how to conduct my mission," he wrote.

HERBERT CARDINAL VAUGHAN (*1832–1903*)

In the year 1860, a young priest in London paced restlessly in his study. "What is the matter with me?" he wondered. "I know that there are not nearly enough priests in England, and yet I am constantly tormented by the urge to devote my life to the foreign missions. Thinking of it gives me no peace."

At last the young priest – Father Herbert Vaughan – decided to unburden himself to the aging Cardinal Wiseman. He was surprised to discover that the cardinal had long believed that England should establish a foreign-mission seminary, but had found no priest prepared to undertake the work. Father Vaughan knew that he could not expect the necessary financial support for his apostolic project from the small Catholic population of England. Having obtained the approval of the English bishops, and the special blessing of Pope Pius IX, he set out to become a beggar for Christ in California and in South America. In two years' time, Father Vaughan was back in England and ready to purchase a site for the seminary.

The Mill Hill Foreign Mission Seminary, in the northwest of London, opened its doors on March 19, 1866, with one student and one professor! More students soon arrived, however; and after some years, Father Vaughan accompanied his first four missioners to the scene of their apostolate. They were to work among the Negroes in Baltimore, Maryland. After those humble beginnings, the activity of the Mill Hill Foreign Mission Society spread to the Philippines, Borneo, Africa, India, and the Dutch East Indies.

Father Herbert Vaughan later became Bishop of Salford and then Cardinal-Archbishop of Westminster. But Mill Hill remained always in the thoughts of that Prince of the Church; and in 1903, when his life was drawing to its close, he returned to his seminary. Cardinal Vaughan asked to have engraved on his monument, in

Mill Hill's little cemetery, the simple epitaph: *Herbert Vaughan, Missionary.*

APOSTOLIC GENEROSITY

Cardinal Vaughan desired that his English Catholic missioners should consecrate themselves to the service of pagans, not for a term of years as did the Protestant evangelists, but without reserve and forever.

MOTHER MARY OF THE PASSION, F.M.M. (*1839–1904*)

Helen de Chappotin, the future foundress of the Franciscan Missionaries of Mary, was born near Nantes in Brittany. In the year 1860, Helen became a Poor Clare; but before long she fell seriously ill and was obliged to return to her home. Two years later, she was accepted into the recently founded Congregation of Marie Reparatrice, and she received the name of Mary of the Passion.

Even before she had made her first vows, the Breton novice was assigned to India. But the congregation she had joined was a semicloistered one, and sharp criticism of an active apostolate among the Indians soon arose. Most of the nuns in India desired the active apostolate, so Mother Mary of the Passion journeyed to Rome with three companions to submit their cause to Pope Pius IX. In January, 1877, the Holy Father decided upon the foundation of a new apostolic congregation, to be called "Missionaries of Mary."

Mother Mary of the Passion became the Mother Foundress of the new congregation. She hastened to place it under the protection of the Franciscan Order, since for her the virtue of poverty had a special attraction. And, in truth, the beginnings of the new congregation were made in the utmost poverty. Far greater trials were the calumnies and misrepresentations about the Mother Foundress, which even caused her to be deposed from her office for nearly a year. In the spring of 1885, after the anxiety of the period of trial was past, the Congregation of the Franciscan Missionaries of Mary began that remarkable expansion that has been continuous ever since.

In the succeeding years, the congregation made new foundations in France, Italy, Corsica, England, Ireland, Switzerland, Belgium, Holland, Malta, Sicily, Austria, Poland, the United States, and South America. Mission activities were undertaken in Africa, Ceylon, China, Burma, the Philippines, and Japan. The congregation had its first martyrs in the year 1900, in Shansi Province, China, when Mother Mary Hermine and her six companions were beheaded by the Boxers.

Mother Mary of the Passion continued to direct and to inspire the Franciscan Missionaries of Mary until her death on November 15, 1904. Of that great missionary foundress, it can be truly said, "Blessed are the dead who die in the Lord . . . for their works follow them" (Apoc. 14:13).

WORK FOUNDED ON PRAYER

Mother Mary of the Passion gave the following instruction to her spiritual daughters: "Seek in prayer the blessing of your apostolate, and in the apostolate the object of your prayer."

FATHER ARNOLD JANSSEN, S.V.D. (*1835–1909*)

In the second half of the nineteenth century, Father Arnold Janssen, an obscure priest in northern Germany, was constantly preoccupied with the idea that Germany ought to found a foreign-mission seminary of its own, as France, Italy, and England had already done. But even Father Janssen's friends did not think that he was the person to undertake a work of such magnitude. He was a small man, of somewhat shabby appearance, and quite wanting in personal magnetism. Furthermore, he lacked influential connections.

At first, Father Janssen did not hope to do more than to spread the mission idea in Germany by means of the Catholic press. In 1875, however, he took more daring action. At that time the German Government was persecuting the Church, so Father Janssen crossed over into Holland and founded a mission seminary in the village of Steyl. The intrepid little apostle met with opposition aplenty. At first few missionary candidates offered themselves. Then some of the early students were not in favor of living under a religious rule as the founder desired.

"God gave me just courage enough to keep trying to carry out my plans," said Father Janssen years later.

The founder called his new missionary congregation "The Society of the Divine Word." After the slow and painful beginnings, it knew a remarkable expansion. Before his death, Father Janssen had approved mission foundations in China, West Africa, New Guinea, Japan, the Philippine Islands, Argentina, Paraguay, Brazil, Chile, and among the Negroes in the United States.

Father Janssen opened branch houses of his society in Rome, Austria, Germany; and at Techny (Illinois) in the United States. He greatly strengthened his society by the addition of Brothers. He also founded a missionary Sisterhood, entitled "The Servants of the Holy Ghost." From the beginning, Father Janssen made wide use of the printing press to secure funds and to help the mission cause in general.

This humble founder of a great missionary organization died in 1909. He attributed the success of The Society of the Divine Word to its special devotion to the Holy Ghost.

UNBOUNDED CONFIDENCE

Father Arnold Janssen had unbounded confidence in God's providence, and his resignation to God's will was so entire that even the most distressing news did not disturb him for long.

ARCHBISHOP ANDREW NAVARRE, M.S.C. (*d. 1912*)

In Auxerre, France, Father Andrew Navarre longed to go the whole way for Christ, so he became a member of the newly founded Society of the Missioners of the Sacred Heart. In 1881, Pope Leo XIII asked Father Chevalier, the founder, to send some of his pioneer subjects to the South Seas. Father Navarre was among the five apostles chosen to pioneer in the immense vicariate of Melanesia and Micronesia. He was then forty-five years of age and in poor health. But during the long journey to the South Seas, it was the superior of the little band, and not Father Navarre, who fell ill.

The leadership of the pioneers was transferred to Father Navarre. The first foothold of the group was established on the island of New Britain. Then, as additional missioners arrived from France, foundations were made successively on Thursday Island, on New Guinea, and on the Gilbert Islands. Protestant missionaries in the islands sought legal barriers to keep the Catholic priests from entering their field of work. Tropical illnesses attacked the pioneers. The natives were cannibals and in a low state of culture. But the Missionaries of the Sacred Heart were not dismayed. Father Navarre was consecrated bishop in 1887, and appointed archbishop the following year.

At the beginning of 1890, Archbishop Navarre was so short of funds that he said to his fellow missioners: "We have no money for food or clothing. Do any of you wish to leave for Australia?" Not one of the archbishop's helpers chose to leave their mission work; but during the following months of want, several of the heroic apostles died at their posts.

Archbishop Navarre himself labored on in the South Seas until his death in 1912. At that time, one third of the islanders among whom his missioners had worked were Catholics. During World War II, the Christian "Fuzzy Wuzzies" were true friends of the Allied soldiers struggling in the swamps and forests of New Guinea.

WITH GOD ALL THINGS ARE POSSIBLE

The obstacles encountered in the South Seas by the pioneer Missioners of the Sacred Heart seemed insurmountable, but they did not abandon God's work. Thus, when Archbishop Navarre was in Rome for the jubilee of Leo XIII, in 1888, the Pope could say: "This apostle brings to me as a gift a world of souls."

FATHER CHARLES DE FOUCAULD (*1858–1916*)

In the early years of the twentieth century, a remarkable man took the ancient camel route out of Tunis into the depths of the Sahara Desert. He halted on the heights of Ahaggar, where he built a small hermitage in the mountains outside Tamanrasset.

Charles de Foucauld belonged to an aristocratic French family. He had served as a distinguished and atheistic army officer in North Africa, and had been an intrepid explorer in the Sahara. Then God had granted to him a profound religious experience. Charles de Foucauld became a priest and an apostle. Although the immense Sahara Desert is larger than all of our forty-eight States together, Father Charles de Foucauld called it for fifteen years his parish; and the ten thousand roaming Tuaregs were his missionary flock.

The proud and warlike Tuaregs are Moslems. The hermit of Ahaggar did not win numerous converts, but he did make himself widely loved by the veiled desert warriors. The missioner often gave a hungry Tuareg the greater part of his own frugal meal, and he always managed to have some little present for his visitors. But in the year 1916, Father Charles de Foucauld was shot by a fanatic of the aggressive Moslem Senusi brotherhood. The Tuaregs mourned the dead missioner as if he had been a member of their own tribe.

A Moslem writer said of him: "The renown of our Marabout (holy man) is great in Ahaggar. The people to whom he did good, and that means all the dwellers in Ahaggar, honor his tomb as if he were still alive."

In 1933, two religious institutes – the Little Brothers of the Sacred Heart and the Little Sisters of Jesus – were founded in Africa to realize the austere ideal of the religious life proposed by the Apostle of the Tuaregs. The missionary activity of these followers of Father Charles de Foucauld has now spread to India, where they share the hard life of the starvation-ridden masses.

THE RIGHT PERSPECTIVE

God granted to Father Charles de Foucauld a vision of the manner of his death, nineteen years before he was slain. Thereafter he meditated daily on this great grace, saying to himself: "Consider that it is to this death that your whole life must tend; think often of this death, in order to give things their right perspective."

FATHER ALBERT LACOMBE, O.M.I.
(*1839–1916*)

Father Albert Lacombe, the son of a sturdy French-Canadian habitant, was one of the intrepid Oblate pioneers in western Canada. He followed his Indians about on the great plains, lived in their smoke-filled tents, endured the bitter winters with them, nursed them in deadly epidemics caused by the white men's arrival, prevented Indian uprisings against officials, and won hundreds of red men for Christ. No wonder that the Crees called Father Lacombe "The Man of the Beautiful Soul"; and the Blackfeet, the mortal enemies of the Crees, addressed him with equal love as "The Man of the Good Heart."

One night Father Lacombe was in the tent of Chief Natous of the Blackfeet when the camp was suddenly attacked by Cree warriors. Until dawn the battle raged; then the missioner advanced alone toward the Crees, calling out: "Attention, you Crees! Your priest is speaking to you!"

But the Crees did not see Father Lacombe in the heavy fog, and finally the missioner was slightly wounded. Roused to fury, the Blackfeet launched a wild counterattack. One of them shouted in a lull of the battle, "You have wounded your Blackrobe, you dogs!"

The Crees were horrified. Could it be that they had wounded their beloved priest? They ceased firing and withdrew in confusion. Such was the power that Father Lacombe had over the hearts of the roaming natives of the Canadian plains.

The officials of the Hudson's Bay Company in the Far West, the pioneer Northwest Mounted Police, and the civic leaders in Ottawa, all held Father Lacombe in particular esteem. The lovable missioner devoted sixty-four years of his long life to his Indians. He also championed the half-breeds and was chaplain for a time to the rough navvies of the Canadian Pacific construction camps.

Father Lacombe was a prominent founder of the Indian school system in Canada. Towns sprang up around the early missions established by him. Many parts of the Old and the New World saw the aging missioner of the plains in the role of an irresistible beggar for his red men. As the years passed, several of Father Lacombe's early companions in the apostolate became bishops; but the "Man of the Good Heart" remained to the end a simple priest.

"A bishop is charged with the administration of one portion of the Church," explained his ecclesiastical superior. "But Father Lacombe has lent himself to all and for all."

A SPEEDY TRUCE

The truce brought about by Father Lacombe between the Crees and the Blackfeet did not require long, exasperating negotiations. The warring Indian tribes stopped fighting in a matter of minutes, because they knew that their wounded apostle cherished them all equally in God.

ST. FRANCES XAVIER CABRINI (*1850–1917*)

Frances Xavier Cabrini, the first citizen of the United States to be canonized, was born in Lombardy, Italy, the youngest of a family of thirteen children. At an early age she desired to become a missioner in China, but her health was so delicate that two religious communities later rejected her plea for admittance. Undaunted, Frances taught in a public school with marked success, and then accepted the position of directress of a school for orphans.

The bishop of Lodi had formed such a high opinion of the young teacher-directress that he asked her to found a new community, the Institute of the Missionary Sisters of the Sacred Heart.

Its first members were orphan girls who had already been under the guidance of Frances Cabrini. The new institute grew in a surprising manner. Mother Cabrini always trusted absolutely in God for material support, and it was never wanting.

In 1887, Mother Cabrini went to Rome to seek the approval of the rule of her institute and to found a house in the Eternal City. Mother Cabrini still thought of China; but while she was in Rome, she was informed of the social, economic, and religious plight of Italian emigrants to the United States. Pope Leo XIII himself counseled her, "Not to the East, but to the West."

With six companions, Mother Cabrini landed in America in 1889. Undismayed by immediate difficulties, she began and energetically extended her work for the Italians in the United States. Her aim was to reinvigorate the Catholic faith of the adults and to provide a sound Christian education for the new generation. She opened schools, colleges, orphanages, hospitals, and free clinics in New York, New Orleans, Chicago, Seattle, Denver, and Philadelphia. As time passed, she extended her institute's activities to Central America, South America, Spain, France, and England. In all, Mother Cabrini opened during her lifetime sixty-six houses of the religious institute she had founded.

The frail but indomitable religious undertook long and repeated journeys, made canny property deals, and proved to constructers that they could not outsmart her. She came to love the United States; and Americans, in their turn, were attracted by her selfless zeal. In 1909, Mother Cabrini obtained United States citizenship.

By 1917, no strength remained in Mother Cabrini's worn body. For her Christmas card that year, she had chosen the text: "Send forth Thy light and Thy truth; they shall lead me into Thy holy mountain and into Thy tabernacles." On December 22, the beloved foundress spent her last day on earth filling bags with Christmas candy for the children in her schools.

SWIFT AND DETERMINED

A journalist in Rome, while enumerating Mother Cabrini's amazing works of charity, described in a single, terse sentence the secret of her sanctity. "She was a swift and determined agent of the Heart of Christ," he wrote.

BISHOP PHILIP AUGOUARD, C.S.Sp. (*1852–1921*)

Bishop Augouard, in his missionary boat equipped with a floating chapel, paddled down a great river in French Equatorial Africa. He went ashore at the village of M'Betu and saw a Negro eating out of a human skull. The cannibal was feasting on the brain of his late victim. The bishop was accustomed to similar sights. Calmly he made his way to the chief's hut and was engaged in friendly conversation with that black potentate when a handsome slave passed by.

"What is the name of that fine fellow?" the bishop inquired.

"You mean that creature?" the chief answered absent-mindedly. "That is only meat."

Bishop Augouard knew all too well that his "parishioners" maintained droves of slaves and of children who were destined expressly for the cooking pot. No wonder that Pope Leo XIII called the zealous prelate of French Equatorial Africa "Bishop of the Cannibals." The fearless, optimistic Bishop Augouard did not consider his Negroes subhuman. He took them as they were, and spent himself to lead their souls to Christ. The black men loved him.

French Equatorial Africa stretches for a thousand miles from the Atlantic Ocean to Lake Chad. In this backward region, about one fourth the size of the United States, live only three million people. Holy Ghost missioners were the territory's first apostles; and among them, the energetic Father Augouard was, in the year 1890, the outstanding pioneer. It is worthy of record that, as early as 1892, a valiant little group of Sisters of St. Joseph of Cluny began doing missionary work among the cannibals of French Equatorial Africa!

Soon after he had landed in Africa, Bishop Augouard ventured many hundreds of miles inland from the coast to found among the Bondjo tribe the mission of St. Paul-of-the-Rapids. The Bondjos had been called by explorers "human hyenas," because of their ferocious cannibalism; but they never harmed their loved apostle.

For over forty years, the sturdy bishop from France journeyed ceaselessly in his floating chapel on the mighty rivers of his immense territory. When Bishop Augouard died, in 1921, he had carried the Light of the World to myriad dark places of Africa.

"QUICKLY, QUICKLY"

In French Equatorial Africa, the natives gave to Bishop Augouard the name of "Quickly, Quickly!" The charity of Christ urged on the French missioner with a drive long incomprehensible to the wondering Negroes.

JAMES CARDINAL CAGLIERO (*d. 1926*)

In Turin, Italy, one of the first boys whom St. John Bosco had taken under his sheltering care was at death's door. James Cagliero lay in delirium, and suddenly the walls of his room seemed to melt away. Very tall and almost naked red men appeared and thronged about his bed. James was not afraid of the savages, for their faces were not fierce. They seemed to be begging the sick boy to come and help them. (Later, Father Cagliero was to see those same faces in far-distant Patagonia!)

Then the Indians disappeared, and in their place James saw his protector, the beloved Don Bosco. "You will not die now, my son," said the saint. "You will become a priest and travel far, far away. In time you will become a bishop, and then a cardinal."

All happened as Don Bosco had foretold. Patagonia, far down in southern Argentina, was entrusted to the care of the Salesians, the religious society founded by Don Bosco. And Father James Cagliero became the outstanding pioneer in that inhospitable region. As priest, and later as bishop, this great missioner was constantly in the saddle, covering immense distances in search of his scattered flock.

Bishop Cagliero labored forty years in South America. He became seasoned to the cold winds that blow all the year round in

Patagonia; but he always watched, with the same delighted interest that he had experienced on his arrival, the swift flight across the plains of the big rhea, the South-American ostrich. The missioner's Indians were very big, too. Most of the men stood well over six feet in height.

"You may be the tallest race on earth," the Apostle of Patagonia would say to his red men. "But you are not tall enough to reach heaven without baptism. That is why I am here among you."

James Cardinal Cagliero was still an active Churchman when he was ninety years of age. He went on his last great journey in March of the year 1926.

NO GREATER THRILL THAN THIS

The service of God is not, as some persons believe, forbiddingly devoid of romance. On his arrival at the southern tip of South America, Father Cagliero discovered in Patagonia the thrilling fulfillment of a boyhood vision of service for Christ and souls.

PART IX

Total Missioners

(1914 TO THE PRESENT TIME)

SINCE the year 1914, two global wars, the ruthless aggressions of Soviet Russia and Red China, and the relentless tension of the "cold war" have mocked the deep yearning of mankind for universal peace. The counsel given by Pope Pius XI to the distressed, confused nations is still largely unheeded.

"Neither peace treaties, nor the most solemn pacts, nor international meetings or conferences, nor even the noblest and most disinterested efforts of any statesman will be enough, unless in the first place are recognized the rights of natural and Divine law," warned the Vicar of Christ.

Marxian Communism has attracted many souls by its claim to universalism, its assertion that it is the true belief of all men. In view of this claim, the present divisions of Christianity are more than ever calamitous, and recent popes have spurred on apostolic efforts toward a united Christendom. With the return to union of schismatic Eastern Churches in mind, non-Latin-rite sections have been instituted in several religious orders. Catholic clergy and laity have been forcibly reminded of their apostolic obligations toward all non-Catholic Christians.

Catholics have suffered bitter persecution in Russia, Mexico,

Nazi Germany, "Loyalist" Spain, and the countries of the Communist bloc. The Communist advance has engulfed China, North Korea, and northern Vietnam, and threatens other mission fields hitherto bright with promise. In the words of the United States Hierarchy: "Christianity faces its most serious crisis since the Church came out of the Catacombs."

This serious crisis can be met only by totally dedicated missioners, and it calls for a selflessly resolute adherence to a fundamental objective of the Catholic apostolate. From the Apostolic age, the normal practice of the Church in evangelizing new nations was to insure the continuation of the work by creating as soon as possible an indigenous hierarchy. Thus it happened in the conversion of the various nations of Europe.

In the seventeenth century, Pope Innocent XI said to a missionary from China: "I would rather see you ordain one indigenous priest than baptize fifty thousand pagans."

But though this primary policy of the Church always remained that of the Holy See, individual missioners, and even some missionary communities, tended to lose sight of it in the great expansion of the white race during the past three hundred years. We have seen how the Papacy reacted against this disastrous loss of vision by creating vicars apostolic, directly dependent on the Holy See, and by approving the establishment of the Paris Foreign Missions Seminary for the express promotion of the development of a native clergy in mission countries.

Recent popes — Benedict XV, Pius XI, and Pius XII — have stressed in masterly encyclicals the urgency of developing indigenous Catholic hierarchies among all peoples; and they have sent apostolic delegates to direct on the spot this crucial apostolic activity. Today, of some twenty-seven thousand priests now working in the foreign missions, strictly so called, eleven thousand are members of the native populations. Moreover, steadily increasing numbers of foreign missioners are working under the direction of native bishops.

During the period since 1914, the missionary activities of Catholic Sisters have continued to expand, notably in the field of medical charity. Pope Pius XI emphasized the important apostolic role of women by proclaiming St. Thérèse of Lisieux patron and protector of all mission fields, together with St. Francis Xavier. Catholic Sisters, also, are concentrating their chief energies on the training of indigenous religious, who will eventually be able to carry on without them.

At present the white race's definite loss of world domination, and the Communists' tendency to exploit for their own ends the mounting nationalism of the colored races, make the duty of the Catholic missioner poignantly clear. He must prepare himself wholeheartedly for work under indigenous bishops, seeking in every way to aid them to develop strong local Catholic leaders among both clergy and laity. His must be the total emptying of self of St. John the Baptist, the Precursor. His role diminishes in outward authority in the measure that Christ grows in the people of his apostolate: "He must increase, but I must decrease" (Jn. 3:30).

THE COFOUNDERS OF MARYKNOLL (*d. 1919 and 1936*)

On June 29, 1908, a decree of Pope Pius X declared that the United States was, canonically, no longer a mission country. The hour had struck for the Church in our nation to pick up, in its turn, the missionary torch. Two American priests decided to do something about it. One — Father James Anthony Walsh — was serving in Boston as archdiocesan director of the Society for the Propagation of the Faith. The other — Father Thomas Frederick Price — had pioneered for a quarter of a century in North Carolina, one of the most strongly Protestant states in the Union.

In the year 1910, both Father Walsh and Father Price were pilgrims to the Eucharistic Congress at Montreal. Father Price got in touch with Father Walsh and said, "I want to know what is in your mind about foreign missions."

As a result of that meeting, the two apostolic priests founded, on June 29, 1911, the Catholic Foreign Mission Society of America

— better known by the name of its headquarters, "Maryknoll." The saintly Pope Pius X gave his blessing to that first distinctly American, Catholic foreign-mission project. Maryknoll stands high above the Hudson, about thirty miles from the skyscrapers of New York. Beginnings were made in humble poverty and in that joy experienced only by those ready to go the whole way for Christ. At the special request of Father Price, Father Walsh was chosen as the first Superior-General of the Society. Father Walsh encouraged and fostered the development of a Maryknoll Sisterhood.

Maryknoll's first little mission band, four priests, went overseas to South China in the autumn of 1918. The superior of the band was Father Price, who became known among the Chinese as "The Holy Priest." Maryknoll's cofounder was the first member of the society to lay down his life in the mission field. He died in Hong Kong, on September 12, 1919, the feast of the Holy Name of Mary.

In the lifetime of the society's first Superior-General, the Maryknoll mustard seed developed amazingly. Maryknollers journeyed to several new fields in South China, to Korea, to Manchuria, to the Philippines, to Hawaii, and to Japan. When Bishop James Anthony Walsh died, on April 14, 1936, the late Archbishop John T. McNicholas of Cincinnati said of his friend of many years:

"With more than human prudence, Bishop Walsh mapped out for himself and his co-laborers the work providentially entrusted to his society. His trust in Divine Providence seemed to me that of a saint. He knew the spirit and genius of America better than any priest I have met. He was convinced of the nobility of American youth and of their capacity for work and sacrifice under proper direction. He served the Lord in joy, and he taught his sons and daughters to be swift and generous athletes of Christ."

THE CATHOLIC VISION

The cofounders of Maryknoll repeatedly told their pioneer subjects to unite shining loyalty to their own society with a truly Catholic appreciation of other religious institutes. On the eve of his death, Bishop James Anthony Walsh drove home this noble thought in a farewell letter to his priests, saying: "I have often urged you to appreciate what is good in other societies than ours."

FATHER MIGUEL AUGUSTIN PRO JUAREZ, S.J. (*1891–1927*)

Miguel Augustin Pro was admitted into the Society of Jesus in Mexico in 1911. Three years later he was exiled from his country, during Carranza's revolution. He continued his studies in California and Spain, after which he was assigned to a period of teaching in Nicaragua. In the summer of 1922, the young Mexican was again ordered to Europe. He completed his studies in Spain and Belgium, and was ordained to the priesthood in the latter country in 1925.

Father Pro was loved for his buoyant gaiety, a happiness undimmed by frail health and bouts of illness. After obedience had brought him back to Mexico, he knew that his life was in constant danger; but he joked lightheartedly about his frequent escapes from the determined pursuit of the government police.

The young Jesuit organized "Communion Stations" in private homes in Mexico City. He heard thousands of confessions, administered the Sacrament of Baptism, presided at marriages, and took Viaticum to the dying. Father Pro, dressed as a student, often rode a bicycle belonging to one of his brothers, and was sometimes accompanied by a large dog which had been given him.

The persecuting administration of Calles was well aware of Father Pro's activities. The Jesuit's brothers, Humberto and Roberto, and a young engineer by the name of Luis Segura Vilchis, had likewise attracted the attention of the persecutors by their tirelessly valiant service of Christ the King. When a bombing attempt was made on the life of ex-President Obregon in November, 1927, the minions of Calles were ordered to arrest and falsely accuse all four of these young men. With them was imprisoned a nineteen-year-old laborer, Antonio Tirado, seized for no better reason than because he had run away at the time of the bombing to avoid being wounded.

Every constitutional and humanitarian guarantee was violated in the case of these prisoners. During the six days they were held in prison, Father Pro converted one of his jailers. He prayed and joked with the other young men, so that the guards marveled at the carefree happiness of the captives.

All of the accused were illegally done to death on the morning of November 23, 1927, with the exception of Roberto Pro, who was reprieved at the last moment by the efforts of a South American diplomat. Father Pro was the first to be led out to die. He asked to be allowed to pray, kissed his crucifix, and, on rising from his knees, blessed his executioners.

The young Jesuit refused an offer to be blindfolded. At the order, "Get ready to shoot," he extended his arms in the form of a cross. The command, "Aim!" followed; and Father Pro died in uttering the solemnly triumphant cry, "Hail, Christ the King!"

FATHER PRO'S PRAYER TO THE BLESSED VIRGIN (1926)

"On life's highway I do not seek the gladness of Bethlehem. . . . My wish, O most sorrowful Virgin, is to stand near thee on Calvary, to strengthen my soul through thy tears, and to complete my offering through thy martyrdom."

FATHERS GODFREY, CLEMENT, AND WALTER, C.P. (*d. 1929*)

Father Godfrey Holbein, from Baltimore, and Father Clement Seybold, from Dunkirk, New York, arrived in the Passionist mission field in Hunan Province, China, in the autumn of 1924. The American Passionists had been in China only three years. Their mission territory was a difficult one, poor and bandit-ridden. The newly ordained Father Godfrey and Father Clement set about mastering the local dialect with the enthusiasm of dedicated youth. The two young Americans became to their Chinese people spiritual fathers, teachers, doctors, and friends, tending the sick and the dying when a famine struck their barren countryside.

They were constantly on the watch for bandits. In 1926, as Chiang Kai-shek began his victorious drive northward from Canton, communistic troops moved up into Hunan. Those Chinese Reds had been indoctrinated with a hatred of everything foreign, and their presence placed the Passionists in continual danger.

Father Godfrey's outstanding characteristic was a boundless generosity. His co-workers accused him of lying awake at night so that all the hardest sick calls might fall to his lot. The steady, quiet Father Clement was often entrusted with thankless, monotonous tasks, because his companions knew that the work would be well and willingly done. So passed for the two young classmates five happy and fruitful years.

In the spring of 1929, Father Godfrey and Father Clement made their annual retreat at the central mission house. When the retreat was over, they started back to their Christians, accompanied by Father Walter Coveyou, from Petoskey, Michigan. Father Walter, who had been a star promoter for the missions in the United States, had just arrived in Hunan Province.

The three young Passionists stopped overnight at the mission of a confrere, Father Anthony. Two days later, as they were riding through mountainous country, lurking bandits seized the three priests and marched them about five miles to a lonely spot. After the outlaws had stripped the Fathers, they shot them and threw their bodies into a deep pit.

One of the Chinese coolies who had been with the priests escaped and made his way back to Father Anthony's mission. The Passionist could hardly believe the terrified man's shocking story. Accompanied by soldiers, Father Anthony rode to the scene of the murders where he saw that the coolie had exaggerated nothing. Father Godfrey, Father Clement, and Father Walter were the first American priests to shed their blood as missioners in China.

GOD'S WAYS ARE NOT OURS

The three young Passionists murdered by bandits in China seemed urgently needed to reap Hunan's harvest of souls. But God's ways are not ours. The supreme sacrifice of the three dedicated apostles became a strong missionary inspiration for American Catholic youth.

BISHOP EMILE GROUARD, O.M.I.
(*1840–1931*)

As a young missioner from France, Father Emile Grouard arrived in the Canadian Far North in 1862. He learned the language of the Montagnais Indians quickly and well, and was destined to become one of the best-known apostles of the Canadian wilderness. Father Grouard was a mighty journeyer for the Lord; and at one time, in the space of two years, he covered over more than four thousand icy miles.

"I like the Montagnais," recorded the sturdy French Oblate. "They are cheerful and pleasant, and even humorous in their own way. I never expected to find Indian women so talkative and so ready to laugh. Human nature is evidently the same the world over."

On August 1, 1891, Father Grouard was raised to the episcopate. He became Vicar Apostolic of Athabaska-Mackenzie. After his consecration, Bishop Grouard continued his gigantic labors. He was a valiant beggar for his mission and a tireless builder. His energy brought sawmills and steamboats to the frozen North.

Bishop Emile Grouard lived to be ninety-one years of age, but the fire of his zeal never grew dim. When the great old Oblate died on March 7, 1931, he could offer to the First Missioner seventy years of the most rugged apostolic labor among Indians near the Arctic Circle.

A VAGRANT FOR CHRIST

Bishop Grouard made light of what others considered his heroic sacrifices for God and souls. "I like what I may call a rough and vagrant sort of life," he said. "I think I have just about enough knowledge and piety to teach the Catechism to the Indians."

FATHER AIMÉ VILLION, P.F.M. (*1843–1932*)

Aimé Villion, of Lyons, France, entered the Paris Foreign Missions Seminary and in 1866, after his ordination to the priesthood, he was assigned to the Orient. From China he was sent to Nagasaki. The missioner from Lyons was to labor for sixty-four years in Japan without ever returning to his loved France.

At the time of Father Villion's arrival, there was a renewal of persecution in Japan. Government officials had recently become aware of the existence of descendants of the proscribed seventeenth-century Japanese Catholics. These heroic descendants and their forebears had secretly kept the Faith for over two hundred years in the mountains behind Nagasaki and in the Goto Islands. The persecution did not cease until 1873.

Meanwhile, Father Villion had been sent to replace a confrere who had died in Kobe. The young apostle found that feeling against foreigners ran high. When cholera struck the city, Father Villion devoted himself night and day to the sick. Numerous conversions blessed his sacrifices, and he transformed his converts into lay missioners. Then his bishop transferred him to Kyoto, the stronghold of Japanese paganism.

As the years passed, Father Villion baptized five hundred people in Kyoto, ancient city of the Japanese Emperors. He accomplished the almost impossible feat of purchasing a lot in the center of the city, and his hope was to build a church on the lot. He had just begged enough money to start building his church when he was transferred to Yamaguchi.

In that city, Father Villion remained for thirty-five years and made many converts. He was eighty-three years of age when his district was turned over to the Jesuits. The intrepid old missioner departed to make a new beginning at Nara. There he bought a fine piece of ground and began again making plans to erect a church.

But on April 1, 1932, the Catholics of Japan heard sad news. The eighty-nine-year-old Father Villion was dead. On his deathbed, he had given thanks to God that his apostolic life had been spent in Japan and that he was a member of the great Paris Foreign Missions Society.

YOUTH OF SOUL

During Father Villion's sixty-four years in Japan, the vigor of his apostolic zeal never declined. Again and again his society felt free to call on him to make new beginnings and to leave the remarkable fruits of his work to others.

ARCHBISHOP GUSTAVE CHARLES MUTEL, P.F.M. (*d. 1933*)

When Father Mutel entered Korea secretly in the year 1880, the peninsula deserved its name of Hermit Kingdom. In those days, Korean rulers had no use for foreigners; and if any intruders persisted in crossing the forbidden boundaries, officials welcomed them by cutting off their heads! Father Mutel managed to keep his head on his shoulders, however, by concealing it under the broad Korean mourning hat, shaped like a huge mushroom.

Two years after Father Mutel's arrival, Commander Schufeldt, an American Navy officer, came with warships and forced Korea to open its doors to the outside world. The first treaty that Korea signed with a foreign nation was one with the United States. Then treaties were also signed with various European nations; and by those treaties, foreign missioners were granted the legal right to enter the country. After that Father Mutel and his French confreres were able to work openly.

Father Mutel was consecrated a bishop in 1890. From Seoul, the capital, he journeyed on horseback all over his immense mission field. He showed his appreciation of the hospitality offered him by poor Korean farmers; and they, in turn, loved this kindly, courteous man of God. Other Koreans, too, were drawn to the apostolic bishop. Diplomats, government officials, businessmen, and travelers enjoyed conversing with the Catholic prelate.

Under the leadership of Bishop Mutel, the Church in Korea grew by leaps and bounds. New missioners arrived in increasing numbers from France, and young Koreans were ordained to the priesthood. Before his death, in 1933, Archbishop Mutel had welcomed priestly helpers from Germany and from Maryknoll, New York. The Gospel was carried to remote sections of the peninsula where it had never been preached. During his long episcopate, the loved archbishop lived to see the blood of martyrs become the seed of almost two hundred thousand Korean Christians.

A CATHOLIC THROUGH AND THROUGH

An American prelate wrote of Archbishop Mutel: "Every inch and at every moment an archbishop, is the Vicar Apostolic of Seoul. Large in outlook and big of heart, Archbishop Mutel is a Catholic through and through."

FATHER EMMET McHARDY, S.M. (*1904–1933*)

Emmet McHardy was born among the mountains of New Zealand, of a Scottish father and an Irish mother. Though he had an unusually strong love for his home, he entered the Marist seminary at Greenmeadows, in his native island. As a priest, in 1929, he volunteered for pioneer work in the North Solomons; and he accepted all the hardships of that primitive region with buoyant zest.

The New Zealander overcame natural repugnance in treating the yaws and other festering sores of his often unwashed flock. He wrote with gaiety of perilous voyages in native boats, of tremendous electric storms, of earthquake shocks, of muggy heat, of drenching rains, and of the difficulties of persuading the naked natives to clothe themselves. On one occasion, when he had to cross a quaking bog that roofed voracious crocodiles, Father McHardy said merely that, for the next time, he would pick a different route!

Father McHardy built up his little mission station in the bush, assembled some seventy native boys at his catechist school, and converted numerous islanders in territory where a census had never been taken. Then he was attacked by an unusually severe bout of malaria. His bishop sent him to Australia, where a doctor in Sydney found that his lungs were seriously affected.

"I am perfectly content. Things like that don't happen without the knowledge of God," the young missioner wrote to his brother.

Father Emmet McHardy was later taken to his native New Zealand where he died on May 17, 1933. In the North Solomons, the American superior of the Marists, Bishop Thomas J. Wade, wrote of his deceased co-worker:

"Father McHardy was peculiarly fitted by nature for foreign missionary work. God gave him to us for a very short period, but in that time he accomplished wonders. Constantly cheerful, he had just the manner to win and to hold the natives. Great was their sorrow when he left them; earnestly they prayed for his return. They simply sighed aloud, when I told them that their missioner had experienced eternal birth."

REAL SANCTITY

"Some biographers of saints would turn a smile into a venial sin. For too many, sanctity lies in the extraordinary. . . . Real sanctity, as the Little Flower tried to show us, consists in being extra-ordinarily ordinary." —*Father Emmet McHardy*

ARCHBISHOP ALEXANDER LE ROY, C.S.Sp. (*d. 1935*)

In the year 1890, one of the great missionary pioneers in East Africa was a Holy Ghost priest, Father Alexander Le Roy. He was the first white man to establish contacts with various African chiefs on the slopes of lofty Mount Kilimanjaro in Tanganyika.

Chief Foumba proposed to the French missioner that they become blood brothers. Incisions were made in the arms of the blood-brothers-to-be. Then Father Le Roy ate a piece of goat's meat dipped in Foumba's blood; and the chief consumed a similar piece of meat moistened with the priest's blood. Soon the whole tribe knew that this white man and their ruler were blood brothers. That made Father Le Roy everyone's friend.

The Holy Ghost missioner became acquainted with Chief Mandara, who was a leader of rare intelligence and consummate villainy. He met, also, the treacherous Chief Sina, who at first tried to murder the French missioners, but who changed his mind when he saw that relationship with Europeans brought material advantages to his tribe.

The vigorous Africans in the Kilimanjaro region admired Father Le Roy for his indomitable courage. This white man was always fair and kept his promises, they said; moreover, he was never hesitant or vacillating. As time passed, Father Le Roy and the other Holy Ghost Fathers founded numerous missions in the beautiful Kilimanjaro country.

Later Father Le Roy was raised to the episcopate. Then he was made Superior-General of his society. Finally the veteran apostle received the pallium of an archbishop. Although his residence was then in France, his heart remained always in Africa; and he continued to promote by every means possible the evangelization of the Negroes.

The great missionary archbishop died on April 21, 1935. Some years before that, the Kilimanjaro region, the scene of his pioneer labors, had been assigned to the care of Holy Ghost Fathers of the American province. This development must have seemed singularly appropriate to Archbishop Le Roy, for in the days of his boyhood, he had first acquired a love for Negroes from his reading of *Uncle Tom's Cabin.*

AN INCENTIVE TO GREATER EFFORT

Archbishop Le Roy looked upon temporary defeat in apostolic work merely as an incentive to greater effort. A young confrere complained that his field of labor was sterile as a rock. "Drill into it, water it with your sweat! You will then see that rock bear fruit for Christ," replied the ardent missionary prelate.

FATHER LEONIDAS FEODOROV (*1879–1935*)

Leonidas Ivanovitch Feodorov, the grandson of a serf, was born in St. Petersburg in 1879. After he had entered the Imperial Orthodox Theological Academy, he read widely and he was increasingly influenced by the works of Peter Chaadaiev and Vladimir Soloviev, who both advocated the reunion of Russia with the Holy See. The courageous Leonidas believed more and more strongly that the Catholic religion was the only true one. He resolved to become a Catholic priest of the Byzantine-Slavonic rite, which was not legally recognized by the Czarist Government.

Leonidas made his way to Rome where he studied for the Catholic priesthood. He was ordained at Constantinople, in 1911, by a Bulgarian prelate of the Eastern rite. The outbreak of World War I found him in Austria, working under the direction of the great Ruthenian Uniate Metropolitan, Archbishop Andrew Shepticky. Father Feodorov returned to St. Petersburg where he was arrested and sent to Siberia. After the fall of the Czarist regime in March, 1917, he set out again for the city of his birth, then renamed Petrograd.

During the following years Father Feodorov, and the five or six priests working under his direction, gave themselves to the organization of Catholic parishes of the Eastern rite in Petrograd, Moscow, and other large Russian cities. The Soviet officials had taken special note of the talented leader of the Russian Catholics of the Slav rite. They arrested him in March, 1923, together with fourteen Catholic clergy of the Latin rite.

The ensuing trial in Moscow was a grim mockery of justice. The Soviet prosecutor declared that Father Feodorov was the most dangerous of the accused, because of his outstanding ability to attract Orthodox Christians to the Catholic Church and thus to form the dreaded "united religious front" against the Proletarian Revolution. Father Feodorov spoke in court with quiet dignity and complete absence of fear.

"Since the moment I gave myself to the Catholic Church, my sole thought has been to bring back my country to the only true religion," he stated.

Father Feodorov was sent to the notorious prison camp in the former monastery of Solovky on an island in the White Sea. There he found condemned members of his Catholic flock and said Mass for them in secret. "We must carry our cross with patience, for we are a burnt offering without which there can be no spiritual rebirth for Russia," he told them.

In 1929, Father Leonidas Feodorov fell seriously ill and was removed from Solovky. He was to spend the remainder of his life in various prisons in northern Russia. Wherever he was, he roused the anger of the Soviet police by fearlessly exercising his priestly functions. On March 7, 1935, he died at Kirov (formerly Viatka), in dire want but in glad acceptance of God's will. With the death of Father Feodorov, the first spring of modern Russian Catholicism came to an abrupt end.

CONSCIENCE IS ABOVE MAN-MADE LAWS

When the Red prosecutor asked Father Feodorov if he obeyed the laws of the Soviet, the Russian Catholic apostle replied quietly: "If the Soviet should wish to force me to act against my conscience, I would not obey its laws."

BISHOP FLORENTINO ASENSIO BARROSO (*d. 1936*)

Father Barroso, the son of a village shopkeeper in Spain, attracted the notice of his ecclesiastical superiors by his great charity in caring for the poor and the sick. In 1919, he was made rector of the Valladolid Cathedral, but he still found time to make daily visits to the needy. Well aware of the increasing unrest among Spain's workers, the zealous rector conducted nightly classes in Christian doctrine for laborers.

In the autumn of 1935, Pope Pius XI named Father Barroso Bishop of Barbastro in the Pyrenees. When the new prelate arrived in Barbastro, he found it already under the political control of Freemasons and radicals. He set to work with great vigor, but the attack on religion was already too far advanced. Civil war reached Barbastro on July 19, 1936. Bishop Barroso was imprisoned and subjected to an infamous "trial," in the course of which the fifty-nine-year-old apostle was barbarously beaten, kicked, and slashed with knives.

At two o'clock on the morning of August 9, Bishop Barroso was taken with several other prisoners to the city cemetery. The captain of the Communist execution squad lined the victims up one behind the other, boasting that he could kill them all with a single bullet; but Bishop Barroso agonized during two hours.

The Communists scoffed as the dying prelate begged God's forgiveness for his murderers. At length, as Bishop Barroso murmured weakly, "My Father, open soon to me the door of heaven!" one of the executioners, less hardened perhaps than the rest, used another bullet to finish off the clerical "enemy of the people."

THE LONGING FOR HEAVEN

Bishop Barroso's many friends in Valladolid were fearful as they saw him depart for Barbastro. "What of it?" the loved prelate told the anxious ones. "If I am killed, I shall only enter heaven all the sooner."

JOSEPH LO (*d. 1937*)

If someone were to ask you who the most apostolic Catholic layman of the first half of the twentieth century was, you could not be far wrong if you should answer: "Mr. Joseph Lo – or, to give him his Chinese name, Lo Pa Hong – of Shanghai. He was known as the St. Vincent de Paul of China."

Mr. Lo belonged to a family that had been Catholic for three centuries. He was essentially a man of prayer, and he had an intense devotion to the Holy Sacrifice of the Mass. Every morning of his busy life, he served Mass and received Holy Communion. His great charitable enterprises had their beginning in the work of Catholic Action which he directed in Shanghai. The members of his Catholic Action Society intensified their own spiritual lives, taught catechism in the outlying districts of the city, visited prisons, aided the poor and the sick, and raised funds to build churches and chapels.

One day in 1911, a sick beggar lying on a street in Shanghai asked Mr. Lo for alms. The businessman put the beggar in his ricksha and took him to a little house on his own grounds. There

Mr. Lo tended the repulsively sick man. Soon other outcasts flocked to the little shelter, and abandoned babies were brought to it. Lo Pa Hong saw that something had to be done. With the aid of his patron, St. Joseph, he founded St. Joseph's Hospice – which developed to include a dispensary, a hospital, a refuge, an orphanage, a school, and a workshop. He brought in, to staff the hospice, the Sisters of Charity; and later, for the boys' school, the Salesian Fathers.

Funds were never lacking for the hospice. Mr. Lo, who liked to call himself "The Coolie of St. Joseph," had made his heavenly patron the treasurer of his institution. So evident was the selflessness of the Christian founder's charity, that the hospice was supported by non-Christian Chinese as well as by Catholics. In the closing years of Mr. Lo's life, St. Joseph's Hospice had a population of about two thousand outcasts.

St. Joseph's Hospice was not the only institution to which Mr. Lo gave his time and his resources. He assumed responsibility for the Sacred Heart Hospital in Shanghai; aided the Home for the Aged, conducted by the Little Sisters of the Poor; and founded in the suburbs a hospital for the insane, the first institute of its kind in the whole of China. Many were the penitent criminals whom Mr. Lo baptized on the eve of execution; and he was always on the alert for an opportunity to make of a dying baby a "thief of heaven." Between August, 1937, and the date of his own death, Joseph Lo personally baptized two thousand wounded Chinese soldiers.

After the arrival of the Japanese in Shanghai, Mr. Lo, a devoted patriot, was falsely suspected of collaboration with the enemy. He was assassinated in December, 1937, as he was going out to buy rice for the starving poor.

TRUE CHARITY

The primary interest of many modern "philanthropists" is the material and temporal welfare of those they aid. This was not the case with Joseph Lo. The essential aim of this Catholic lay apostle was to save souls through his multiple charitable enterprises.

PIUS XI, *Pope of the Missions* (*1857–1939*)

From the time when Pius XI became the Vicar of Christ, in 1922, he agonized over the multitudes of human beings still in darkness and in the shadow of death. "Again and again, the mere thought of that staggering mass of one billion pagans prevents us from resting!" the great Pontiff cried.

With bold authority, Pope Pius XI set to work to make all Catholics mission-minded. He urged bishops in Christian lands to encourage unselfishly the development of missionary vocations in their dioceses. He pleaded with the Catholic laity to give unstinted prayerful and financial support to the mission cause. He pointed out to the missioners themselves their essential duty, which is to train an indigenous clergy wherever they labor. Then, when the native clergy is ready to take over the indigenous Church, the missioners must move on, to pioneer anew elsewhere.

Pius XI centralized the financial resources of Catholic missions. He strengthened the bond uniting Rome with the most distant missions, by appointing apostolic delegates to countries of the Far East and to Africa. In the Holy Year of 1925, he organized the grand display of the Vatican Mission Exhibition. Two years later, the Pope of the Missions rejoiced over the creation in Rome of the *Fides* news agency – a service to collect world-wide Catholic mission news and to distribute it through the press.

Unceasingly, Pius XI urged the multiplication in mission lands of hospitals, orphanages, and schools. A vital need was a greater number of seminaries for the training of indigenous priests. The missions should develop religious congregations of their own for both sexes. But not all the Catholic works should be grouped in one mission center, lest such centralization should immobilize too many missioners in one spot.

During the seventeen years of the pontificate of Pius XI, the numbers of Catholics in mission countries grew from twelve million to more than seventeen million, while the number of mission territories was increased by one third. The apostolic Pope consecrated with his own hands Chinese, Japanese, and Indian prelates;

and he entrusted over thirty mission territories to the care of an indigenous clergy.

Pius XI was the fearless exponent of the mission vocation in all its purity: "All for Christ; nothing for self."

From the year 1936 onward, the Pope of the Missions was in failing health. But he refused to take any repose, saying on the contrary: "We pray that We may be able to die working." On February 10, 1939, the mourning nations learned that the great laborer for Christ had begun his eternal rest.

TOTAL DEDICATION

Pius XI said of the society of priests founded by the renowned missioner in China, Father Vincent Lebbe, for the express purpose of working under indigenous bishops: "They are at the very center of the missionary vocation. There is no missionary vocation purer or more total than theirs."

FATHER VINCENT LEBBE (*1877–1940*)

Father Vincent Lebbe, a young Vincentian missioner from Belgium, began his work in China in 1901. Already he knew the course that he must follow. "I wish to become absolutely Chinese!" he declared. Father Lebbe wore a Chinese gown and a queue; and he made constant use of his Chinese name, Lei Ming Yuan, which in English is "Thunder That Sings in the Distance."

Father Lebbe was not satisfied with preaching to the Christians; he also reached out with burning charity to the pagan multitudes. He converted entire villages. In the large city of Tientsin, he inaugurated conference halls, where the Faith was preached to thousands of non-Christians. Mass conversions followed. Father Lebbe founded Catholic Action and a Catholic press in his beloved China. But as it happens to all precursors, he met with misunderstanding.

In the year 1920, the great Belgian missioner left the land and the people he had served so ardently, and he did not know when or how he would return to them. During the following years, Father Lebbe worked among Chinese students in France and in Belgium, winning some three hundred future leaders for the Church in China. On October 28, 1926, Father Lebbe had the immense happiness of witnessing, at St. Peter's in Rome, the consecration of six Chinese bishops by the Holy Father himself.

Soon afterward, one of the newly consecrated Chinese prelates asked that Father Lebbe return with him to China. The Belgian apostle thus became the first European missioner to work under a Chinese bishop. Before leaving Europe, Father Lebbe founded in Belgium a society of priests whose special vocation is to place themselves under the orders of indigenous bishops in mission lands.

On his return to China, Father Lebbe became a naturalized citizen of the country, in order to be wholly one with his adopted people. In 1928, he opened a monastery for Chinese monks; and in the following year, he founded a similar community of Chinese nuns. Father Lebbe's religious were to be "Trappists in their monastery, and missioners outside of it."

When Japan attacked China, Father Lebbe's monks served as volunteer stretcher-bearers. Father Lebbe himself organized hospital work and carried on an apostolate among the soldiers. Several of the Chinese monks were put to death by Communists. In 1940, the founder himself was taken prisoner by the Chinese Reds, and he fell mortally ill of the hardships then endured. Generalissimo Chiang Kai-shek sent his private airplane to fly Father Lebbe to Chungking. There the missionary abbot's life ended, on June 24, 1940.

When Father Lei Ming Yuan died, Chiang Kai-shek decreed a day of national mourning; and he said of the apostle, "His memory is immortal." Never, since the time of the seventeenth-century Matteo Ricci and his Jesuit successors, had the highest civil authorities of China manifested such esteem for a Catholic priest.

NOTHING MORE, NOTHING LESS

Asked to put into writing his instructions for the training of members of his Society of Auxiliary Priests for the Missions, Father Lebbe summarized his thoughts as follows: "That which surpasses infinitely all the rest is that you be saints! Nothing more, nothing less. It seems to me that all can accept this program, the Gospel put into practice: absolute renunciation, true charity, constant joy."

BISHOP AUGUST DE CLERCQ, I.H.M. (*d. 1940*)

In the year 1893, Father August de Clercq was a pioneer missioner in the Kasai district of the Belgian Congo. The Africans called the young Belgian priest "Sharp Knife." Their name for the missioner was a compliment: they meant to say that Father Clercq's mind was as keen as a sharp blade.

Father Clercq set himself to learn the dialects and the customs of the Africans of that region of the Belgian Congo. Not only did he master the dialects of the Kasai district, but he also coined new words in those dialects, words to express the truths of Catholic doctrine. Thus he prepared vocabularies for his apostolic successors in that part of Africa.

Father Clercq was religious superior of the Kasai Mission from 1904 to 1907. Then he was recalled to Belgium, where he remained for twelve years in various important posts in his Society of the Immaculate Heart of Mary. He thought constantly of Africa, and he used every moment of his spare time to increase his knowledge of Congolese dialects. In the year 1919, Father Clercq was consecrated a bishop, and he returned to Africa as the first Vicar Apostolic of Kasai.

Much progress had been made in the mission since Bishop Clercq had last seen it. The number of Catholics had increased to sixty thousand. The missioners had journeyed through the entire district, instructing and baptizing converts and building chapels. But Bishop Clercq perceived that this gigantic effort lacked solidity. At once, he pointed out the cause: there were not enough Catholic schools. He started immediately to make adequate provision for the Catholic education of the young people.

Two decades later – in 1940 – Bishop Clercq died of exhaustion. By that time, his territory had more than three thousand mission schools; and in those schools, over one hundred and twenty thousand African boys and girls were receiving an excellent Catholic education. Bishop Clercq was, indeed, the founding "Sharp Knife" of apostolic endeavor in the Belgian Congo.

THAT SOLID BASIS

The keen mind of Bishop Clercq was not deceived by surface prosperity in missionary endeavor. He knew that a converted people could not be thoroughly grounded in Catholic doctrine and morals, without the solid basis of a thoroughgoing Catholic education.

FATHER MAXIMILIAN KOLBE, O.F.M.Conv. (*1894–1941*)

"When our Lady appeared to you, what did she say?" Mrs. Kolbe asked her ten-year-old son.

"She held out to me two crowns, one white and one red; and she asked me which I would choose," answered the boy. "The white crown signified that I would always be pure, and the red that I would die a martyr. I told the Blessed Lady that I chose both crowns! She smiled and disappeared."

From then on, Raymond Kolbe resolved to consecrate his life to the service of the Immaculate Mother of God and to win souls for Christ through her aid. Raymond's father was a weaver, and his family lived near Lodz, in Poland. Raymond and his two brothers joined the Franciscan Order of Friars Minor Conventual; and the young client of our Lady received the religious name of Friar Maximilian.

Friar Maximilian was sent to Rome to complete his theological studies and was ordained to the priesthood there in 1918. In the Eternal City, also, he recruited the first members of *The Militia of Mary Immaculate*. Its initial activity consisted in prayer and the distribution of the Miraculous Medal. The Militia was blessed by Benedict XV and Pius XI, and the latter Pontiff elevated it to the status of a Primary Union. At present there are units of the Militia in Italy, Poland, Rumania, Holland, Belgium, America, and Japan.

Father Maximilian, the originator of this great work for our Lady, was a small, frail man, early attacked by chronic tuberculosis. In the face of considerable lack of understanding and opposition, he succeeded in establishing a great Marian center near Warsaw. In 1938, no less than 762 Franciscan Conventuals were engaged there, in printing and circulating almost a million copies of Father Maximilian's review, *The Knight of the Immaculate.* Nine other Marian reviews were likewise published at this Polish center. Father Maximilian inspired his co-workers with his own spirit of selfless dedication to the salvation of souls through our Lady's potent intercession.

In 1930, Father Maximilian and four of his confreres journeyed to Japan. They were welcomed by the Japanese Bishop of Nagasaki, and established a Marian center in the suburbs of that city. Father Kolbe's Japanese center was not destroyed by the atomic explosion in August, 1945. His confreres are now printing some 70,000 copies of *The Knight of the Immaculate* in Japanese, and they have opened a large orphanage.

Father Maximilian was recalled to Poland in 1936. When the Nazis invaded Poland, he was twice arrested. Finally, he was sent to Oswiecim, the terrible "concentration camp of death." In July, 1941, a prisoner escaped from Oswiecim; and in retaliation, the Nazis condemned ten other Poles to death by starvation. Father Maximilian offered himself in the place of one of the ten, a young man with a wife and small children. The knight of our Lady died a martyr of charity on August 14, 1941. He had won his red crown on the vigil of the glorious feast of the Assumption.

CHARITY IS A DIVINE MAGNET

Even the SS guards were not immune to the influence of Father Kolbe's Christlike charity. They watched him for two weeks, while he was starving to death and leading the other condemned in the recitation of the rosary and the singing of hymns to the Blessed Lady. "This priest is really a gentleman. We have never before seen a prisoner like him," they said wonderingly.

SISTER BLANDINA SEGALE, S.C. (*1850–1941*)

In 1876, there was a gun fight in Trinidad, Territory of Colorado, in the United States. An outlaw of Billy the Kid's gang shot a rival, and was himself seriously wounded. The wounded outlaw was thrown into an empty hut and left there to die. Everyone was afraid to approach him – everyone, that is, except Sister Blandina, a Sister of Charity and teacher in Trinidad's adobe public school. Sister Blandina cared for the outlaw and talked to him about the mercy of Christ. One day Billy the Kid and several of his gangsters met the young Sister in their sick comrade's room.

The terrible Billy shook Sister Blandina's hand and said: "At any time my pals and I can serve you, Sister, you will find us ready."

It would be hard to discover a more authentic and thrilling piece of Catholic Americana than Sister Blandina's journal, *At the End of the Santa Fe Trail.* It affords a graphic picture of pioneer days in our Southwest: the heroic priests and Sisters, the lawlessness of frontier mobs, the constant threat of Indian raids, and the injustices done to the natives by land-grabbers from the Eastern States. From the terse narrative there emerges a revelation of the forthright sanctity, prudence, and courage of Sister Blandina herself.

Sister Blandina Segale was born of devout Italian parents. She was assigned to the Southwest in 1872, when she was only twenty-two years of age. She labored for souls in Trinidad, Territory of Colorado; and later in Santa Fe and in Albuquerque, New Mexico. Fearless in her love of God and souls, this small Sister met all emergencies.

Sister Blandina influenced the lives of her pupils for good, helped with her own hands to erect new school buildings, cared for the sick and the needy, visited prisoners, pacified Indians on the war-path, defeated the schemes of wily politicians and land-grabbers. In all her activities, her Christlike charity drew many souls to God. It was Sister Blandina who, by her holy courage, dealt the first blow to lynch law in the Territory of Colorado.

After twenty-one years of missionary work in the Southwest,

Sister Blandina was recalled to her mother house in Cincinnati. During the following thirty-five years, she worked among the numerous Italian immigrants in that city. This tireless Catholic missioner died in 1941 at the age of ninety-one years.

INTREPID COURAGE

The late Archbishop of Cincinnati, John T. McNicholas, wrote of Sister Blandina Segale as follows: "No work was foreign to her, provided it was God's work. One knows not which to admire the more, her instant grasp of a difficult situation or the coolness and resourcefulness with which she met it."

ARCHBISHOP ALOYSIUS MARIA BENZIGER, O.C.D. (*d. 1942*)

Bishop Aloysius Benziger, spiritual ruler of the diocese of Quilon, in southwestern India, was the brother of Louis Benziger, one of the founders of the well-known firm of Catholic publishers. This Swiss missioner, who ranks among the foremost modern apostles of India, was simple in his ways. He was at one and the same time strict and kind with his flock. He was gifted with unusual foresight in solving the many local problems of his apostolate.

Bishop Benziger built orphanages for the thousands of homeless little ones in his diocese and established schools for the teen-age boys. He secured Sisters to care for the sick in his mission hospitals, and the charity of those nursing religious won for Christ many a dying pagan. However, the bishop realized that the Church could not become truly indigenous in India without the existence of numerous Indian priests, so he built two seminaries for the training of Indian "other Christs."

This zealous missionary prelate developed a strong convert movement in his diocese. It was Bishop Benziger who converted the schismatic Jacobite prelate, Mar Ivanios. After his conversion, the dynamic Mar Ivanios led thousands of his followers to reunion with Rome.

During his episcopate, Bishop Benziger saw the number of Catholics in his diocese mount from eighty-nine thousand to two hundred and twenty thousand. The Holy Father made the spiritual head of Quilon an archbishop in recognition of his great services to the Church in India. Archbishop Aloysius Maria Benziger died on August 17, 1942.

FIRST THINGS FIRST

Archbishop Benziger laid undeviating emphasis on developing native priests in his Quilon Diocese. Not only did a strong convert movement take place as a result of this policy; but the zealous Swiss apostle could rest assured that the Church in his field would hold its own, after the passing of white rule in India.

FATHER JAMES GERARD HENNESSY (*d. 1942*)

Father James Hennessy was a distinguished priest of the Boston Archdiocese who had made brilliant studies in Rome. He conceived the idea that the lack of priests in foreign missions might be remedied if a number of priests on the home front would volunteer to give a few years of service in foreign fields. With the permission and the blessing of Cardinal O'Connell, Father Hennessy left Boston in 1936, to work under Bishop Wade in the Solomon Islands in the far South Pacific.

The particular work undertaken by Father Hennessy in the North Solomons was the establishment of a catechetical school. He also developed a model farm to feed the future catechists. In the course of time, Father Hennessy sent well-trained native catechists to various islands of the vicariate, to assist the missioners in their apostolic labors.

A number of Father Hennessy's "boys" were executed during the Japanese occupation of the Solomons, because they had refused to give up their catechetical activities. Two of the young men who escaped studied for the priesthood after the close of hostilities. These first Solomonese to be raised to the Catholic priesthood,

Father Aloysius Tamuka and Father Peter Tatamas, were ordained in December, 1953. Father Tamuka is a young hereditary chieftain, whose ancestors were notorious head-hunters.

When bombs fell on Pearl Harbor, Father Hennessy was temporarily in charge of a mission on Buka Island. In March, 1942, Japanese warships arrived off the coast of Buka. Officers landed and took the American priest aboard one of their ships. Father Hennessy was tried by court-martial at sea and he was condemned to death. He was not executed at once but was imprisoned for three months on the island of New Britain.

On the wall of his prison, Father Hennessy carved the words: "In Thee, O Lord, I have hoped. I shall never be confounded."

In June, 1942, Father Hennessy was placed on a Japanese vessel, together with more than a thousand other prisoners of war. The ship had reached a point north of Luzon Island, in the Philippines, when it was torpedoed by an American submarine. All on board the Japanese ship were lost. So died the heroic young volunteer from Boston. But Father Hennessy had shown the way; and other diocesan priests have since followed in his footsteps, by serving for limited periods in mission lands.

GROWTH BY SACRIFICE

A principal reason for the flourishing condition of the great Boston Archdiocese is the missionary zeal of its prelates, priests, and Catholic laity. Its pulsating Catholic life calls once again to mind the truth: "God is never outdone in generosity."

BISHOP JOSEPH SHANAHAN, C.S.Sp. (*1871–1943*)

The work of the pioneer Holy Ghost missioners in Nigeria, West Africa, was much hampered by the virulent paganism of that region. The pagan priests worked hand in hand with slave traders. Ibo Negroes who went to consult the oracles at the Long Ju-Ju Temple were kidnaped and sold into slavery. Human sacrifices were not uncommon at the unholy shrine. But all those horrors had been wiped out by the British when Bishop Joseph Shanahan became Prefect Apostolic of Southern Nigeria in 1905.

The new prelate was a young Irishman of sturdy frame, keen mind, vigorous will, and burning zeal for the conversion of the blacks. His plan was to go out to the people in the remote villages, and not to wait for the Ibos to come to the central mission. Bishop Shanahan animated his priestly helpers with his own enthusiasm. He stressed the training of Ibo priests after discovering promising candidates in many villages. To compensate in some measure for the current lack of indigenous priests, he sent able catechists far and wide. Conversions began to multiply.

With his keen understanding of the Ibos, Bishop Shanahan sensed their eagerness for education. When, in 1906, the Nigerian Education Board was formed, the Catholic prelate was one of its members. This gave Bishop Shanahan the opportunity of pushing forward his educational projects in the best possible way. The zealous organizer did not forget the Ibo women and girls. He journeyed to his native Ireland and founded there a community, the Sisters of the Holy Rosary, to teach in the schools for Nigerian girls.

The outstanding modern apostle of the Ibos spent twenty-nine years in the service of his beloved blacks. Bishop Joseph Shanahan died on Christmas Day, 1943.

THE THIRST FOR SOULS

It was an agony to Bishop Shanahan to see the Ibo crowds going by without the missioners to preach to them. He begged the Eternal Father to let him be broken at will, as His Son had been broken; but not to let the poor blacks miss eternal life, through the paucity of human instruments of salvation.

FATHER HUGO MENSE, O.F.M. (*1879–1943*)

One day, early in his work among the Mundurucu Indians of the Amazon jungle, Father Hugo Mense showed a picture of the Crucifixion to some of the boys and tried to explain the Passion to them. The little Indians listened stolidly; and the missioner feared he had made no impression. The next day, however, when Father Hugo looked at the picture he had used for illustration, he was startled to see that his primitive listeners had savagely mutilated the faces of the Saviour's persecutors. Those small Mundurucus, descendants of Mato Grosso head-hunters, left no doubt about the intensity of their reactions!

Hugo Mense was the son of a German blacksmith of Paderborn, Westphalia. In his youth he entered the Franciscan Order and volunteered for mission work in Brazil. He spent seven years accustoming himself to the sweating jungles among the Indians on the Lower Amazon. Then his superiors sent him far into the interior of Central Brazil, east of the Mato Grosso, to found his mission in the wilderness among the tattooed Mundurucus.

The Franciscan traveled on the Amazon by wood burner to Santarém; then he sailed south on the mighty Tapajós and founded his San Francisco Mission on the Cururu River, a tributary of the Tapajós. Gradually he won the confidence of the Mundurucus, mastered their language, and entered wholly into their simple lives.

Father Mense grew to appreciate all that was good and beautiful in the Mundurucus' tribal religion, customs, art, and dances. He admired their patient fortitude in their unending struggles with hunger, heat, torrential rains, and jungle animals. The Franciscan never tried to make Europeans of his "children"; his one desire was to renew their souls in the likeness of Christ. His ministry reached out to include the "civilized" Brazilian rubber cutters, so often cheated by unscrupulous traders.

After a while other priests, and Brothers and Sisters, joined Father Hugo Mense at Mission San Francisco. Vegetables and fruit trees were planted. Grass was imported, and then cropped by healthy cattle. Mundurucu children received a sound Catholic education in the mission schools, while Christianity became the most vital element in their parents' lives.

During twenty-seven years Father Hugo labored on the Cururu River, before the jungle took its toll. Then, deaf and shaken with malarial fever, the aging apostle was obliged to spend the last six years of his life in Rio de Janeiro. After Father Hugo Mense's death, his mission continued to be a light in the jungle; and every time its chapel bells sounded, the Mundurucus thought with loving remembrance of their "old Father" in God.

ONE IN CHRIST

Father Hugo Mense entered so deeply into the hearts of his Indian flock, that their chief performed a ceremony hitherto unknown among them. He inducted the white man into the Munducuru tribe, making the missioner a member of his own clan.

SISTER XAVIER BERKELEY (*1861–1944*)

Agnes Mary Philomena Berkeley was born in a family of the old English Catholic nobility. The family was a devout and charitable one, and the children were encouraged to join the recently founded Society of the Holy Childhood. One day the six-year-old Agnes, studying the famous picture of the Sisters of Charity in China rescuing abandoned babies, said, "When I am older, I will go to China and save babies, like those Sisters."

Agnes Berkeley never wavered in that early resolve. She grew up tall and strong, gifted with much common sense, and loving God with a fearless simplicity. Three weeks before her twenty-first birthday, she left her beautiful home forever and became a Sister of Charity. Her first work was in an orphanage in Plymouth, England.

In 1890, Sister Berkeley was assigned to China. At Kiukiang, in Kiangsi Province, she worked in the recently established hospital and dispensary. Her heart went out to the terrible sufferings of the Chinese poor; and she applied herself with ardor to the study of the language, without which "nothing can be done for their unfortunate souls." The following year, the English Sister was sent to Ningpo, in Chekiang Province, where she was to remain during the next two decades.

At Ningpo, Sister Berkeley visited the poor in the city and the riverside villages. She found countless opportunities for baptizing dying babies. She organized a new work for boys and young men, who became designers and silk or satin weavers, according to their capacity. Through her many friends in England, Sister Berkeley secured a market for the beautiful products of the mission workrooms.

In 1911, Sister Berkeley was made superior of the House of Mercy on Chusan Island, which lies to the south of Shanghai, off the coast of Chekiang Province. She found great poverty and dilapidated buildings. With determined zeal and calm trust in God, she developed the mission on Chusan into a model of charity for the Christian world. Even the brigands and the pirates respected the "white-hat Sisters," for when any of those rough men were ill in prison, the Sisters of Charity nursed them and gave them nourishing food.

World War II and the Japanese occupation of the Chusan Archipelago brought many anxieties to Sister Berkeley. She suffered much when supplies ran out and the occupants of the House of Mercy had to remain hungry. Her own strength failed when she was eighty-three years of age. On March 9, 1944, she died, soon after having said: "I am so weary, so weary! I can do no more."

Sister Xavier Berkeley was buried in the Chusan mission garden. One day two Japanese officers of high rank marched out to the simple tomb, took off their hats, and saluted with three deep bows. Enemies though they were, they had come to pay their respects to the "Mother of the Orphans and the Poor."

A FOUNDER'S IDEAL

The late Bishop James Anthony Walsh, cofounder of Maryknoll, the Catholic Foreign Mission Society of America, wrote to Sister Xavier Berkeley: "Your House of Mercy is my ideal – simple, modest buildings for the Sisters, and with the poor Chinese around you all day long. It is real mission life, such as I wish our American Sisters to live."

ARCHBISHOP JOSEPH RAPHAEL CRIMONT, S.J. (*1858–1945*)

Joseph Crimont was small and frail. His parents in Amiens, France, were so poor that they could not give him nourishing food. Later, after Joseph had become a Jesuit scholastic, he was attacked by acute anemia, and his life was despaired of. Just at that time, St. John Bosco came as a guest to the Jesuit house in which Joseph was studying. The founder of the Salesians was already known for his miracles. Joseph told Don Bosco of his longing to become a missioner, and begged the saint to pray that he might live long enough to fulfill his desire.

"You will obtain that favor, my son," promised Don Bosco.

Joseph did not die, and some years afterward he volunteered for missionary work in America. He was ordained to the priesthood by Cardinal Gibbons in 1888. For a time he labored with marked success among the Crow Indians, in Montana; then he was assigned to Alaska.

Father Crimont lost his heart at once to the lonely vastness of Alaska. He loved its Eskimos, its Indians, the rough white traders and miners, and his heroic brother missioners. The frail priest thrived and grew strong amid the rigors and privations of rugged Alaska.

Ten years after his arrival in the far North, Father Crimont was appointed Prefect Apostolic of Alaska. Thereafter, the chief burden of the Alaskan missions rested for over forty years on his slender shoulders. In 1917, Pope Benedict XV raised the head of the Alaskan missions to the episcopate. The new prelate continued as before to live in utter poverty, giving away all the presents he received from friends. He journeyed unceasingly from one of his far-flung missions to another.

The veteran apostle of Alaska died on May 20, 1945, at the age of eighty-seven years. One who had been close to Archbishop Crimont said of him: "He was a man with a gentle soul and a great spirit. You felt better for having known him."

THE CHRISTLIKE HEART

Archbishop Crimont was so generous in his friendship that he continued to love even those who had proved unworthy of his affection. "God goes on loving people, doesn't He? He loves His saints, but He loves sinners, too," the gentle apostle would point out.

FATHER LOUIS LIANG (*1918–1947*)

In December, 1936, when the Chinese Communists made Yenan in northern Shensi Province their headquarters, Spanish Franciscan missioners had developed in that ancient city a flourishing Christian community of some ten thousand Catholics. The eighteen-year-old Louis Liang was one of their most promising seminarians. At the end of a few months, Mao Tse-tung drove the Franciscans out of Yenan. Louis Liang escaped to neighboring Shansi Province, where he was ordained to the priesthood in 1940.

After his ordination, the young Chinese priest made brilliant studies at the University of Peking; and his Franciscan bishop counted on him for important educational work. But Father Liang thought more and more frequently of the shepherdless Catholics at the Communist headquarters. In 1945, he obtained permission to return to Yenan and almost certain death.

The Communists agreed to allow Father Liang to stay in Yenan, where he found that terror and persecutions had thinned out the Catholic community to a small group of heroic faithful. From the first, the Reds surrounded the Chinese priest with spies; and in 1947, they haled him four times before a people's court. During these so-called trials, Father Liang was suspended from a beam and cruelly beaten. The Communists would no doubt have proceeded to his execution; but just then they were obliged to flee before the Nationalist troops approaching in force from the south.

In the course of their flight, the Reds abandoned their priestly prisoner in a village hut. Because of the tortures Father Liang had suffered, he was a very sick man. A Nationalist soldier found the priest and cared for him. But the Nationalists' victory was not permanent; and when the Communists returned to the village, a spy told them that the sick priest had been helped by a Nationalist soldier.

"So you were a running dog of the Nationalists all the while!" the Reds triumphantly stated to Father Liang. They killed the helpless priest on April 15, 1947. They had seen that no amount of "brain-washing" would ever obliterate this twenty-nine-year-old apostle's belief in God and in eternal life.

A CATHOLIC PRIEST IN ETERNITY

When the Communists ordered Father Liang to apostatize, he told his persecutors: "Not only am I a Christian, I am also a Catholic priest. Even if you cut off my head, I shall always be a Christian and a Catholic priest in eternity."

BISHOP VICTOR ROELENS, W.F. (*d. 1947*)

Victor Roelens was ordained to the priesthood in 1889 by Cardinal Lavigerie, founder of the White Fathers. Four years later, Father Roelens was appointed superior of a vast territory in the Belgian Congo. There were only two mission stations in a territory eight times the size of Father Roelen's native Belgium.

Eight years passed before a single adult African was baptized in the mission of the Upper Congo. The people had often seen the missioners baptize dying babies, and they thought that the inevitable result of baptism was death. At length, one young man was so eager to become a Christian that he was willing even to incur the risk of death. The brave youth was baptized under the name of Primo, as the first convert. Primo did not die, and he became an exemplary Christian. A few years later, thanks to zealous catechists and school children, Christian teachings spread far and wide, and many Africans began to ask for baptism.

Meanwhile, in 1896, Father Roelens had been consecrated a bishop. He was an organizer of genius and truly a man of God. Under his able guidance, mission works developed rapidly, in spite of insufficient personnel and lack of funds. Bishop Roelens secured

White Sisters and Franciscan Sisters to educate the African women and girls and to care for the sick. In 1922, he founded a native Sisterhood.

Long before that – in fact, in 1897 – Bishop Roelens had begun to train African boys for the priesthood. The old men in the villages laughed and said: "An African Catholic priest? That is impossible!"

In 1912, the "impossibility" became a reality, when Stefano Kaoze was ordained to the priesthood. In 1933, Father Kaoze founded the first mission to be operated exclusively by African priests in the Upper Congo territory.

As the years passed, Bishop Roelens was attacked by the dread black-water illness no less than eighteen times, but his robust constitution resisted each onslaught. The great pioneer died on August 5, 1947, at the age of eighty-nine years. During his long apostolate, the number of African converts in his vicariate had increased from one – the daring Primo – to almost fifty-four thousand!

IT TOOK A SAINTLY APOSTLE

The flame of zeal must burn high in the missioner's heart before it can communicate itself to others. It took a saintly apostle to inflame the untutored African, Primo, with a desire of baptism so ardent that he surmounted the fear of physical death in order to obtain it.

BISHOP MAXIMILIAN KALLER (*1880–1947*)

On July 19, 1947, exiled priests from East Prussia wept as they stood around an open grave in West Germany. They watched the cheap coffin that held the body of their bishop being lowered into the earth, and then sang the funeral hymns of home. The bishop of the expelled East Prussian refugees had gone to his eternal reward.

All his life, the apostolic Bishop Maximilian Kaller had spent himself in caring for scattered Catholics of the German diaspora. As a young priest, he was sent from a flourishing parish in Upper

Silesia to the spiritual desolation of the Isle of Ruegen. During eleven years of strenuous pioneering, he succeeded in building up an active Catholic community on that neglected outpost. He devoted himself to the special service of the uprooted Polish seasonal workers on the island; and they came to return his love for them.

His experiences in Ruegen gave Father Kaller courage for his following labors in Berlin. He organized in that big Protestant city a vigorous Catholic lay apostolate, and thus was able to distribute food to hundreds of the poor during the days of famine after World War I. He was the first priest to lead a Corpus Christi procession through the streets of Berlin.

In 1930, Father Kaller was made Bishop of Ermland, an extensive region in central East Prussia. A particularly close friendship linked the new prelate to his large East Prussian diaspora and its priests. Bishop Kaller's long years of labors among the scattered Catholics of northeastern Germany had given him a keen understanding of their special problems. He secured numerous priests from West Germany to work among his flock, and he organized them under the title of The Wandering Church.

When the Nazis began to arrest his priests, Bishop Kaller did everything in his power to aid his co-apostles. At one time he offered himself as chaplain for Catholics imprisoned in a Jewish concentration camp, but the apostolic nuncio could not accept his offer. In 1945, the Gestapo drove Bishop Kaller from Ermland. He made his way back after the German defeat, only to be ignominiously expelled from his see by the Poles. Pope Pius XII then gave the exiled prelate a task for which God had prepared him through his long years of experience among the Catholics of the German diaspora. He became the bishop and father of the East Prussian refugees.

Within a few months his work extended all over West Germany. Owing to political circumstances, his flock had been refused entry to many of the more Catholic regions of Germany, and their spiritual needs were appalling. Bishop Kaller did not complain about lack of understanding or grinding destitution, but sought only the

blessing of God on his almost superhuman efforts. No wonder the exiles wept, as they stood beside his grave in 1947. But they were also uplifted in soul, inspired by the desire to imitate him in his selfless sharing in the Passion of Christ.

BEARING HIS REPROACH

Bishop Maximilian Kaller saw in the catastrophes which overtook the nations of central Europe a judgment of God on current disbelief, complacency, and spiritual sloth. At the same time, however, he recognized in these disasters a divine challenge to expiate the guilt which had caused the catastrophes and to serve Christ, crucified anew in His wandering, exiled followers. "Let us go forth therefore unto him without the camp, bearing his reproach" (Hebr. 13:13).

BISHOP TEOFIL MATULIONIS
(*1873–c. 1948*)

When Teofil Matulionis was born in a Lithuanian village, his country was under Russian rule and every effort was being made by the Czarist authorities to Russify his people. Teofil's devout Catholic parents sent him to St. Petersburg for higher studies; and in 1895, the young man entered the central seminary for Latin Catholics in the Russian capital. His associates admired his intellectual brilliance and his intense piety. The Lithuanian seminarian was ordained to the priesthood in 1900.

Father Matulionis began his priestly work in Latvia, then part of the immense Russian Catholic Mogilev Archdiocese. In his zeal for souls he baptized the child of a Catholic mother and a Russian Orthodox father, so the Russian Government imprisoned him for a year. On his release, he was assigned to a parish in the industrial area of St. Petersburg, where he ministered to Poles, Lithuanians, Latvians, and White Russians. The Lithuanian priest readily recognized the sterling qualities of the Russian masses, and he longed for the reunion of this great people with the Holy See.

After Lithuania had regained her independence, following World

War I, Father Matulionis continued to remain with his precariously situated Catholics in Russia. They were devoted to their saintly priest and unaffected by Soviet antireligious propaganda. In vain the Soviets sought to bribe Father Matulionis to spy on his brother priests. He was arrested in March, 1923, and held during two years in solitary confinement in Moscow. Released in 1925, he returned to his parishioners.

Pius XI raised the heroic Lithuanian apostle of Russia to the episcopate in 1929. That same year, Bishop Matulionis was again arrested and subjected to torture. In 1930, he was sentenced to ten years of forced labor on the frigid Solovky Islands in the White Sea. He and his fellow priests in the prison camp said Mass secretly. They were betrayed by a renegade Catholic who acted as a Soviet spy. Bishop Matulionis was transferred to slave labor in the vicinity of Leningrad; but the Lithuanian Government negotiated his release in 1933 in exchange for the return of a Soviet political prisoner.

During 1935 and 1936, Bishop Matulionis visited Lithuanian Catholic parishes throughout the United States. Everywhere he ceaselessly urged prayers for the conversion of Russia. The following year, the Holy See appointed him bishop of a Lithuanian diocese. In 1940, the Soviet Union annexed Lithuania, and Bishop Matulionis saw repeated in his own country the determined attack on religion that he had previously witnessed in Russia.

Then came the Nazi occupation, followed in 1944 by the furious return of the Soviet troops. Three years later, Bishop Matulionis was taken at night from his episcopal palace and deported to Russia. The exact manner, time, and place of his death cannot be verified; but it is believed that he consummated his martyrdom in 1948 in a Siberian prison camp.

SUCH LOVE IS FROM GOD

When the Lithuanian Government negotiated the liberation of Bishop Matulionis, in 1933, he pleaded to remain with his Catholics in Leningrad. Only after the Soviet authorities had said that he must either leave Russia or return to prison did he agree to depart.

FATHER IGNATIUS LISSNER, S.M.A.
(*1867–1948*)

"Father Lissner, we are sending you to work among the Negroes of Georgia in the United States," said the Superior-General of the Society of African Missions one day in 1907.

Father Lissner's society was founded at Lyons, France, in 1856; and its missioners go chiefly to West Africa and to Egypt. Father Lissner himself, a native of Alsace, had previously labored in Dahomey, French Guinea, the Gold Coast, and Egypt. He would have preferred another assignment to Africa, but he set off at once for the land of the Stars and Stripes.

Father Lissner rented a room at a boardinghouse in Savannah, and began to map out his apostolic campaign. When the Alsatian priest arrived in Georgia, there was only a handful of widely scattered Catholics among a Negro population of one and one-quarter million souls. Within seven years, this pioneer apostle, aided by a small group of priests and Sisters, had preached Christ to the Negroes in every important center of the State. He considered that the Catholic school is an all-important factor in the conversion of the Negro. Today some two thousand Negro children attend the schools of Father Lissner's society in Georgia.

At Tenafly, New Jersey, Father Lissner founded an American Province of his society in 1922. After his labors in Georgia, he opened Negro missions in Los Angeles, California, and Tucson, Arizona. He believed that the Negroes should have priests and Sisters of their own race. He founded in Georgia a Negro Sisterhood, called Franciscan Handmaids of the Most Pure Heart of Mary. Those Sisters now conduct a school and a day nursery in Harlem, and have a novitiate on Staten Island. For the training of Negro priests, Father Lissner opened a seminary at Tenafly.

The zealous apostle from Alsace organized three-day retreats for

Negro professional and businessmen. Until his death in 1948, at the age of eighty-one, Father Lissner continued to work for the spiritual, social, and economic advancement of the American Negro. His name must henceforth be ranked among the missionary great in the United States.

A PIONEER OF GENEROUS VISION

Father Ignatius Lissner pioneered in the training of Negro priests and Sisters in the United States. Though there are still too few of these invaluable apostles among their own race, they have already demonstrated their indispensable role in the conversion of American Negroes to Catholicism.

ARCHBISHOP HENRY STREICHER, W.F. (*1863–1951*)

Archbishop Henry Streicher stands high among the great prelates who have left their mark on the Church in Africa. He was born in Alsace in 1863. As a young White Father, he was assigned to the mission field of Uganda, in Central Africa. Like most truly great men, Archbishop Streicher was very simple; and he spoke frankly of the humble beginnings of his flourishing Uganda seminary for African priests.

"Bishop Hirth showed me a letter from Rome," he recalled. "It said, 'A mission ripe enough to produce martyrs must be ripe enough to give priests to the Church.' There was no answer to that argument. So I rolled up my sleeves and got busy.

"First of all, we had to teach our lads how to read and write. By way of writing paper, I used the envelopes of the letters that our missioners received from Europe. 'Write on both sides of the paper, and write small; these envelopes have to last!' I told those pioneer seminarians."

The Uganda seminary grew steadily, and today it is housed in fine buildings. Out of the pioneer students, two finally reached the goal of the priesthood. They were ordained by their first teacher—for Father Streicher had received episcopal consecration in 1897.

One of the African priests then ordained by Bishop Streicher was called to Rome in 1939 and was consecrated a bishop by the Holy Father himself. Pope Pius XII invited Archbishop Streicher to the Eternal City to see the consecration of Bishop Joseph Kiwanuka of Uganda. Teacher and pupil had traveled a long way from the days of those writing lessons on the backs of used envelopes!

When Bishop Streicher was placed over the missions of Uganda, there were thirty thousand Catholics in his care. There are now in Uganda well over one million Catholics. In the evening of his life, the grand old man among the White Fathers of Uganda entrusted his administrative burdens to a young Canadian successor. Then Archbishop Streicher went out to a mission in the bush, to finish his apostolate in the same way in which he had started it so many years ago.

THE UNENDING SERVICE

Few secular executives in business or industry would care to return in advanced old age to the strenuous labors with which they began their career; but this is exactly what Archbishop Streicher did. The direct apostolate had always been the work nearest to the heart of the grand old missioner. Moreover he was serving, not his own ambition, but a Master for whom he could never do all that he desired.

FATHER FRANCIS XAVIER TUAN (*1919–1950*)

In 1919, a son was born to Catholic Vietnamese parents in a village not far distant from the imperial city of Hue. At the suggestion of their French pastor, the Tuans named their son after the Apostle of the Orient. When Francis Xavier was ten years old, the French missioner told the Tuans that he thought their son had the makings of a catechist, perhaps even of a priest. The boy accordingly joined a group of Vietnamese lads who were preparing in the missioner's own residence for the service of God.

After five years in the missioner's residence, Francis Xavier was sent to the minor seminary. As his knowledge of the history of the Catholic Church in his own country grew, he felt increasingly proud of it. He was told that there was now in Vietnam one indigenous priest for every thousand Catholics – a higher ratio than in any other mission country.

Francis Xavier received his diploma as catechist after six years at the minor seminary. Under the direction of a priest, he did catechetical work for another six years; and then, at length, he was ready to enter the theological seminary. Meanwhile Communism had been growing strong in his country under the leadership of a remarkably gifted native, Ho Chi Minh. Violent hostilities between the French colonial forces and Ho's troops broke out toward the close of 1946.

Ho's followers, the Vietminhs, attacked French and Spanish Catholic missions and native Catholic villagers accused of collaboration with the foreigners. Foreign missioners were imprisoned, while Vietnamese Catholics were executed after having refused to give up their Faith. There arose, nevertheless, a strong convert movement throughout the land. Non-Christians were drawn to the Church by the steadfastness of Catholics in the midst of a general confusion.

Francis Xavier Tuan was ordained to the priesthood in June, 1950, and gave his blessing to his happy parents. The French ordaining bishop warned: "The present situation in Vietnam demands complete confidence in God and a constant spirit of sacrifice. We must be ready for anything, even to the giving of our life's blood."

A few days later, Father Tuan set out on his bicycle to offer his First Solemn High Mass in his native village. As he crossed a stretch of the road skirting the foothills, Communists shot him from ambush. That afternoon, farmers discovered Father Tuan's bloodstained body lying by the wayside. The festive decorations in the village church were changed to funeral trappings.

Profoundly shocked, the villagers said again and again: "He prepared during twenty years to be a Catholic priest, and now he has been murdered only a few days after his ordination."

NO PAINS ARE SPARED

The long training of Catholic priests in Vietnam is paralleled in other mission countries. The foreign missioners spare no pains to insure that the Catholic communities growing up in pagan surroundings shall have "other Christs" worthy of their sacred vocation.

BISHOP BONIFACE SAUER, O.S.B. (*1877–1950*)

In May, 1949, as thousands of Catholics from Communist-held North Korea were fleeing south of the 38th parallel, Bishop Boniface Sauer and some seventy of his priests and Brothers were arrested and imprisoned in Pyongyang, the Red Korean capital. The foreign Benedictine Sisters were likewise arrested, while the Korean Sisters were sent to their homes and ordered to wear lay garb.

Bishop Sauer was born in the diocese of Fulda, Germany. He had been in Korea since 1909; and his monastery at Tokwon, on the bay of Wonsan, was one of the best-equipped Catholic institutions in the Far East. Bishop Sauer also established mission stations with resident priests and Brothers, scattered far and wide in his extensive Wonsan Vicariate in northeastern Korea.

The Communists declared the great missionary prelate guilty of "conspiring with reactionary persons in South Korea." Bishop Sauer and some other members of his community were held in the Pyongyang jail, while a number of Benedictines were sent northward to slave labor in desolate country.

The seventy-two-year-old prelate was in poor health at the time of his arrest. He was kept in solitary confinement, without any possibility of his offering the Holy Sacrifice. The food was bad and scanty. When Bishop Sauer became seriously ill in December, 1949, a Benedictine Brother was permitted to stay with him. The end came on February 7, 1950.

"Why did the old bishop say that he was going home, just before he died?" the prison guards asked one another. "We all know that the foreign reactionary's home was in Germany, many thousands of miles from here."

MISSIONARY SEED DIES HARD

The Korean Communists did not succeed in annihilating Bishop Sauer's Benedictines. Some of his Korean seminarians, Brothers, and Sisters were eventually evacuated by the American forces to the safety of Pusan in southeastern Korea. Korean Reds were not the first to discover the death-defying properties of missionary seed.

FATHER ANTHONY COLLIER (*1913–1950*)

The first Catholic priest killed in South Korea by the invading Reds was a thirty-seven-year-old Irish missioner, Father Anthony Collier, of the St. Columban's Foreign Missionary Society. Father Collier was stationed in Chunchon, about twenty-five miles below the 38th parallel. He had been in Korea since 1936, and was greatly loved by his Catholics.

On June 27, 1950, Communist soldiers arrested Father Collier, together with his young Korean language teacher, Gabriel Kim. The Reds ordered their captives to "confess" that they had acted as spies in Chunchon. When both the prisoners denied this absurd charge, their arms were tied and they were roped together. The soldiers then marched Father Collier and his language teacher toward the river, with the apparent intention of drowning them.

Soon, however, the Reds halted, and shot their captives from behind. Thinking that both their victims were dead, the Communists went away; but Gabriel Kim still lived. During a day and two nights, the young Korean strove feebly to free himself from Father Collier's corpse. At last he succeeded and made his way into the neighboring hills, where a compassionate old man dressed his wounds.

THE GOOD SHEPHERD DOES NOT FLEE

American Army officers had warned the St. Columban priests of the imminent peril to their lives. The missioners had replied according to the immemorial tradition of their calling: "Our place is here. We cannot leave our Christians."

BISHOP PATRICK J. BYRNE, M.M. (*1888–1950*)

"We can relax a bit, now that Patrick Byrne has been ordained," said the Sulpician professors at St. Mary's Seminary in Baltimore, in 1915. No other student in their memory had enlivened the theology classes with such searching, difficult questions, put with irrepressible wit and humor, as this young man from Washington, D. C.

During that same summer, Father Byrne went straight to Maryknoll, New York, the young Foreign Mission Society of America. He longed to spend himself in active work for souls on the mission field; but as a pioneer member of his society, his great talents made him indispensable at the center in the United States. At last, in 1923, he was appointed first Maryknoll superior in Korea.

Never physically strong, Father Byrne smiled through the hardships of the Korean beginnings. He wished to have another Maryknoller appointed superior in his stead, so that he could devote all his energies to actual mission work. The Maryknoll Superior-General did not accede to this request; and in 1929, Father Byrne's unwanted honors increased when he was named Prefect Apostolic of Pyongyang. That same year, a worse blow fell: Father Byrne was elected to the council of his society and recalled to the United States.

In 1934, Father Byrne was assigned to Japan, where three years later he was named Prefect Apostolic of Kyoto. This was probably the happiest period of his life, but then came World War II. The Maryknoller gladly resigned as Prefect Apostolic of Kyoto, in favor of Monsignor Furuya, a Japanese. Father Byrne remained among his beloved Japanese; and when the American occupation was about to begin he addressed them by radio, reassuring them as to the intentions of the conquerors.

But Father Byrne was to finish his work for Christ in the country where he began his mission labors. The Holy See appointed him

Visitor Apostolic to Korea in 1947, and made him Apostolic Delegate two years later. In 1949, Father Byrne was raised to the episcopate at Seoul.

In July, 1950, the Reds arrested Bishop Byrne and his secretary, Father William Booth, a Maryknoller from Rockville Center, New York, who was liberated in 1953. Together with other foreigners and captured UN soldiers, the Maryknollers were taken north. On the last day of October, the prisoners were forced to begin a long march of one hundred miles, because the Communist guards feared they would be rescued by American troops. Bishop Byrne was getting steadily weaker, but he remained patient through all the sufferings and tried to help others.

The first Apostolic Delegate to Korea died of pneumonia on November 25, 1950, in a hut as poor as Bethlehem itself. Just before his death, he said to his fellow prisoners: "After the privilege of my priesthood, I regard this privilege of having suffered for Christ with all of you as the greatest of my life."

A BRAVE SPIRIT

Bishop James E. Walsh, M.M., who pioneered with Bishop Byrne during the early days at the Maryknoll center, said of his confrere: "Maryknoll has had no braver spirit, no more generous, self-forgetting soul, among its sons than Bishop Byrne – no more acute mind, either; and these were the qualities which helped to forge him into a champion of Christ."

CHAPLAIN EMIL JOSEPH KAPAUN, *U. S. Army (1916–1951)*

Father Emil Joseph Kapaun was born on a farm near Marion, Kansas. During World War II he was a chaplain in the China-Burma-India theater. Then he served for two years as parish priest at Timken, Kansas. But Father Kapaun had seen and deeply understood the stark need of soldiers for the ministrations of a priest, so his apostolic heart led him to return to the Corps of Chaplains in 1948.

Lieutenant Ray M. Dowe, a graduate of West Point and a fellow prisoner with Father Kapaun in Korea, wrote of him in *The Saturday Evening Post,* January 16, 1954, "so that the folks at home can know what kind of man he was, and what he did for us, and how he died."

Long before Chaplain Kapaun was captured by the Reds, he had become a legend among the troops in Korea. Outwardly he was all G.I., tough of body, and with a farmer's flair for homely, pithy speech. His parish was the battle front and the battalion aid station close behind the lines. There he would comfort the wounded and say the prayers of the Church over the dying men, whatever their faith. He seemed to have no fear of being killed, and rescued wounded men under fire so thick that his pipe was shot out of his mouth.

Father Kapaun was captured by the Reds at Unsan in November, 1950, because he refused to leave the wounded. After his capture, he served as a stretcher-bearer during the long march over frozen, slippery roads to the prison camp. "Carrying a litter was agony. Father never ordered a man to carry. After a rest he'd just call, 'Let's pick 'em up,' and all down the line the guys would bend and lift, and follow him."

When it became obvious that the prisoners must either steal food or slowly starve, Father Kapaun, in the presence of all the captives, said a prayer to St. Dismas, the Good Thief, asking for his aid. Then the chaplain became the most accomplished food thief of them all; it seemed he could not fail. He always tossed his stolen food into the common pot. Some other men, who had been keeping what they stole for themselves, were shamed by his example and the private hoarding stopped.

The Reds refused Father Kapaun permission to tend the wounded; but he sneaked into their wretched shelter just the same. He brought them clean bandages and washed the old ones, foul with corruption. He held them in his arms like children when delirium came upon them. Above all, he inspired them with a renewed will to live. When a POW died, the chaplain from Kansas always volunteered for the dreaded burial detail.

Father Kapaun was an unbending enemy of Communism. When the Reds tried to brain-wash him, he told them to their faces that they lied. In his sermons he urged the men, above all, not to sell their immortal souls by yielding to the false doctrines of their captors. He related the sufferings that Christ endured to those that the prisoners were forced to bear. As Christ had endured, so they, too, must endure until the resurrection from the prison camp, he told them.

On the first Sunday after Easter, Father Kapaun fell gravely ill. The Reds saw their opportunity to get rid of the man they both hated and feared, so they said he must go to their "hospital." Father Kapaun told Lieutenant Ralph Nardella, who knew the prayers of the missal, to keep on at all costs holding services for the prisoners. Then he turned to Lieutenant Dowe.

"Don't take it hard, Mike," he said. "I'm going where I've always wanted to go. And when I get up there, I'll say a prayer for all of you."

A few days later, in May of 1951, Chaplain Kapaun went to God from the Reds' foul pesthouse. His body was lost in a mass grave beside the Yalu River; but the soldiers who loved him knew that "he and the things he believed in can never die."

HIS FAITH SUSTAINED THEM

Lieutenant Dowe says of Father Kapaun: "He was, I think, the bravest man I ever knew and the kindest. . . . Because of his sermons, which gave us hope and courage, and the food he stole for us, and the care he gave us when we were sick, many of us came back who would never have survived our long ordeal without him."

FATHER BEDA CHANG, S.J. (*d. 1951*)

When the Communists took Shanghai, in May, 1949, the Sorbonne-educated Chinese Jesuit, Father Beda Chang, was rector of St. Ignatius College at Zikawei and professor of Chinese literature at Aurora University. The Reds forced their distinguished opponent out of St. Ignatius College; and in August, 1951, they placed him under arrest. Father Chang was then a man forty-six years of age, in flourishing health.

In the course of the succeeding months, the Communists announced that Father Chang had "joined" the schismatic Church sponsored by the Reds; but no one gave the slightest attention to this crude lie. On November 11, Father Chang's brother was summoned to the place of the priest's imprisonment. There he found the Chinese Jesuit's blackened, wasted, and naked corpse lying on the prison floor. The Catholic priest had died suddenly of a "brain tumor," the jailors said.

The Reds forbade a solemn funeral procession for their victim; but to their amazed anger, thousands of Christians thronged to all of the city's Catholic churches the following morning as Requiem Masses were sung throughout Shanghai. Two hundred priests in Shanghai that day privately celebrated the Martyr's Mass in red vestments for the soul of their heroic confrere.

THEY COULD NOT SILENCE HIM

After the Reds had deprived Father Beda Chang of the rectorship of St. Ignatius College, he continued fearlessly to preach to large congregations that "the true Church is one, holy, catholic, and apostolic." The slaying of the confessor of the Faith by the Communists served merely to give his words a more sacred authority in the hearts of men of good will.

BISHOP FRANCIS XAVIER FORD, M.M. (*1892–1952*)

The twelve-year-old Frank Ford put in the collection basket a nickel, at that time the sum total of his wealth. Then he repeated to himself the closing words of a fiery appeal in broken English, just delivered by a veteran European missioner on behalf of his Chinese lepers: "My one ambeesch is to die a martyr!" muttered the boy, and suddenly realized that he meant it.

Francis Xavier Ford was born in Brooklyn, New York. His literary parents were devoted to the cause of Irish independence.

Mr. Ford hoped that, among his eight children, the talented Frank would be the one to continue his parents' literary battle for Irish freedom. This hope was not realized, because Frank Ford remained faithful to his early desire to become a foreign missioner. In 1912, he was the first student to join Maryknoll, the newly founded Catholic Foreign Mission Society of America.

Father Ford went to South China in 1918, a member of Maryknoll's initial mission band. From the first he gave his heart to the people and the land of his apostolate, so that the Chinese who knew him remember him above all as one who truly loved them. After some six years in the market town of Yeungkong, on the southern seacoast of Kwangtung Province, Father Ford became the first superior of the Maryknoll Hakka mission field, in mountainous country to the north of the Yeungkong area. He was consecrated a bishop in 1935 by the Superior-General and cofounder of Maryknoll, Bishop James Anthony Walsh.

Among his beloved Hakka Chinese, Bishop Ford put into effect the apostolic plans that had been maturing in his mind during the Yeungkong years. Chinese youths received a sound training for the priesthood in his preparatory seminary. The Hakka Catholic laity were taught to undertake apostolic work on their own part. Bishop Ford emphasized the direct apostolate among the people for both the priests and the Sisters under his guidance. The Papal Internuncio in China requested that Bishop Ford's plan for the Sisters' direct apostolate be adopted by heads of missions all over that vast land.

When the Communists set up their regime in the Hakka area, in 1949, Bishop Ford urged his missioners to persevere in their apostolate with full confidence in God's aid. The Reds placed Bishop Ford under house arrest two days before Christmas, 1950. During the following April, the American prelate was condemned by a people's court, together with a Maryknoll Sister who had served as his secretary. The two Maryknollers were then taken to the provincial prison in Canton.

During the stops in the journey, Bishop Ford was beaten, stoned, and knocked down by mobs egged on by Communist agitators. Each time the bishop rose and continued calmly on his way. He was silent, and not once did he try to defend himself.

Just before her own liberation, Bishop Ford's secretary was taken to an old public cemetery outside Canton and was shown her leader's grave. She was told that he had died "of old age" on February 21, 1952. Among Bishop Ford's last recorded words were the following ones, addressed to his fellow prisoner, Sister Joan Marie: "We must not hate the Communists. They are acting according to their lights."

It was the immemorial apostolic echo of the charity of the Crucified First Missioner: "Father, forgive them, for they know not what they do" (Lk. 23:34).

AN ACCEPTED OFFERING

"Grant us, Lord, to be the doorstep by which the multitudes may come to worship Thee. And if, in the saving of their souls, we are ground underfoot and spat upon and worn out, at least we shall have served Thee in some small way in helping pagan souls; we shall have become the King's Highway in pathless China." — *Bishop Ford's Prayer*

Epilogue

THE world wars and the vast spiritual catastrophes of the present age have served to discredit the smugly complacent nineteenth-century belief in inevitable human progress, the vapidly conceited concept of man lifting himself by his own bootstraps. In the present frightening uncertainty and confusion, those outside the Church yearn more than ever before for world peace and the unity of human brotherhood.

If we tell them that true unity is to be found only in the Mystical Body of Christ, in the Church that He established, they will not fail to point out the great scandal of disunion among Christians themselves — the schismatic Eastern Churches, and the multiple, widely differing groups of Protestants.

"And how do you account for the almost one billion and a half pagans in the world at present?" they will ask. "Your Church has had over nineteen centuries to unite mankind, yet today seventeen out of every twenty men on earth do not belong to it."

If we are honest with ourselves, most of us Catholics will have to admit our share of culpable negligence as a factor in the grievous delays in the unfolding of God's plan of salvation for humanity. The divine plan for the unity of all nations in the Mystical Body of Christ was a mystery of God's loving mercy before the creation of the world and it has been unfolding throughout the existence of men on this earth. Christ revealed to us that it is now in its final phase — the period between His Ascension and His Second Coming, when at the end of time He will introduce all humanity into the Kingdom of God. Why is this final phase so painfully protracted?

It is because most of us Catholics do not love God with that selfless faith which would make us dedicated witnesses to Christ. Yet so to bear witness is the essential destiny of every Christian.

Our Lord has sent down upon each of us the Holy Ghost, His Spirit of Love, so that we might be enabled to manifest Him to all men. God's Kingdom is one of love. He will not force it on humanity. It will not come until a vast kindling of the apostolic spirit among Catholics shall urge them on to fill up at last in the Mystical Body "those things which are wanting of the sufferings of Christ" (Col. 1:24).

The missioners we have glimpsed in this book were invincible in love and faith because their apostolic zeal was centered primarily in God. Nothing mattered, except that they should further to their utmost the coming of the perfect paean of praise that all humanity, gathered at last into the Mystical Body, shall render to God at the end of time. They were joyfully selfless witnesses of Christ, even to martyrdom.

Only in their spirit of total dedication to God and souls can Catholics meet the challenge of our times with the Christian intrepidity of the late Holy Father, Pius XI. "Let us thank God that He makes us live among the present problems. . . . It is no longer permitted to anyone to be mediocre," said the great Pope of the Missions.

> Send forth Thy Spirit, and they shall be created;
> And Thou shalt renew the face of the earth.
> Come, O Holy Spirit, fill the hearts of Thy faithful;
> And kindle in them the fire of Thy love.

Index of Names